POCKETFUL
of MIRACLES

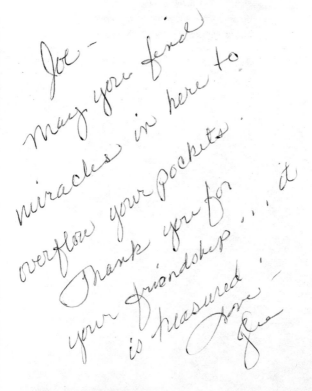

Joe —

May your fence
miracles in here to
overflow your pockets.

Thank you for
your friendship . . . it
is treasured.

love,
Gia

Also by Joan Borysenko

Fire in the Soul
On Wings of Light
Minding the Body, Mending the Mind
Guilt Is the Teacher, Love Is the Lesson

POCKETFUL *of* MIRACLES

PRAYERS, MEDITATIONS, AND AFFIRMATIONS TO
NURTURE YOUR SPIRIT EVERY DAY OF THE YEAR

JOAN BORYSENKO, Ph.D.

WARNER BOOKS

A Time Warner Company

Copyright © 1994 by Joan Borysenko, Ph.D.
All rights reserved.

Warner Books, Inc., 1271 Avenue of the Americas, New York, NY 10020
New York, NY 10020

Visit our Web site at http://warnerbooks.com

W A Time Warner Company

Printed in the United States of America
First Printing: November 1994
10 9 8 7 6

Library of Congress Cataloging-in-Publication Data
Borysenko, Joan.
　　Pocketful of miracles / Joan Borysenko ; illustrated by Miron Borysenko.
　　　　p.　cm.
　　ISBN 0-446-39536-6 (pbk.)
　　1. New Age devotional calendars.　I. Title.
BP605.N48B673　1994
299'.93—dc20　　　　　　　　　　　　　　　　　　　94-11588
　　　　　　　　　　　　　　　　　　　　　　　　　　　　CIP

Cover design by Julia Kushnirsky
Cover illustration by Raul Colon

Book design by H. Roberts

DEDICATION

For the children—yours and ours.
May they live in a world of peace.
May they live in a world of beauty.
May they live remembering that
there is only One of us here.

ABOUT
POCKETFUL OF MIRACLES

Pocketful of Miracles is a guide to remembering the loving Source from which we come. Each one of us has moments of remembering, when we find ourselves present to the beauty of a sunset, the smile of a baby or the light in the eyes of a stranger. At those moments we feel most at home in our skin; confident, happy, grateful, loving and connected to the seamless web of life. We are present in our essential nature, what you may think of as the Higher or Spiritual Self. At other times that connection fades and we adopt a more limited perspective. Fear of loss, abandonment and the withdrawal of love form a shell around our hearts and obscure the light of the Higher Self which is always present, always calling us to remember who we really are.

In spite of the inner drive to wake up to our essential nature, there is another force of mind working to keep us asleep—the ego. As a psychologist, I think of this aspect of personality as the "conditioned self." It arises in response to the conditions of life that threaten to separate us from love. As we grow up, we don a variety of masks that we show to the world in an attempt to be lovable, or at least powerful. The masks help us feel safe. Paradoxically, they are informed by fear and keep us separate from the only true source of love—the Divine Mind. In spiritual systems, the fear-based conditioned self is called the ego. This is different from ego as it is used in psychological parlance to denote a healthy, independent sense of self.

The miracle that this book refers to is the shift in perspective out of the fear-based nature of the ego into the timeless love and wisdom of the Higher Self.* This miracle is the basis of what writer and philosopher Aldous Huxley called the Perennial

*This definition of "miracle" was adopted from *A Course in Miracles,* a modern statement of the Perennial Philosophy that has inspired hundreds of thousands of people. (Foundation for Inner Peace, 1975.)

Philosophy—the esoteric, or hidden, core of all religions. The Perennial Philosophy consists of four fundamental doctrines:

- The world of relative reality in which we live is the manifestation of a Divine Mind without which nothing would exist.

- Access to the Divine Mind is not a matter of knowledge or doctrine, but a direct experience of the numinous.

- Each one of us has a dual nature: the ego and the Higher Self. The Higher Self is the Divine Spark within. The ego is the provocateur that leads us to discover that Higher Self.

- The purpose of human life is to discover our union with the Divine Mind, not by transcending this life, but by becoming fully alive here and now, through the giving and receiving of love.

Pocketful of Miracles is a collection of daily practices, drawn from all the world's great spiritual traditions, that are meant to bring the reader into a direct experience of the Divine. The peace, wisdom, creativity and love that make up the essential nature of the Higher Self can then shine forth as a blessing to all. Peace on earth begins with peace in our own souls. It is with this objective, to bring forth peace and compassion upon the earth, that *Pocketful of Miracles* is written.

The time pressures of modern life are such that few of us can engage in long periods of daily prayer and meditation. Although our hearts may call us to a contemplative life, the need to earn a living may pull us in the opposite direction. It may also be that we are so confused by the number of spiritual practices available that we don't know where to start, or that it's just plain difficult to maintain enthusiasm for spiritual practice by ourselves. Even if we have a spiritual practice, at times it becomes dry and lifeless.

We need inspiration to bring it to a deeper level. It is my hope that *Pocketful of Miracles* will provide the inspiration and framework for a spiritual practice that fits easily into most schedules. The daily lessons can generally be completed in ten minutes or less, although at times you might want to spend longer.

The "Spiritual Supermarket"

The Dalai Lama once heard that America was a kind of "spiritual supermarket." When the term caught his imagination, and he began to refer to our great spiritual supermarket in lectures, someone took him aside and explained that the term was actually derogatory. His holiness disagreed. He asked whether shopping at a supermarket wasn't infinitely more advantageous than frequenting a small corner store where only a few stale tubes of toothpaste could be found.

Indeed, we're living in unprecedented times in which the esoteric or hidden spiritual wisdom of many cultures has come into mass consciousness. In the mid 1940s, the Dead Sea Scrolls and Nag Hammadi manuscripts were discovered, casting new light on early Christian/late Jewish thought, and providing a number of gospels to augment those in the New Testament. The terrible holocaust that the Chinese perpetrated on Tibet in the 1950s has likewise resulted in the broad distribution of previously little-known Tibetan Buddhist texts and practices. And a new awareness of and respect for Native American culture has accompanied mounting concern over ecological damage to the earth.

In addition to the surfacing of ancient wisdom, medical technology has inadvertently created a large group of modern-day mystics— people who have reported near-death experiences after being snatched back from the gates of the unknown. Their message is the same as mystics from both the East and the West—that the purpose of life is in learning how to give and receive love. Their philosophy becomes one of peace and lovingkindness, which is the measure of success in any religion or philosophy.

Pocketful of Miracles is a little bit like a spiritual supermarket in that it draws on the richness of all the world's spiritual traditions—from Judaism to Gnosticism, from the Cherokee wisdom fires to the life of Jesus, from Bahai to Islam, from Buddhism to Vedanta, from *A Course in Miracles* to the depth psychology of Carl Jung. It is my hope that this book will augment whatever your primary path may be, bringing your spiritual practice to life.

Twelve Gates to the Kingdom

There's an old spiritual that goes, "Three gates to the east; three gates to the west; three gates to the north; three gates to the south. Twelve gates to the city, halleluljah." These gates, I believe, are the twelve months of the year. The three months of spring comprise the Eastern Gate; the three months of summer the Southern Gate; the three months of fall the Western Gate; and the three months of winter the Northern Gate. The city to which they give access is the inner kingdom, the Spiritual Self, which is a direct reflection and extension of Divine Mind. As more and more people enter the gates of that inner city, our outer cities will come to mirror the peace within. Clearly, the time for inner and outer transformation is now. The seeds of peace are within each one of us and the season for their cultivation is at hand.

The most ancient spiritual wisdom was centered around the predictable shifts in seasonal energies. Rituals revolved around sowing, reaping and the cycles of light and darkness. The four cardinal points of the spiritual year were summer and winter solstice—the longest and shortest days of the year respectively— and spring and autumn equinox, when the hours of light and darkness are equal. Many of the Judeo-Christian holidays are variants of these more ancient earth-centered rituals. Hannukah and Christmas, both festivals of light, are outgrowths of winter solstice celebrations. Passover and Easter are celebrations of the annual resurrection of life that occurs at the spring equinox. Other important points on the Medicine Wheel of the year are the "cross-quarter days" midway between solstices and equinoxes: Imbolic in February, Beltane in May, Lammas in August and Samhain in November.

The seasonal rhythms correlate with our bodily rhythms. Women tend to menstruate on the full moon. Bears hibernate in the winter, and humans, too, put on an extra layer of fat as metabolism slows. Our dreamlife and inner life grow more insistent in the winter darkness, while the dramatic light of summer favors outward-directed activity. In the fall, the Western Gate of death and rebirth stands open. The Jewish high holy days, Yom Kippur and Rosh Hashanah, honor this energy of retrospection and completion. The old year is put to bed, one's business is finished, and the harvest of spiritual maturity is reaped as wisdom and forgiveness. In the spring we rejoice at the return of the light. We are freed from the prison of darkness, emerging from our winter dens with greater clarity, love and purpose.

The seasonal energies of earth and heaven are available to help us awaken from the ego's ancient sleep. These energies have been known from the beginning of time by a variety of names. Angels are one of those names.

A Mandala of Angels

Several years ago, I was researching Sabbath rituals with which to begin a women's weekend spiritual retreat. Quite unexpectedly, I unearthed an ancient Jewish meditation that involved an invocation of the angels. This meditation is delightfully similar to the Native American practice of calling upon the energies of the Four Directions.

In Cherokee tradition, the energies of the Four Directions are called Adawees, or great cosmic protectors. In Hebrew, the Adawees are known as the four archangels; Uriel, Gabriel, Raphael, and Michael. Although these names are often used for males, they are in fact genderless derivations of Hebrew words.

- *Uriel,* the Archangel of the East, means "Light (or fire) of God." This is the energy of clarity, rebirth and new beginnings. It is the seasonal gateway of spring.

- *Gabriel,* the Archangel of the South, means "Strength of God." This is the energy that supports overcoming fear, so that we can bring our divine purpose into manifestation. It is the seasonal gateway of summer.

- *Raphael,* the Archangel of the West, mean "Healer of God." This is the energy of death and rebirth, of transcending the opposites and coming to Wholeness. It is the seasonal gateway of fall.

- *Michael,* The Archangel of the North, means "How like unto God." This is the energy of wisdom and love. It is the seasonal gateway of winter.

In both Eastern and Western traditions, one faces East while praying or meditating. In this way, East (Uriel) is in front of you, South (Gabriel) is to your right, West (Raphael) is in back of you, and North (Michael) is to the left of you. In the Sabbath meditation in which I was first introduced to the Archangels, after invoking them on all four sides of the body temple, one then imagines the Light of God (the Shekhinah, or Divine Feminine Presence) above one's head. The Light washes over you and through you, revealing the light within your own heart. This second part of the meditation—the washing with light—is very similar to Tibetan Buddhist practice. In time, this Jewish/Buddhist/Native American meditation became an important part of my daily practice and was accompanied by a number of mystical experiences. I hope it will also become a tranformative aspect of your own daily practice. As you progress through the year with the the guidance of these archangelic presences, you will find them a constant source of support. I often feel that I am the center of a wheel, surrounded by the archangels on all sides, a part of a cosmic mandala.

In *Pocketful of Miracles,* each season is introduced by a mandala—a circular, geometric design—that captures the energy of the season in visual form. Mandalas are archetypes, or cosmic blueprints, for the Higher Self. They have been used for thousands of years, in both Eastern and Western traditions, as means for awakening. There is a famous mandala maze at Chartres Cathedral in France. One walks through the maze mindfully, while singing sacred music. The result is a parting of the clouds of confusion and fear that obscure the Higher Self. In Tibetan Buddhist tradition, mandalas are considered to be the vibrational fields of deities. In meditating upon them, one aligns with that sacred energy. Swiss psychiatrist and mystic Carl Jung discovered that when his patients created mandalas, they were often lifted out of depressed and fearful states into the peaceful connectedness of the Higher Self.

My husband, Miroslav—whose name literally means "celebration of peace"—found that peace and reclaimed his birth name in part through drawing mandalas. He created the four mandalas in this book using a technique that he learned from the artist Judith Cornell, called drawing from the light within. The images appear to come directly out of light or darkness, effectively transcending the polarity of darkness and light and leading to the experience of a higher unitive Source. They are a wonderful focus for open-eyed meditation.

A delightful synchronicity occurred during the time that Miroslav was creating the mandalas for this book and I was writing the text. As he sat drawing from the light within, and bringing forth the autumn mandala, the phone rang. It was Judith Cornell.

A MANDALA OF THE ANGELS

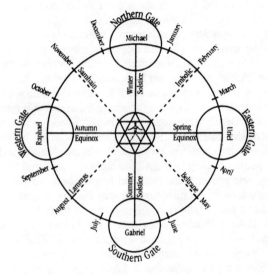

She knew of Miron's (the short form of Miroslav) interest in mandalas and wanted us to write the foreword for a book she was writing on creating mandalas from the light within! When Miron came upstairs to tell me about the synchronicity of her calling while he was using her technique to create the very mandalas she was writing about, I happened to be reading a part of Jung's autobiography that dealt with a synchronous experience he had while creating a mandala. Synchronicities are such a delight—little messages from the Universe that we're on the right track!

How to Use This Book

Each month contains daily lessons organized around a specific theme that is explored for the entire month. The daily lesson consists of two parts, a **seed thought** for contemplation and an accompanying **prayer or practice** that will help you *realize*, or internalize, the lesson so that it becomes part of you. Many days have instructions for bringing the lesson alive in daily life. Meditation, for example, is more than a brief harbor of peace in the busy stream of responsibilities; it is a way of perceiving and being part of the flow of life. The Tibetan Buddhist teacher Sogyal Rinpoche defines meditation as being spacious. Through practice it becomes progressively easier to let thoughts come and go like birds flying through the sky of clear mind. We become less prone to grab onto a stray thought that pulls us out of the spacious, peaceful present. Once we know how to maintain spaciousness in meditation, we can bring it into the rest of life. For example, when you're driving down the highway and a needless train of worried thinking grabs your attention, you can take a deep breath, let the thoughts go, and return to the peace of spacious awareness. Your life becomes a meditation.

In just this way, the thoughts and practices for each day are meant to become an integral part of how you live, helping you attain the miracle of shifting out of the ego's limitations and living instead in the infinite love and creativity of the Higher Self.

Pocketful of Miracles is different from most books of daily thoughts and prayers because the practices build on one another. The foundation practices taught in January cultivate the ability to use the breath as an aid to concentration and a means of shifting from the small mind of ego to the Big Mind of God. If you have had relatively little experience with meditation, it is best to begin with January even if you first pick up the book in October. You can then skip ahead to November, or whatever month it actually is, once you have completed the January practices. Since several different approaches to prayer and meditation are taught throughout the year, you may find reference to a practice that you have not yet learned, or have forgotten. In that case, refer to the section called Index of Spiritual Practices, and review the lesson in which the practice was first given. There is also an appendix of meditations at the end of the book.

January, February and March provide grounding in basic spiritual principles as well as a number of meditative practices. Beginning in April, the daily lessons become more substantial. If you are just beginning to explore spiritual principles, you may wish to read through the first three months' seed thoughts in addition to doing the January practices before beginning any of the other months.

Pocketful of Miracles is created as a lasting guide to spiritual practice that can be used year after year. As you change, your perception of the daily lessons will change, and the depth at which you experience the practices will also change. My hope is that this book will be a faithful companion for you, wherever you are along the way. Use it joyfully and gently. If you miss a day or a week or a month, so be it. If you do the practices in the morning and forget to apply them to the rest of the day, so be it. This book is not about perfection, but about the wholeness and graciousness that arise from an open heart. I offer it to you with great respect and love for who you are, and for your intention to nourish the seed of peace and awakening in this world.

—Joan Borysenko
Boulder, Colorado
Winter 1994

INDEX OF
SPIRITUAL PRACTICES

Each of these practices can also be found in the Appendix of
Meditation Practices at the end of the book.

MONTHLY THEMES

JANUARY: The Foundations of Spiritual Practice
FEBRUARY: Lovingkindness
MARCH: Courage
APRIL: Freedom: Moving from the Ego to the Higher Self
MAY: Gratitude and the Divine Feminine
JUNE: Miracles of Light: Prayer and Spiritual Healing
JULY: Creativity, Vision and Purpose
AUGUST: Spiritual Maturity
SEPTEMBER: Dreams, Intuition and the Inner Life
OCTOBER: Taking Stock
NOVEMBER: Grieving, Forgiveness and Completion
DECEMBER: Kindling the Light Within

NORTHERN GATE

Archangel Michael

WINTER

JANUARY

The Foundations of Spiritual Practice

The lessons and practices this month are designed to awaken the longing
within our hearts for reunion with Our Divine Beloved.
Through prayer, meditation and breath awareness we will set our
intention to
become aware of the limiting, fearful thoughts
that obscure our awareness of the Divine Presence,
and to transform them into fuel for awakening our hearts to love.
Having considered our ideas about God, we will move into the
experience of that Divine One through meditation, centering prayer and
an ancient practice called the egg of light.
We are not alone in our search for Divine Union.
The angels of night and morning are always by our sides.
The great Archangel Michael guides us Home to the heart of love.
This month we will begin working with Michael
and cooperating with the energies of the unseen worlds.
The darkness of winter beckons us inward so that
we may discover the seed of peace lying ready within our hearts.
Hear the words of the Ancient Ones as they echo through the
long winter nights:

Brother Bear is in his den,
re-creating in the Earth Mother's womb.
The Medicine Wheel
is fully open
to the Northern Gate.
Archangel Michael
instructs us in the foundation
practices through which
we will realize our
birthright
of
Divine Wisdom
and Love.

Seed Thought

You have known us, Divine One, since before the foundation of the world. You are closer than hands and feet. Truly, as it is said, in You we live and move and have our being. Yet so often we feel alone, like strangers in a strange land. Although the mind may forget its Divine birth the heart yearns ceaselessly to remember.

Prayer/Practice

Divine Spirit, thank you for the gift of a new day and for awakening my mind that it may follow the longing of my heart. This month I ask for the help of Michael, whose name means Like unto God, in remembering that I am a part of the mind of God, and therefore a part of All. May I see You in the sky and in the clouds. May I see You in the frozen waters. May I see You in the darkness as my soul rests and grows in winter's quiet womb. May I learn to live in the present where You are.

Close your eyes and take a deep breath. Become aware of the stillness deep within you and affirm,

My Divine Beloved and I are One.

Repeat this practice two or three times today.

January 2

Seed Thought

A drop of water can never be separate from the vast ocean which is its mother. For even as the drop circulates through clouds and plants and the cells of human beings, bringing the blessing of life to many forms, it will reunite one day with its Source, the great ocean of Love that creates and sustain the wholeness of life.

Prayer/Practice

Divine Spirit, thank you for the gift of life made new this morning and for awakening my mind today so that I can deeply appreciate how every person, every tree, every drop of water is the perfect expression of Your love in action. Throughout this day help me remember to see every object with new eyes and affirm,

"This chair, this cloud, this person, this—is the creative energy, the mind of God, in form."

Repeat this awareness two or three times today.

January 3

Seed Thought

"Be still and thou shalt know God" is one of the oldest mainstays of spiritual wisdom. Stillness is always right there inside us, only a breath away. There is sanctuary within, available twenty-four hours a day.

Prayer/Practice

Great Spirit, thank you for the gift of life and renewal that is always available to me and within me. Sometimes my mind is so turbulent that I forget about the silent place of healing within. Please help me remember to keep letting go of mental turmoil so that I may enter the inner sanctuary where Your healing presence dwells.

Several times today take a deep breath, let go and enter the place of inner stillness.

January 4

Seed Thought

The breath is the lifeforce itself, the holy spirit that binds us to the mind of God. Known as Ruach in Hebrew and Pneuma in Greek, the breath controls the winds of our energy body and the activity of our minds. Control of breath is the cornerstone for health and for letting go of our small mind and entering the Big Mind of God.

Prayer/Practice

Every breath is a form of prayer. Become aware of your breathing now. Is it shallow and irregular or deep and slow? Take a big breath in and let it go slowly, like a sigh of relief. Let the next breath come in slowly and feel how your belly expands. When you exhale, feel how your belly relaxes. As you breathe diaphragmatically from your belly, notice how both mind and body come to rest.

Several times today remember to take a letting-go breath and shift your awareness to belly breathing for a minute or two.

January 5

Seed Thought

Awareness of breath is the cornerstone for developing control of the bodymind. When breath is shallow and fast, body responds with an increase in heart rate, blood pressure and fear hormones. Mind responds with fantasies of loneliness, unworthiness and negativity. When breath is long and slow, body becomes peaceful and relaxed. Mind stops churning and comes to rest in its own true nature, the Big Mind of God.

Prayer/Practice

Great Spirit, thank you for making me new this morning and for increasing my attention to breath, body and mind. Help me form the habit of noticing the quality of my breathing throughout the day, shifting to belly breathing as often as I can. Help me let go of fear by control of my breath so that I might rest in the peace of Your Mind, which is the true nature of my own mind.

Several times today, notice the quality of your breathing. Shift to belly breathing as often as you can, repeating "Letting go of small mind" on the inbreath and "I am one with Big Mind" on the outbreath.

January 6: Epiphany

Seed Thought

Control of the mind requires concentration and awareness. Breath is the key to learning these skills. Learning to let go of small mind and entering the presence of Big Mind is called meditation. Breath and mind control are the basis of meditative awareness. The first step in exiting small mind and entering God's Presence (Big Mind) is developing the ability to concentrate.

Prayer/Practice

Take a letting-go breath, a big sigh of relief. Now shift to belly breathing. One the next outbreath, mentally concentrate on the number four. One the next outbreath, three, then two and one on successive outbreaths. Start counting down from four again and continue for five minutes. Whenever thoughts come to mind, just notice them and let them go as soon as possible, returning your attention to breathing and counting.

Repeat this exercise two or three times today.

January 7

Seed Thought

The nature of the mind is to think and create, so the mind naturally wanders during meditation. The demoralizing thought that only *your* mind wanders while other meditators are sitting there in bliss is a major reason why people give up meditation practice. All people think when they meditate. What distinguishes the novice from the skillful meditator is the attitude of detached awareness that the skillful meditator maintains toward thinking.

Prayer/Practice

Great Spirit, thank you for a new day and a new beginning. Help me adopt a healthy attitude toward my wandering mind during meditation, smiling at its antics like a loving mother, while firmly bringing it back to the object of concentration.

Practice concentration on breathing and counting for five minutes, as in yesterday's practice. Repeating this exercise two or three times daily for a week will strengthen your concentration tremendously.

January 8

Seed Thought

Meditation is a form of mental martial arts. If we resist thoughts they will overpower us. But if we just step lightly out of their way, letting them come and go like birds flying overhead, we can use their energy to further focus our minds.

Prayer/Practice

Take a big letting-go breath and take up concentration on breathing and counting, as in the last few days' practice. Let part of your awareness watch for thoughts, and when they arise just let them subside, continuing to focus on breathing and counting. Continue for five minutes and repeat once or twice more during the day.

January 9

Seed Thought

Mind and body are so intimately related that they form a bodymind unit. When the body is relaxed, the mind slows down. When the mind slows down, the body relaxes. Before meditation and throughout the day, remembering to stretch the body allows the mind to be spacious.

Prayer/Practice

Before prayer and meditation, and throughout the day when you feel stressed or fatigued, take a moment to stretch. Inhale and gently stretch back, then exhale and round your back forward, dropping your chin to your chest. Inhale and stretch your arms above your head, then exhale and let them float down as though you were making a snow angel. Gently move your head from side to side, then drop it front to back. Stretch your face with a big yawn.

Take a good letting-go breath and meditate for five or more minutes. Notice how your body feels two or three times today. Then stretch, and observe how your body and mind respond to your attention.

January 10

Seed Thought

Centering prayer is a form of meditation that is a conscious letting go of small mind and its continuous self-centered fantasies. In this form of prayer, popularized by Father Thomas Keating, we shift awareness away from the thoughts that Keating compares to boats floating down the river of consciousness to the river itself. The river is Big Mind, Divine Presence.

Prayer/Practice

Focus your mind by counting back from four to one on successive outbreaths. Continue for two or three minutes. Now let go of counting and let your awareness focus on the feelings of peace and tranquility that naturally arise as small mind quiets down. When you begin to think, mentally repeat a word or phrase of your choice—a prayer word. Thank you, peace, shalom, Kyrie Eleison . . . are examples of prayer words. As soon as your mind quiets down again, let go of the word. Your intention is just to sit quietly in the peace of God's Presence. Continue for a long as you like.

January 11

Seed Thought

The mind can be either our staunchest ally or our greatest enemy.
If we learn to control the mind, practicing the art of staying present,
then the Divine Presence reveals itself in each moment as peace,
beauty, insight and joy. If the mind controls us, we are at the
mercy of our imagination and out of conscious contact with God's
Presence.

Prayer/Practice

*Take a few letting-go breaths and remember a time when you
felt present in the moment—absorbed in a sunset, marveling
at fresh-fallen snow, enchanted by the smile of a baby. . . . Enter
the memory with all your senses . . . remember the sights and
colors, the smells, the position and movement of your body, the
emotional or felt sense. . . . Now let the memory go and
meditate for a few minutes on what remains—the stillness and
joy of your awareness of God's Presence. Every moment that
you are in the present is a holy moment.*

January 12

Seed Thought

John Milton wrote that "The mind is its own place, and in itself can make a Heav'n of Hell, a Hell of Heav'n." Living in heaven or hell is a choice that we make moment by moment, depending on how we use our minds. Choosing the present is a choice for the love and peace of heaven. *Choosing to dwell in past and future fears opens the doors of the mind to an internal hell.*

Prayer/Practice

Great Spirit of love and wisdom, thank you for a new day and for the deepening awareness of how I use my mind. I gratefully accept Your help today, and the help of Michael and the angels of awareness, in reminding me to notice where my mind is and to make the consistent effort to bring it back to the heaven of the present moment.

Practice a few minutes of centering prayer as learned on January 10. Remembering a holy moment as we did yesterday is a good way to enter the stillness of centering prayer.

January 13

Seed Thought

Every moment is a holy moment if we are present in it. Peace and stillness, love and wisdom, joy and creativity are the fruits of the present. Fear and negativity exist outside the now and naturally disappear when we realize that now is the only moment that really exists.

Prayer/Practice

Divine Beloved, thank you for the indescribable gift of life, of consciousness, of creativity. Thank you for sharing your Mind with me. Please help me to appreciate life, to remember You, to serve others by increasing my motivation to learn the ancient practice of the Present Moment.

Several times today stop and take a letting-go breath, bringing your mind to focus. Enter the moment with all your senses, taking time to fully taste and smell, hear and see, feel and move. Be as aware as a panther stalking her dinner.

January 14

Seed Thought

What am I doing on earth, so far from Home? I can no longer remember the bright fields from which I came, except in dreams. And even these I forget upon awakening. My heart's desire is to awaken from the dream of this life, in this life, that I may rejoice in the Divine Union here and now. I am ready to wake up now.

Prayer/Practice

Divine Spirit, thank you for a new day. Just as I awakened this morning from the dreams of night, please help me awaken from the dreams of the day that keep me separate from You. Today, each time I find my mind dwelling on worries of the past and future, let me pray,

I am ready to wake up now. Heaven is right here, in this moment.

Then take a letting-go breath and switch from the worried small mind to the loving, spacious presence of Big Mind. Stay aware and awake!

January 15

Seed Thought

Developing awareness and waking up from the dreams of small
mind so that we can enter the wise and loving ocean of Big
Mind requires the intention to do so. A strong intention is the single
most important requirement to bring about growth and change,
because intention provides the energy that motivates our continuing
efforts.

Prayer/Practice

Great Spirit, I come to you this morning with gratitude for the
intention to awaken and become one with Your compassionate heart.
Thank you for strengthening my motivation for love and service
both through the sweet revelations you bring and through the
suffering and difficulties that make me search for a better way to
live.

*Spend a few minutes in centering prayer, for there is no better
motivation to seek God's Presence than a taste of the peace, stillness
and love of the Divine.*

January 16

Seed Thought

A woman told me about a near-death experience she had when she was a child. After she left her body, traveled through a long tunnel and was surrounded and washed clean by the Great Light of God, a Being of Light took her on a tour of the Other Side. At one point she saw a gray room full of depressed, lonely souls. All around them were Beings of Light, who, she was told, were ready to help but could do nothing unless they were asked, because our freewill is inviolable.

Prayer/Practice

Divine Beloved, thank you for the incredible universe you have created to bring us into the fullness of Your Mind that we may become true helpmates, growing edges of Divine Consciousness. I am particularly thankful for the help that is always available to me from the angels, the beings of light, and I pray to become more aware of them and to learn how to ask for their help.

January 17

Seed Thought

There are four Archangels available to help us at all times. In addition, during different seasons of the year, our energy fields are particularly attuned to the awareness of different angels. Michael, who is often represented wearing robes of snow, is the archangel of winter, the guardian of the Northern Gate on the Great Medicine Wheel of the yearly cycle.

Prayer/Practice

Great Spirit, thank you for the gift of life on this midwinter morning. May the frozen lakes of the north be mirrors for my soul, so that I can see myself more clearly, letting go of old habits of mind that keep me out of conscious contact with You. I call upon the Archangel Michael—angel of wisdom and love—to be with me throughout the day and to help me awaken to the love that is my own true nature.

Two or three times today, take a deep breath and enter the moment with mindful awareness. Call upon the Archangel Michael to help you sense the beauty of the world.

January 18

Seed Thought

We are never alone. The angels are always present as helpers for our evolution and awakening. Michael, as the embodiment of love and wisdom, is particularly helpful when you need insight on a particular issue or when your heart feels closed and you need a little help opening it back up again.

Prayer/Practice

Take several letting-go breaths until you feel your bodymind becoming more still and focused. Place your awareness to your left—the North side of your body temple—and ask to feel the loving presence of Michael. Be patient, and whether you are aware of that Presence now or in six months from now, don't doubt that it's there.

Throughout the day, when you become aware that your heart is closed, ask for Michael's help in opening it up.

January 19

Seed Thought

Angelic beings are always around us, ready to help us awaken so that we can dwell in God's Mind and attune to the bigger picture of God's Will—the Divine Plan. They repeatedly try to get our attention by focusing loving energy on us throughout the day, the angelic equivalent of grabbing someone's arm and saying, "Look at that. It's important. Pay attention!"

Prayer/Practice

Great Spirit, thank you for opening my senses, both physical and subtle, to a greater awareness of your Presence and the Presence of your angelic helpers. Michael, I am ready to open my heart and mind to the help of the Beings of Light. Please help attune me to these messages throughout the day.

Take several letting-go breaths and when you begin to feel yourself coming to a relaxed, still focus, place your attention on your left, the North side of the body. Welcome Michael's Presence and ask for what you need. Spend a few minutes in meditation.

January 20

Seed Thought

We can deepen our spiritual practice by forming a more personal relationship with God. This puts us face to face with the mystical paradox that God is both an impersonal, mysterious force present everywhere and at the same time a personal, exquisitely intimate friend, lover and guide to each soul.

Prayer/Practice

Contemplate your relationship to God. In what form or aspect do you know the Sacred Mystery? Can you best relate to God as Mother and Father, or through Buddha or Allah, Mary or Shiva, Tara or Innana, Great Spirit, The Light, The nameless and formless One, Shakti or Ishwara, Ram or the Void, Jesus or Jehovah? Like the facets of a jewel, each aspect of the Divine is a perfect expression of the Whole. Which aspect are you drawn to?

January 21

Seed Thought

God is one of the most loaded words in the English language. It has often served as a screen for our projections of fear, inadequacy and intolerance. A mature spirituality grows most easily when old ideas about God are examined, and thrown out if found lacking. Any idea of God that is less than loving, merciful, forgiving, tolerant and nurturing is a reflection of small mind and its fears. God is like the perfect mother, always interested in our growth and wellbeing.

Prayer/Practice

Great Spirit, thank you for the new day and for the deepening relationship with You. Help me reach beyond any limitations of mind that separate me from accepting the ceaseless flow of your love. Archangel Michael, spirit of love and wisdom, please help me develop a more personal relationship with God. Throughout the day help me remember to stop, breathe and pray.

Come to me, Divine Beloved.
Reveal your sweetness to me.

Spend a few minutes in centering prayer to strengthen your awareness of God's Presence.

January 22

Seed Thought

My mind takes the shape of whatever it dwells upon. And my body conforms to that mold. When my mind is fearful and grasping my body is tense and exhausted and it is hard to let go and feel God's love. Old habits of mind overwhelm me, and once again I feel separate and alone. If I learn to rest in the Divine Presence, my body will take the shape of a perfect smile.

Prayer/Practice

In the space before you, imagine whatever form of the Divine you relate to most easily. Feel streams of Divine Love and Light flowing down over you and washing though your body, carrying away any fatigue, fear, or negativity. As all the darkness washes out of the bottoms of your feet, imagine that the light in your heart shines more and more brightly, filling you and extending around you like an egg. Allow the egg of light that you are to merge and become one with Light of the Divine Presence. Rest for a few minutes in that Presence.

Two or three times today, surround yourself with the egg of light, think of your Divine Beloved and affirm, "I am one with thee."

January 23

Seed Thought

Things that we think of as solid are actually comprised mostly of space. The distance between the atoms in our body is like the distance between the earth and the sun. We are mostly space traversed by streams of energy. Our real body is made of light. That light radiates outward and affects things around us. In turn, we are affected by the light of others.

Prayer/Practice

Imagine whatever personal form of the Divine you are working with as above your head and slightly in front of you. Feel the light of the Divine radiating down over you and running through you, washing you clean of any negativity and revealing the light within your heart. Feel that light expanding around you, merging with the Divine light, and encasing you in a cosmic egg of protection. Affirm that only loving thoughts can be released from your egg of light, or penetrate it from the outside.

During the day, whenever you feel lonely or afraid, surround yourself with the egg of light and call upon Michael for help.

January 24

Seed Thought

Because there is only One Mind in which we are all joined, the thoughts of other people affect us whether we are aware of them or not. Likewise, we affect other people with our thoughts of them. It is important to be aware of our thoughts so that we can eliminate judgment and anger and increase thoughts of encouragement and love.

Prayer/Practice

Divine Beloved, thank you for this new day and for my growing awareness of the power of mind. Help me to use my mind lovingly, both in thoughts about myself and in the thoughts I send out toward others.

Meditate on the Divine Beloved and place yourself in the egg of light. Affirm your intent to send forth thoughts of love and encouragement to all those whom you meet or think about today. Be aware of your thoughts today. When judgmental or fearful thoughts come up, let them go. If it's hard to do that, place yourself in the egg of light and ask the Archangel Michael to wash you clean of old patterns of judgment and fear.

January 25

Seed Thought

Everything in the Universe has its own song. A chorus of frogs. The wind in the trees. Songs inspire the soul to remember how to love. Ave Maria opens the heart to compassion. Kyrie Eleison awakens forgiveness. Shalom Aleichem beckons the tired soul to rest. Om restores harmony and unity. Music is a powerful connection to our Source.

Prayer/Practice

Think of a song or a chant that inspires you, awes you or opens your heart. Play or sing it until your body responds with peace, love, compassion, gratitude or devotion. Sit quietly in the feelings that the music evoked. Conclude by placing yourself in the egg of light and affirming your intent to send thoughts of love to all those you meet in person or in mind today. Feel the Presence of Michael to your left and ask for whatever help you need in being loving.

January 26

Seed Thought

If loving thoughts are expressions of God's creative energy, so also are negative thoughts. It is easy to find Union with God through love. But how hard it is to see the Divine in anger, jealousy or fear. Yet God must be there, too, for there is nowhere the Divine Presence is not. We can use the intense energy of painful emotions to impassion our desire to live in God's Presence and attune to the Divine Will.

Prayer/Practice

Divine Spirit, thank you for the gift of a new morning, a new body and a new mind. Thank you for helping me transform the creative energy locked in negative emotions into fuel for the fire of my love for You. Each time I feel the passion of painful emotions today I can call upon the Archangel Michael for assistance and offer my pain to You, praying:

Divine Beloved, take the fire burning in my heart and transform it to the Fire of Love for You.

Then take a letting-go breath and switch out of small mind into the Present-centered awareness of Big Mind.

January 27

Seed Thought

We learn to transmute negativity by recognizing that all thoughts
of fear and separation are the Heart calling out to remember its Divine
Beloved. Every thought of separation—guilt, anger, sadness or fear,
blame, judgment or hopelessness can be reframed as reminders
to *stop* and remember our Oneness with the Divine Source.

Prayer/Practice

Divine Beloved, thank you for the gift of a new day and for the
awareness that every thought of separation is a call from my Heart to
remember You. Every time I feel out of the moment, out of the
flow, I will call upon the presence of Michael, the archangel of
love and wisdom, and affirm,

I am One with the Heart of Love.

*Then take a letting-go breath and find the still center within you,
expanding your attention to everything around you and
practicing mindful awareness of the present moment.*

January 28

Seed Thought

How shall we come home to You and rest in the peace and love of
Divine Mind? In the Torah it is written that we can remember You by
writing Your Name on the doorposts of our house and on our gates.
By thinking of You when we come into our homes and when
we go out. How often we forget you, Divine Beloved.

Prayer/Practice

Great Spirit, thank you for the new day and for helping me to
remember You as I come and go, playing my role in the drama that
You have created for the growth of my soul. I call upon the help
of Michael and the heavenly hosts in reminding me to practice
being in your Presence through awareness of my comings and goings
today, affirming each time:

*"Thank you, God, for my safe arrival (or departure). I am going
about your business."*

January 29

Seed Thought

The autistic eleven-year-old child of a friend of ours told her parents that the first lesson in spiritual growth was to remember God every hour. A few days later she told them they were ready for the second lesson. Remember God every hour.

Prayer/Practice

Divine Beloved, thank you for this new morning and for the spiritual longing that opens my heart even more to You. Today, help me to remember You at every coming and going, and every time I (choose a cue like looking at your watch). Michael, great angel of wisdom and love, please help me remember the loving Source in which I live and move and have my being.

January 30

Seed Thought

A resplendent angel guards the gate of the night and yet another the gate of the morning. Before sleep you can call upon the angel of night to help you retrospect your day, offering thanks for the wisdom gained and the things you learned from your mistakes. Upon arising you can call upon the angel of day to help you remember that every thing you do and every thought you think is an act of service to others and a reflection and extension of God's love.

Prayer/Practice

This morning, reflect on your upcoming day, thinking of the opportunities that will present themselves for you to be of service in little as well as in larger ways. Think of the difference you can make with a smile, an extra moment or a kind word. Call upon the angels to help you remember God moment by moment, for that is the greatest motivation to loving service. Spend a few minutes in centering prayer.

January 31

Seed Thought

Shakespeare said, "Pretend a virtue if you have it not." Most of us are still locked up in the petty, self-centered concerns of our egos. Nonetheless we feel the ancient longing of our soul to move beyond ego to union with the Divine. It doesn't matter if our motivation for Divine union falters, or if selfish concerns predominate. If we just pretend the virtue of longing for God and being of service to others, eventually those virtues will arise spontaneously. As my husband puts it, "Fake it till you make it."

Prayer/Practice

Divine Beloved, thank you for the light of morning and another day to learn, to love and to grow. Whether I am aware of the fire of love in my heart, or whether my spirit feels cold and lifeless, let me continue to practice loving You and being of service. I call upon Michael and all the Heavenly Host to help me internalize these ideals so that they will become as familiar as the air I breathe.

Spend a few minutes in the egg of light or in centering prayer strengthening your awareness of the Divine Presence.
Throughout the day, call upon Michael for help in becoming "Like unto God"—the Hebrew meaning of Michael.

FEBRUARY

Lovingkindness

The lessons and practices of February comprise the Way of the Heart.
Jesus, and the line of rabbis from which he came,
summarized the spiritual life with elegant simplicity.
"Love the Lord Thy God with all thy heart, with all
thy soul and with all thy mind, and love thy neighbor as thyself."
A precious thought that is easier said than done.
This month we will deepen the doing.
Through ancient meditations including the Buddhist practice of
Metta, or lovingkindness,
through awareness and owning of our projections,
through the help of the angelic realm,
and through our intention to love and serve,
we will remember how to open our hearts
and let go of the poison of self-hatred that keeps
our souls in bondage.
In this way we will restore our place in the Great Web of Life
that we may treat the earth and all her children
with the greatest respect and love.
February is the perfect time for the flowering of compassion.
Listen to the voices of the Ancient Ones as they penetrate
the winter stillness:

The seeds are beginning to stir
in the dark womb of the Earth Mother.
Days grow longer and Brother Bear stretches
in his den.
As our hearts likewise stir
and open in love and wisdom,
Archangel Michael
and the energies of the North
support us
in the practices of
lovingkindness
and the birth
of
compassion.

February 1

Seed Thought

In the wintery darkness of February, new growth is beginning to stir beneath the frozen ground. Just as plants grow in the darkness, unnoticed, so do our souls continue to grow, even though we may not see the progress day by day. One day we will awaken, and our leaves will lift out of the darkness and touch the sky.

Prayer/Practice

Divine Beloved, thank you for the start of a new month, a new day and a new morning. Each day I awaken a new person, different from the day before, yet often I cannot see the changes. I call upon Michael and the legions of Love to help me see myself rightly, as a being who is growing and flowering in my own season.

Spend a few minutes in centering prayer and then contemplate the rightness of how you are unfolding.

When thoughts of self-doubt or self-criticism arise during the day, take a letting-go breath and call upon Michael for help in seeing the rightness of your growth and of your being.

February 2: Imbolic or Candelmas Day

Seed Thought

Today is a cross-quarter day, halfway between the winter solstice and the spring equinox. The sun is becoming an ever greater presence; the days are growing longer. The seeds beneath the earth are struggling to break their shells, and the Godseed within our hearts is likewise swelling and reaching for the light.

Prayer/Practice

Take a deep breath and let go into the inner stillness. Imagine that you are a seed, nestled in the womb of mother earth. Feel the stirring of life within your heart and the gentle opening of the heart's protective coat. You are starting a new cycle of growth. Give thanks to Michael, ever present on the North side of your body temple, and to the Divine Beloved.

February 3

Seed Thought

The images in our minds create the reality in which we live. If we imagine ourselves as hard-hearted, stuck or unforgiving, then small mind closes like a fist around that image. If we imagine ourselves as caring, compassionate and open-hearted, then we invite the Big Mind of God to fill that form. The old adage "Charity begins at home" means that we need to have a loving, growing image of ourselves.

Prayer/Practice

Divine Beloved, thank you for this new morning and the new growth upon the earth and within myself. Please help me open my heart to myself so that the Godseed within can grow into a worthy offshoot of You.

Imagine the Divine One in the space directly above you and in front of you. Feel streams of nurturing love in the form of Light cascading over you and washing though you. Let the Light of God wash away any darkness around your heart, revealing the Light within your heart—the Godseed—in radiant brightness. Give thanks that the Divine Consciousness dwells within you, and pledge to nurture that Godseed with kindness and love.

When thoughts of self-judgment arise during the day, feel the light of the Divine One wash over you and through you, watering the radiant Godseed in your heart.

February 4

Seed Thought

Open-heartedness is a physical feeling as well as an attitude. Since the bodymind is one whole, whenever we create the physical sensation of open-heartedness our thoughts automatically shift to reflect the body's reality.

Prayer/Practice

Great Spirit of Love and Wisdom, I come before you this morning grateful for a new beginning in opening my heart, that I may truly reflect your compassion, creativity and blessing in all my relationships.

Close your eyes, take a few letting-go breaths and go to the place of inner stillness. Now go back to your storehouse of special memories, choosing one in which your heart opened—whether to the beauty of a flower, the sound of music, the birth of a child, a moment of love or forgiveness . . . bring all your senses to the memory, recalling the sights . . . the sounds . . . the fragrances . . . the movements of your body and the physical/ emotional sense of your heart opening. Meditate on the sense of open-heartedness for a few minutes.

During the day, whenever your heart feels closed, bring back the memory or just the feeling of your heart opening.

February 5

Seed Thought

It is natural for the heart to open and close rhythmically like the petals of a flower, many times throughout the day. The times when we are most aware of the heart opening is when it has been closed. The opening is like a gift of grace, a moment of heightened awareness when we lift out of small mind and soar in the limitless sky of the Big Mind of God.

Prayer/Practice

For today, dedicate yourself to an awareness of whether your heart feels open or closed. Periodically, at intervals you select (perhaps before each meal, snack or drink), notice whether or not your heart is open. If it feels closed, call upon the Archangel Michael to help you open it and then pause to take a few deep breaths and bring back a memory of a time that it was open, as we did in yesterday's practice. It is important not to be attached to the results—your heart may or may not feel open. The important thing is the awareness you bring to the exercise.

February 6

Seed Thought

It is often easier to open our hearts to nature, animals, children or other people than it is to ourselves. From the time of birth most of us have been bombarded with messages from parents, teachers, peers, clergy, ads and the media about how we have to look, act and feel in order to measure up. Our heart gradually hardens against ourselves, and we enter a vicious cycle of self-judgment and the projections of those judgments onto others.

Prayer/Practice

Divine Beloved, I come into Your Presence with gratitude and a humble heart. I have so much to learn about love and compassion. With the help of Michael and his angels of awareness, I ask that I become mindful today of the self-judgments I inflict on myself that keep the Godseed within from sprouting. I sincerely ask Your forgiveness for indulging in the poison of self-hatred which keeps us apart.

Spend a few minutes in the egg of light. Allow the light of the Divine Beloved to envelop you the way a mother holds her newborn child.

February 7

Seed Thought

Eliminating the mind-habit of self-hatred is a prerequisite for
spiritual growth. Swami Vivekananda, who brought Vedanta to the West
at the first world parliament of religions in 1893, said, "Our first
duty is not to hate ourselves."

Prayer/Practice

*Today, make a commitment to become aware of self-judging,
self-hating thoughts. Awareness is the first step to change.
Whenever you catch yourself indulging in self-abusive thinking,
immediately pray, "Dear God, I'm so sorry for turning my
back on you. Please let the rays of your Divine Love wash away
the pain and ignorance that keeps me separate from my own
heart's light, the Godseed within."*

February 8

Seed Thought

Our mind is like a field in which many seeds germinate. Some of these seeds are blown in by the wind. Other seeds are deliberately planted. We must become good stewards of our mental garden, weeding out seeds of self-hatred and planting and nurturing seeds of self-love.

Prayer/Practice

Great Spirit, I enter the garden of your Divine Mind this morning with a greater awareness of my responsibility to love myself so that I will truly be able to love others. I need your help and the help of Michael and the angels of the awareness of love's presence to plant and nurture the seeds of self-love that will bloom into compassionate action on behalf of all beings.

Spend a few minutes in the egg of light, bathing yourself in God's love and in the love that emanates from your own heart more each day as the mind-habits of ignorance are dissolved, revealing the light of your own true nature.

February 9

Seed Thought

If we are thinking self-denigrating thoughts, then by definition we
are trapped in the ego, in small mind. The tendency of small
mind is then to become self-critical of our self-criticism: "There I
go again, putting myself down. I'm a hopeless case." This vicious cycle
can be broken with the awareness that every self-judgment is actually
a request from your soul for love.

Prayer/Practice

*Take a few letting-go breaths and settle into the inner silence.
Bring a heart-opening memory to mind, entering into it with
all your senses. Give thanks to God that you are remembering
the Divine Presence within you and around you more each
day.*

*Today, each time you catch yourself in self-judgment, affirm,
"Oh, my soul, I hear your call for love. I'm sorry for forgetting you
and obstructing your awareness of God's Presence."*

February 10

Seed Thought

When the ancient Jewish rabbis were asked to sum up the spiritual path, they replied, "Love the Lord Thy God with all thy heart, with all thy soul and with all thy mind and love thy neighbor as thyself." Jesus was one of the greatest rabbis of all time, and when asked what the most important of his teachings was he replied, "Love the Lord Thy God with all thy heart, with all thy soul and with all thy mind and love thy neighbor as thyself."

Prayer/Practice

Divine Beloved, I come to you made new this morning, bathed in Your sweet Presence. Teach me to live by the wisdom of the rabbis, the teachers, the Great Ones like Jesus who have realized their unity with you and claimed their sonship and daughtership by living the mystery of love.

Take a few letting-go breaths and place your awareness on your left side, the Northern Gate of the energy field that surrounds your body. Ask for the help of Michael in realizing deeply the meaning of Jesus' and his predecessors' words. Contemplate what it would mean to love the Lord thy God with all your heart, with all your soul and with all your mind and to love your neighbor as yourself. Put your realizations into action as you go through the day.

February 11

Seed Thought

The Buddha, which means "the Awakened One," left a road map,
a set of spiritual practices that are the fulfillment of the Judeo-
Christian principle, "Love the Lord Thy God with all thy heart, with
all thy soul and with all thy mind and love thy neighbor as thyself."
One of these is called *Metta*, or lovingkindness meditation.

Prayer/Practice

*Begin by taking a few letting-go breaths and then enter the inner
sanctuary of stillness. Imagine the light and love of the Divine
Beloved pouring over you and washing through you, revealing
the purity of your own heart, extending beyond you and
merging with the Divine Light. See yourself totally enclosed in the
egg of light, and then repeat these lovingkindness blessings
for yourself:*

May I be at peace, May my heart remain open,
May I awaken to the light of my own true nature,
May I be healed, May I be a source of healing for all beings.

*Repeat these blessings for yourself anytime during the day when
you feel alone, afraid or out of touch with the Light within.*

February 12

Seed Thought

We can only love others to the degree that we have opened our hearts to ourselves. It is not selfish to bless ourselves first, because if our heart remains closed we have nothing to give. The most selfless prayer is to awaken so that we can serve others and help alleviate the suffering that comes from ignorance of our unity with the Big Mind of God.

Prayer/Practice

The second step of Metta extends blessings to our loved ones. Repeat yesterday's practice of wishing the lovingkindness blessings for yourself, and then bring a loved one to mind. See them in as much detail as possible, imagining the Light of God shining down on them and washing through them, revealing the light—the Godseed—within their heart. See this light grow brighter, merging with the light of God and enclosing them in the egg of light. Then bless them:

May you be at peace, May your heart remain open, May you awaken to the light of your own true nature, May you be healed, May you be a source of healing for all beings.

Repeat this for as many people as you wish. If worried thoughts about loved ones occur during the day, take a minute to send them a lovingkindness blessing rather than a fearful thought.

February 13

Seed Thought

"Love thy neighbor as thyself" is an unqualified statement. It doesn't say love your good neighbors and your best friends. To love our neighbor is to extend the wish for enlightenment to everyone, including those we might hold in judgment or think of as our enemies.

Prayer/Practice

The third step of Metta extends blessings to those who might be a little or a lot hard to love. Start with those who are just a little hard to love, rather than invoking your archenemy. Easy does it!

Place yourself in the egg of light and repeat the lovingkindness blessings for yourself as given on February 11. Place one or more loved ones in the egg of light and repeat the blessings for them given on February 12. Place someone that you have some problems with in the egg of light, and see the light washing away all their negativity and illusion, just as it did for you. Bless them:

May you be at peace, May your heart remain open,
May you awaken to the light of your own true nature,
May you be healed, May you be a source of healing for all beings.

If judgmental thoughts about others occur during the day, take a minute to send lovingkindness blessings first to yourself, and then to them.

February 14: Valentine's Day

Seed Thought

All around the world there are people in need of love. Rather than feel helpless about their plight, we can take action on two levels. On the outer level we can be socially and politically active, give money to alleviate suffering, and teach tolerance and respect to our children. On the inner level, we can extend our practice of *Metta* to neighborhoods, cities, countries, all the people with AIDS or cancer, or any group of people that our heart reaches out to.

Prayer/Practice

Place yourself in the egg of light and practice Metta for yourself, for your loved ones and for the "petty tyrants" in your life. Now think of a group of people that your heart really goes out to and repeat the blessings for them:

May you be at peace, May your heart remain open,
May you awaken to the light of your own true nature,
May you be healed, May you be a source of healing for all beings.

Happy Valentine's Day! You have learned several practices for opening the heart. Remember to use them today.

February 15

Seed Thought

Our precious planet is at a time of transition, a dark night in our collective soul when old structures are crumbling and new structures have yet to be born. This transition time is a moment of great danger if world consciousness is overtaken by fear, and great opportunity if the thought-form of love predominates. Practicing Metta for our world can help the birth of a more compassionate consciousness on earth.

Prayer/Practice

Place yourself in the egg of light and repeat the lovingkindness blessings of January 11 for yourself, continuing with as many of the other steps of Metta as you wish, and ending by imagining our beautiful planet enveloped in light—the green continents, the blue waters, the white polar caps. The two-leggeds and four-leggeds, the fish that swim and the birds that fly. Bless all:

May there be peace on earth, May the hearts of all people be open to themselves and to each other, May all people awaken to the light of their own true nature, May all creation be blessed and be a blessing to All That Is.

February 16: The Day of Buddha's Awakening

Seed Thought

Jesus used the metaphor "My father's house has many mansions" to refer to the different realms of existence in which our souls sojourn while gaining the love and wisdom needed to unite with Big Mind that we may align ourselves with Divine Will and become fully awakened co-creators. The last step of *Metta* extends our blessings to all beings on all planes of existence. It can also be used at the end of any period of prayer, study or meditation to dedicate the merits of our practice for the enlightenment of all.

Prayer/Practice

The following dedication is modified from traditional Buddhist practice as taught by the Tibetan Lama Sogyal Rinpoche:

First, practice whatever components of Metta you wish to this morning, remembering that the practice always begins with yourself. When you are finished, add:

By the power and the truth of this practice
May all beings have happiness and the causes of happiness
May all beings be free from sorrow and the causes of sorrow
And may all live in equanimity without too much attachment
    and too much aversion
And live believing in the equality of all that lives.

February 17

Seed Thought

Practicing kindness toward ourselves, we begin to think and act with greater kindness toward others. Training our minds in lovingkindness is a two-part program:

- With Metta we plant and nurture the seeds of compassion.

- By owning our negative or limiting projections, we weed our mental gardens of unkind thoughts. The negativity we see in others is a clue to the qualities we are afraid of acknowledging in ourselves.

Prayer/Practice

Divine Beloved, I awaken with heartfelt gratitude that you have given us the teachings needed to open the heart and escape from the trap of the ego. I ask for increased awareness today of the judgmental thoughts I have about others so that I may gain a greater awareness of the hidden ways in which I judge myself.

Practice the egg of light meditation and whatever steps of Metta you wish. Remember to dedicate the merits of your practice for the enlightenment of all beings, as we learned on February 16. Maintain an awareness throughout the day of the kind of judgments you have about others. Do you judge appearance, motivation, intellect? What categories do your judgments fall into?

February 18

Seed Thought

Ram Dass teaches an excellent method for owning our projections and becoming more aware of the judgments that separate us from one another, from ourselves and from God. His instruction is quite simple. Every time you catch yourself judging another person own your projection by saying, "And I am that, too."

Prayer/Practice

Contemplate the judgments you made about other people yesterday. Did they tend to be about one subject or many? If you missed yesterday's lesson, think about what your commonest judgments of others are. Consider Ram Dass's lesson, thinking about those judgments in reference to yourself and stating, "And I am that, too." Today, whenever you find yourself judging someone, immediately own the projection "And I am that, too."

February 19

Seed Thought

The great quantum physicist Erwin Shrödinger said that if we could
measure the sum total of the number of minds in the universe,
"there would be just one." Likewise, Einstein commented that "The
illusion that we are separate from one another is an optical
delusion of our consciousness." Consider the possibility that everyone
you see around you is like a character in a dream. They are all
projections of yourself. More properly, we are all characters in the
dream of the One Great Dreamer.

Prayer/Practice

Great Spirit, You are indeed the One who gives the illusion of having
fragmented into the many so that You can know Yourself and Grow
Yourself through us. Help me realize my unity with You and all
other beings by seeing that everyone I meet is a mirror of some
aspect of myself. Let me learn from my friends, and particularly let
me learn from my enemies and those I hold in judgment.

*Practice Metta, concentrating on those people whom you have
held in judgment over the last several days.*

February 20

Seed Thought

The practice of lovingkindness extends to all creation. In 1854, when Chief Seattle gave up his tribal lands in the Pacific Northwest, he made an impassioned plea for us to be good stewards of the land, to honor the sacredness of life because "all things are interconnected. What befalls the earth befalls the sons and daughters of the earth. We did not weave the web of life; we are merely a strand in it. Whatever we do to the web, we do to ourselves."

Prayer/Practice

Great Spirit, may a greater awareness of the sacred web of life dawn in my heart. May I walk in beauty and harmony, honoring the Earth Mother and all her children, taking care of this beautiful planet as a trust for future generations.

Place yourself in the egg of light and practice Metta for the trees, for the animals, for the rivers, for the seas.

February 21

Seed Thought

A man who had a near-death experience following a heart attack
returned to his body, and the first thing he saw in his hospital
room was a rose. He experienced seeing a rose as for the first time,
realizing that he was intimately connected to that flower. Now,
when he walks through the forest, he feels as though he is one with
the trees. He has realized directly his participation in the web
of life. The secret of happiness, he says, is twofold: to realize that
all things are interconnected, and to send love along those
connections.

Prayer/Practice

Divine Beloved, let my heart awaken this morning to a new level
of gratitude for all things and all people. I call upon dear Michael,
angel of love and wisdom, and ask for help in feeling the
interconnectedness of all things and help in learning to see
things freshly without the filter of preconceptions and judgments.
This is how I can send love along the connections I share with
all things.

*Keeping your eyes open, take a deep breath and let go, feeling
your body and mind begin to relax. Shift your attention to
belly breathing. Look around and select an object to contemplate.
Keeping an awareness of your breathing, see the object with
the eyes of a child, as if you were seeing it for the first time. See
with wonder, delight and absorption. This is called mindfulness, or
moment-by-moment, non-judgmental awareness. Practice
mindfulness two or three times today.*

February 22

Seed Thought

When we are mindful, experiencing the world around us freshly with all our senses, we leave the judgments of small mind behind and enter the web of interconnectedness, the Big Mind of God. Happiness, joy, peace and gratitude arise spontaneously from within our hearts.

Prayer/Practice

Today, practice mindfulness with a renewed awareness of its importance to compassion and happiness. Several times today, stop and take a letting-go breath. Enter the moment with all your senses, taking time to taste and smell, hear and see, feel and move. Feel your connectedness with all things. Begin with a moment of mindfulness right now.

February 23

Seed Thought

The knowledge that all things are interconnected is a first step toward spiritual awakening. A second step is putting that knowledge into action through good stewardship of personal and planetary resources. When the Lakota medicine man Wallace Black Elk was asked how we might heal the earth, he answered that the earth can heal herself; all we have to do is stop making her sick.

Prayer/Practice

Great Spirit, I awaken this morning with a heart full of gratitude for all the gifts of the material world. The gifts of food, of clothing, of shelter. The objects of beauty that uplift my soul and the objects of utility that make my life easier. Help me be a good steward of these gifts so that resources will remain for our children and our children's children for all time.

Spend a few minutes in centering prayer or other meditation and think of one way in which you could conserve and protect the web of life. Can you compost your kitchen waste, recycle your bottles, give your old clothes to charity, or forget about buying that electric can opener unless a condition like arthritis prevents you from using your hands?

February 24

Seed Thought

A Hindu teacher, Swami Chidvilasananda, begins each of her public lectures with this greeting: "With great respect and love I welcome you all with all my heart." A friend of mine who is one of her students once sent me a card inscribed "with great respect and love." I wept when I read it. To be loved and respected is one of our deepest longings. To offer love and respect is one of our greatest gifts.

Prayer/Practice

Great Spirit, thank You for the limitless respect and love that You shower upon me regardless of the mistakes I make, my oversights, and the many small acts of ego that keep me separate from You. You are like a constant sun, always shining Your love and good wishes upon me. Help me open to these gifts and feel them more intensely by offering respect and love to everyone I meet.

Place yourself in the egg of light and practice Metta for at least two people whom you will be coming in contact with today or this week.

February 25

Seed Thought

One of the most important ways we can show our respect and love is by listening carefully when another person speaks. When we interrupt, no matter how important our contribution may seem, we're damming up the flow of energy and giving the other person the nonverbal message that their thoughts and feelings are less important than our own.

Prayer/Practice

Close your eyes and take a few letting-go breaths. Let your mind rest and enter the sanctuary of inner silence. Feel into that place by noticing the natural peace and stillness that is always there inside you. Speak to God from your heart, as if that Great Spirit were your dearest friend. When people speak to you today, listen with that same patience, respect and love. Be mindful of any urge to interrupt, and do your best to be patient, waiting until the other person finishes before you speak.

February 26

Seed Thought

There is a subtle channel, like a vein in which energy flows, extending
from the heart out through the eyes. You can communicate
great love through your gaze, speaking directly to your own soul
or the soul of another person.

Prayer/Practice

*Get a mirror and look into your face. See yourself without
judgment. Forget the wrinkles, the freckles, the beauty or its
lack that small mind is attracted to or repelled by. See yourself
through the eyes of a child, without judgment. See yourself as
a child, the Divine child who is always worthy of your love and
respect. Look deeply into your eyes and tell yourself silently,
"I love and respect you." Tell yourself whatever else you would
most like to hear, from a person who truly wishes you to
awaken and find the Divine within your heart and in your life.
As you go through the day, speak to others through your heart,
allowing respect and love to flow out of your eyes and into
their souls.*

February 27

Seed Thought

Love is a verb, not a noun. It can only be experienced when it is flowing. When we become a source of love, when it flows through our eyes, our voice, our prayers and the selfless acts of lovingkindness that we offer to others, then we feel happiness.

Prayer/Practice

Great Spirit, teacher of love, please help me to become a source of love. Michael, Angel who has become the embodiment of God's love and wisdom, help me give love away so that I can receive love in the giving and experience happiness.

Today, practice giving respect and love to others through the power of your gaze. You can do this only if the channel between heart and eyes is open. So, first open your heart through mindfulness, the recollection of a heart-opening memory, by calling upon the Archangel Michael, by recalling the physical feeling of open-heartedness, or in any other way. Then imagine that a stream of loving light is coming out of your heart through your eyes as you speak to that person verbally or silently.

February 28

Seed Thought

There is a wonderful movement afoot called "random acts of kindness." What a refreshing change from random acts of violence that so trouble our world. Kind acts are things such as feeding a parking meter when you see the red flag up, paying the toll for the person in back of you, doing the dishes when it's not your turn, or leaving a love note. The possibilities for random acts of kindness are limitless.

Prayer/Practice

Divine Beloved, You practice random acts of kindness for all beings at all times. Just as the rain falls on all plants, whether or not they've done something to deserve it, your love rains down steadily on us all. I am so grateful, because if I can do nothing to earn your love, I can do nothing to lose it. Help me love the way that You love, limitlessly and with no strings attached.

Today, practice at least one random act of kindness.

February 29: Leap Year Day

Seed Thought

Perhaps you know the old Shaker song called "Simple Gifts." It is most appropriate for this day of grace when the cosmic timekeeper grants us an extra day to reflect on life's gifts and on how we need only turn around to accept them in gratitude and humility.

'Tis the gift to be simple, 'tis the gift to be free
'Tis the gift to come round where we ought to be
And when we find ourselves in the place just right
It will be in the valley of love and delight.

When true simplicity is gained
To bow and to bend we will not be ashamed.
To turn, turn, will be our delight
Till by turning, turning, we come round right.

Prayer/Practice

Sing "Simple Gifts" if you know it. Spend a few minutes in meditation and contemplate the idea that waking up is not so hard after all. You are coming round just right.

MARCH

Courage

The theme for March is the uncovering of faith and courage
through the letting go of fear.
We have a choice in how we deal with the images in our minds.
By practicing the egg of light, using prayers of protection,
being mindful of our breathing, invoking angelic help and
paying attention to our motivations, we can awaken the twin flames
of courage and compassion that are our heart's true light.
Patience, surrender and the faith that all things work for the best
help form the foundation for deep peace of mind.
When we realize that the attitude we have toward our work
is more important than the results,
we begin to cultivate the seeds of patience and nonattachment.
March is a month of awakening.
Listen to voices of the Ancient Ones as they rise on the warming winds
of spring:

The Medicine Wheel turns
and
opens to the Eastern Gate.
Father Sun returns and draws forth life
from the Earth Mother.
Brother Bear awakens.
The Archangel Uriel
and the angels of clarity
provide the energy that pierces
the veil of fear
and allows us to
raise our sails
to the winds
of grace.

March 1

Seed Thought

March is a month of coming and going, the changing of the guard. Winter gives way to spring. Darkness gives way to light. Fear gives way to courage. We are asked to fast from the ego's fearful thinking and fill ourselves instead with faith. The Muslims mark this change with Ramadan, the Jews with Purim, the Catholics with Lent. The energy of the earth supports us in piercing the veil of fear.

Prayer/Practice

Great Spirit, thank you for a new day and for a new month. Day by day the coldness of winter gives way to the warmth of spring, as the first shoots of new life appear from beneath the barren ground. Likewise may I begin to see new growth in myself as I approach old fears with greater courage and the faith that all situations, seen rightly, are an opportunity for growth in love and wisdom.

Spend a few minutes in the peace of centering prayer, or the egg of light.

March 2

Seed Thought

My mother died on a wintery day one March when the days were growing longer. As the sun set on her for the last time in this life, we shared two precious gifts: mutual forgiveness and the exchange of soul qualities. She willed me her courage. I gave her my compassion. We had not yet realized that they were two sides of the same coin.

Prayer/Practice

Great Spirit, thank you for the new awareness that is dawning in my life. As I open my heart to myself and others, I open to Divine Mind. In Your Mind there is no fear or separation, only the sweet interconnectedness of all things. It is this realization that is the cornerstone of faith and the substance of courage.

Spend a few minutes in centering prayer or in the egg of light. Contemplate the relationship of courage and compassion.

March 3

Seed Thought

The word *courage* comes from the French *coeur*, the heart. Courage and compassion are the twin flames of wisdom that emanate from the Godseed within our hearts, our own true nature or Higher Self. We do not have to learn courage, for it is part of who we already are. We have only to unlearn fear.

Prayer/Practice

Divine Beloved, sometimes I feel connected to life, but at times I feel so separate and alone. Help me understand that these anxious, lonely moments are opportunities to learn to let go of small mind and open to your Divine Mind. Even if I cannot do this myself, please help me *know* that angelic help is always available. I am never alone.

Direct your attention to your left, the Northern Gate of your energy body, and call upon Michael, whose compassionate presence still presides over the waning weeks of winter. Be still and notice whatever you can about the angelic presence. Contemplate the fact that you are never alone. Help from the unseen world is always available to you.

Throughout the day, whenever you feel alone or afraid, place yourself in the egg of light and/or call upon the Archangel Michael.

March 4

Seed Thought

There are different types of fear, and each one is a gift of spirit. The fear that accompanies physical threat shifts the bodymind into high gear and allows us to survive challenging situations. The fear of inadequacy and rejection can lead us to heal old emotional wounds and claim their wisdom. The fear that the Universe is unfriendly or punitive can launch the search for true faith.

Prayer/Practice

Today, notice the types of fear that come up. Categorize them into those that you can take some action on, those that you are powerless over and those that you can let go of instantly by taking a big letting-go breath and switching to belly breathing for five or ten breaths.

March 5

Seed Thought

A friend of mine living with AIDS went through a period when he suffered intense panic attacks. He wrote that he had come out of it "wiser and broadened. I could spend days talking about it and what I learned, but it boils down to just accepting it and letting it go, 'it' being anything in life. Easier said than done, but I'm working on it." We're all working on it.

Prayer/Practice

The serenity prayer of Reinhold Niebuhr is a classic. Say it with all your heart and let its wisdom penetrate your mind:

God give me the courage
to change the things I can,
the serenity to accept the things
I can't and the wisdom to
know the difference.

Sit for a few minutes in centering prayer or the egg of light and allow yourself to surrender to the serenity of the Divine Presence.

When fear arises during the day, place yourself in the egg of light, call upon the Archangel Michael or repeat the serenity prayer. Try these practices with mindful awareness—noticing what changes each one brings about.

March 6

Seed Thought

Surrender to the things that can't be changed is one of the keys to peace of mind. How often has worry about situations beyond your control destroyed your serenity and thrown your bodymind into a fearful uproar? Years ago, when I was caught by worried mind, a friend had a dream about my situation. She found herself in just the trouble I had hoped to avoid, accepted it and affirmed, "What is is and I can handle it."

Prayer/Practice

Great Spirit, thank you for a new day and a deeper commitment to awareness and letting go of worried mind. When I find myself obsessing about things I can't change, give me faith and true surrender. Archangel Michael, whenever I lose myself to worry please help me catch myself and affirm, *"What is is and I can handle it."*

March 7

Seed Thought

Albert Einstein was once asked what the most important question
was that human beings needed to answer. He replied, "Is the universe
a friendly place or not?" Most people don't think much about this
question when life is running smoothly. It's when we hit a
snag—illness, divorce, loss—that heart and soul resonate with the
question "Why?" If the universe is a friendly place, why do bad
things happen?

Prayer/Practice

*Place yourself in the stillness of meditation. Then contemplate the
question "Why do bad things happen?"*

March 8

Seed Thought

Psychological research on pessimism reveals that pessimistic thinking revolves around three reasons about why bad things happen: "It's all my fault; I mess up everything; and bad things keep happening to me." This attitude creates helplessness, low self-esteem and chronic worry. But consider the worse plight of the religious pessimist who adds, "God must be punishing me."

Prayer/Practice

Think of a time when something very difficult happened. What were the reasons you gave yourself? Are you a pessimist, or do you see difficult situations as opportunities for growth? Let go of all thinking and let the motherly arms of God surround you in a few minutes of centering prayer.

March 9

Seed Thought

The story of Job is the archetype of bad things happening to a good person. Job was the kindest, most loving man in all the land and then his children died, his crops burned, his whole life was pulled out from under him. For a week he tried to answer the question "Why me" and finally concluded that the universe was unjust and that God was a petty tyrant. Suddenly God appeared out of a whirlwind and asked Job where he was when the foundations of the world were being laid, that he could possibly believe he knew the divine plan.

Prayer/Practice

Great Spirit, I come before you with a humble heart, wishing to empty it of the belief that I can ever know Your Divine Plan. Dear One, grant me the gift of surrender and the knowledge that every difficulty is an opportunity to grow in love and wisdom. Grant me true spiritual courage.

March 10

Seed Thought

We cannot know why particular events occur in our lives because our spiritual sight is too narrow. Perhaps the very thing we thought of as a disaster was exactly the circumstance that we or another needed to grow. Leo Tolstoy gave us a wonderful way to view difficulties when he said, "The only thing that we can know is that we know nothing, and that is the highest flight of human wisdom."

Prayer/Practice

Imagine the highest form of the Divine above you and slightly in front of you. Let waves of loving Light wash over you and through you, cleansing you of any belief in a punitive God or a senseless universe. Feel the light within your heart shining more brightly as the veil of ignorance and pain is washed away. Let the twin flames of courage and compassion that are your heart's true light merge with the Divine Light. Sit for a few minutes in the peace of the Divine Presence.

March 11

Seed Thought

Ask and it shall be given you;
Seek, and you shall find;
Knock, and it shall be opened to you.

For whoever asks, receives; and
he who seeks, finds; and to him who
knocks, the door is opened.

—Jesus (Matthew 7: 7, 8)

Prayer/Practice

Great Spirit, thank you for the faith that is dawning in my heart
and for the realization that my prayers are heard. Please give me the
patience and maturity to know that my calls for help are answered
in many different ways. I may not always get what I want, so
let me trust that I am getting what I need.

*Throughout the day, if you are perplexed, worried, ill or irritated,
ask the angelic Beings of Light for help. Call upon Uriel for
clarity, Raphael for healing, Michael for wisdom and love and
Gabriel for strength. Even the generic "Help!" opens the door
between the worlds.*

March 12

Seed Thought

The same lifeforce that grows an oak from an acorn, a mountain from the earth's molten core, a stream from the spring thaw, a child from an egg and a sperm, an idea from the mind of a human being is present in all things, all thoughts and all experiences. There is no place where God is not.

Prayer/Practice

Divine Beloved, thank you for a new morning, a new body and a new mind. Help me to see your Presence in all circumstances, good and bad, and to regard all situations as opportunities to learn to trust in love rather than to practice fear.

Be aware of fearful thoughts today. Can you breathe and let them go? Can you practice surrender, "What is is and I can handle it?" Can you call for angelic help? Practice, practice, practice letting go of fear!

March 13

Seed Thought

The egg of light meditation that we have been practicing since January 23 is one of the oldest forms of becoming aware of and invoking Divine Protection. In addition to placing yourself in the egg of light each morning, you can invoke it in a shorter form any time you need courage.

Prayer/Practice

Imagine a star of living Light in the air just above your head and slightly in front of you. Allow streams of liquid loving Light to cascade over you and wash through you, cleansing you of any fear, negativity or illusion that veils the light within your heart. Let your heartlight expand and become one with the Light of God, wrapping you in a great egg of light. If you like, repeat the Unity Church Prayer of Protection:

The light of God surrounds us, the love of God enfolds us, the power of God protects us, the presence of God watches over us. Wherever we are God is and all is well.

March 14

Seed Thought

There's a Hasidic folk song that goes, "All the world is just a narrow bridge. And above all is not to fear, not to fear at all." Did you ever walk a plank easily on the ground and then think about how terrifying it would be to do the same thing a hundred feet up in the air? If we truly had faith that the Universe was supporting us, we would be able to walk the narrow bridge of this life with much greater ease.

Prayer/Practice

Great Spirit, thank you for supporting me, even when I think I am alone. In order to help me find courage, you create many illusions. The illusion of death, the illusion that you could ever forsake your children. Even Jesus fell prey to that illusion on the cross, when he called out, "Father, Father, why have you forsaken me?" Yet you were always there and Your Divine Plan was unfolding exactly as it should.

Place yourself in the egg of light and contemplate whatever difficulties you are experiencing in your life at present. Think about what you are learning from these situations.

March 15

Seed Thought

Pain is the Great Awakener that puts us in touch with the need for and substance of faith. The Buddha was once the Prince Siddhartha and lived in great luxury until he left the palace grounds and came face to face with the reality of suffering: sickness, poverty, old age and death. He committed himself to find the path to overcome suffering, not only for his own liberation but for the sake of all beings.

Prayer/Practice

Take a few letting-go breaths and place your awareness to your left side. Call upon the Archangel Michael for insight concerning how we create suffering. Contemplate what it would be like not to suffer, what life might be like if you let go of the past and had no attachment to what the future might bring. What would a quiet mind feel like? Spend a few minutes in the stillness of centering prayer. Throughout the day, notice when you have been pulled into fear, and try to let go by using the breath, the serenity prayer, angelic help, surrender or the egg of light and prayer for protection. You do have choices!

March 16

Seed Thought

Faith is an attitude that allows us to do our best without being attached to the results. We want the best for our children, so we love them, teach them right from wrong and make whatever plans are necessary for their wellbeing. But if we can only be happy if they grow up to be a doctor or a dancer, live in a certain place or marry a particular type of person, we will create suffering through our attachments.

Prayer/Practice

Great Spirit, thank you for this new day. Help me to live in the moment, to be mindful of what is, to let go to the flow of your love. If I hold on to anything—expectations, regrets, resentments— I obstruct the flow and create suffering. Help me understand how to make necessary plans to live responsibly without attachment to the results.

Spend a few minutes in centering prayer, the egg of light or whatever meditative practice you most enjoy. Give yourself over to God's flow. Throughout the day, notice the attachments that pull you out of the flow. Practice letting go.

March 17: St. Patrick's Day

Seed Thought

Anthropologist and writer Angeles Arrien cites four rules for life:

- Show up

- Pay attention

- Tell the truth

- Don't be attached to the results

I'm doing pretty well with the first three, but, as the Buddha pointed out, the fourth one is the hardest and represents the path beyond suffering.

Prayer/Practice

Think of the things that you have planned today. Thank God for the opportunities for love, growth and service that have been given to you. Pray for the strength and courage to carry out all your affairs with clarity, integrity and commitment—and without attachment to the results. Affirm:

I have faith in Your Divine Plan. Whatever the outcome of my efforts may be, I dedicate them to You and for the benefit of all people.

March 18

Seed Thought

Saint Paul was a most interesting character. He had lots of zeal, which he applied with great singlemindedness to whatever he did. He was rushing to Damascus to persecute followers of Jesus in the name of what was "holy," when he was suddenly overtaken by a Light so bright that it temporarily blinded him—the Light of God. Fortunately, Paul let go of his attachment to his previous plans and became the hub of the early Christian movement. He taught that "faith is the substance of things hoped for and not seen."

Prayer/Practice

Great Spirit, thank you for the grace that is helping me to awaken and the faith that I, like all your children, am on a journey back Home to You. Although, like Paul, I may sometimes take the wrong road, may my sincere desire to awaken and be helpful to others always bring the power of your divine grace to my rescue, converting my errors into learnings.

Spend a few minutes in the meditation of your choice.

March 19

Seed Thought

Throughout the ages, there have been many stories about the unearned and unsolicited action of grace. Grace is a gift that is independent of our good works or grievous errors. Like the sun, it shines freely on all. The great Hindu saint Ramakrishna put it very nicely when he said that the winds of grace are blowing all the time—we just have to raise our sails. When we do, those tender winds propel us quickly Home to God.

Prayer/Practice

How do we raise our sails to grace? Through faith and sweet surrender. Through sinking into the inner silence and becoming present to Divine Mind. By being mindful of the present moment so that our hearts are at peace and we can hear the still, quiet voice of the Inner Navigator who is steering us Home across the vast ocean of this world.

Take a few deep breaths and sink into the silence of centering prayer—asking nothing, hoping for nothing, without attachment to any "results"!

When seeming attachments come up today, practice discernment. Is your desire for a particular outcome propelled by fear or self-interest, or is it the activity of the Higher Self prompting you to use your special gifts according to the Divine Plan? How to tell? Enter the silence and ask for guidance. In time, that guidance will be clear if you persist in getting quiet, asking and patiently listening.

March 20

Seed Thought

For three months the Archangel Michael has guarded the Northern Gate of winter. Although Michael's presence is with you throughout the year whenever you invoke it, the constant angelic presence of spring is the Archangel Uriel. *Uriel* is Hebrew for "the light (or fire) of God." That fire brings us to the Eastern Gate of the Medicine Wheel, the house of the rising sun and new beginnings.

Prayer/Practice

Take a few letting-go breaths and enter the place of inner stillness. Direct your attention to your left, the Northern Gate of your body temple, and thank the Archangel Michael for the insight and wisdom of winter. Ask Michael's continued presence throughout the day and the year. Now shift your attention to the space directly in front of you, the Eastern Gate of your body temple. Invoke the presence of Uriel and give thanks for spring, for the return of the outer light and the inner light of clarity. Sit quietly in Uriel's Presence and become familiar with that energy.

Two or three times today, become aware of the space in front of you and ask for Uriel's presence. If you need clarity about some situation, ask for Uriel's input.

March 21: Vernal Equinox

Seed Thought

Today is a point of balance in the mandala of the year when the hours of light are equal to the hours of darkness. We are called to remember the ever-shifting balance within ourselves, the impermanence of our inner seasons, which, like the outer seasons, are always and forever changing. We are called to accept both our light and our shadow.

Prayer/Practice

Great Spirit, how magnificent is the cycle of the seasons and the coming of the spring. As I awaken from my winter sleep, let me seek balance in my inner life and outer life. Let me value equally the part of me that is healed and in the light, and the difficult traits in my character that are grist for the mill of growth.

Enter the inner silence through a few minutes of belly breathing or meditation, and invoke the presence of Uriel in the space in front of you. Ask for clarity about your "dark" traits of character. Finish up by letting go and resting in the Divine Presence.

March 22

Seed Thought

In 1945, 53 ancient manuscripts were unearthed in Egypt at the site of a second-century Christian monastery. They contained a wonderful poem, "The Thunder, Perfect Mind," written in the voice of a feminine wisdom:

For I am the first and the last.
I am the honored one and the scorned one.
I am the whore and the holy one.
I am strength and I am fear.
I am war and I am peace.

This poem, which continues for seven pages, is similar to a song Jesus sang at the last supper, according to the Apocryphon of John. Jesus, too, claimed to be both war and peace, betrayer and betrayed.

Prayer/Practice

Divine Beloved, Great One who has fragmented into many, how many roles we must play in Your theater of soulgrowth. Though I prefer the role of the honored one, let me honor also the place of scorn. Though I prefer strength, let me honor fear. Though I prefer peace, let me understand that it is through the pairs of opposites that the world comes into being.

Spend a few minutes in the peace of meditation which transcends the pairs of opposites. During the day, if you experience scorn, think about how it teaches the importance of honor (respect). If you feel fear, reflect on how it helps you value peace. Become spacious enough to hold the opposites.

March 23

Seed Thought

The Swiss psychiatrist and mystic Carl Jung often discussed the
shadow—that hidden part of ourself that is the home of both unspoken
fears and unexpressed creativity. Dr. Jekyll's problem was that he
tried so hard to be good that he disowned all his natural impulses
to risk, to rebel, to be passionately alive. These disowned parts of
himself took on a life of their own in the form of the very
objectionable, destructive Mr. Hyde.

Prayer/Practice

Great Spirit, I thank you for a fresh spring morning and for the
courage to become whole by accepting with clarity both my
darkness and my light.

*Today, pay close attention to the judgments you have about other
people which are clues to what lies hidden in your own shadow.
Is that person too joyful? (Whatever happened to your own joy?)
Is that person too angry? (How do you handle your own
anger?) Be sure to own your projections about others with the
affirmation we learned February 18, "And I am that, too."*

March 24

Seed Thought

The poet Robert Bly refers to Jung's shadow as a long bag we drag behind us containing all the discarded parts of ourself that parents, teachers, peers, clergy or society told us weren't good enough. Bly says, "We spend our life until we're twenty deciding what parts of ourself to put into the bag, and we spend the rest of our lives trying to get them out again." It takes courage to re-own our lost parts, but authentic spirituality requires that we make the shadow visible and that we make that which is divided whole.

Prayer/Practice

I loved to sing as a child, but my mother used to joke that I had a voice like a ruptured crow. I became ashamed to sing and for years could hardly produce a note above a whisper. I finally decided to pull my voice out of the bag and sing. It's been fun, challenging and very healing.

Take a few letting-go breaths and move into the place of inner stillness. Think of some creative impulse that you denied somewhere in your first twenty years. Spring is a very good time to let your creativity out of the bag.

March 25

Seed Thought

These words were carved on the gates of the oracle at Delphi:
"Moderation in all things and all things in moderation." Even our
strong points, when taken to their extreme, can become weaknesses.
Confidence can turn to bravado, competence to workaholism.
An ability to let go and move with the flow can turn to laziness.
The desire to grow spiritually and find God can become rigid fanaticism.
I can laugh now as I look back and think of the times when I was
sure I had found "The Truth," and thought that I was doing
other people a favor when I imposed my rigid beliefs on them.

Prayer/Practice

Divine Beloved, how delighted I am to awaken from my winter's
sleep with renewed confidence, deeper faith and greater balance. Today
I call upon your help and the help of Uriel and the angels of clarity
to help me bring moderation to my strengths.

*Spend a few minutes in meditation, and then contemplate your
two greatest strengths and the ways in which these can become
weaknesses when you get out of balance.*

March 26

Seed Thought

Self-discipline is a quality of mind that is based on clarity and balance. Clarity requires an understanding of the big picture. What is most important to accomplish in this lifetime? Once we are clear on our priorities, then we need to approach them steadfastly, but with the flexibility born of self-acceptance and patience.

Prayer/Practice

Spend a few minutes in the stillness of meditation or centering prayer, and then place your attention on the Eastern Gate of your body temple, the area right in front of you. Call upon Uriel and the angels of clarity to help you reflect on your biggest priority. What is the most important thing you will take with you from this lifetime, and what is the most important legacy you will leave for others? What attitude do you most need to cultivate, and what action do you most need to pursue in order to accomplish your goal?

March 27

Seed Thought

The word *discipline* comes from the Latin root *discipulus*, a learner.
Disciple, one who learns from a master teacher, comes from the
same root. If we thought of self-discipline as Self-discipline, the true
meaning would be "to learn from our Higher Self." Too often
we think of self-discipline as cracking the whip to make ourselves
toe the line. How different the real meaning is.

Prayer/Practice

Great Spirit, thank you for helping me learn from the infinite well
of wisdom that has always been present within me. Today I will
pay attention to the inner teacher, noticing the hunches, the
promptings of spirit that instruct me in how to live and take
my co-creative role in this great universe.

*Take a deep breath and let go to the place of inner stillness. Ask
yourself, "What do I need to pay attention to right now?"
Whether there is an immediate answer or not, you are opening
the lines of communication to the teacher within. Repeat this
exercise several more times today.*

March 28

Seed Thought

The application of self-discipline is twofold:

- Keeping our priorities in mind so that our thoughts and actions are in accord with our intentions.

- Noticing and eliminating those habits of mind and patterns of behavior that get in the way of actualizing those intentions.

The Muslim holy days of Ramadan and the Catholic holy days of Lent concern self-discipline and giving up those things that block our ability to love, to serve others and to fulfill our life purpose.

Prayer/Practice

Divine Beloved, thank you for this new season of awareness and a renewal of my faith, courage, balance and self-discipline. For the remainder of March, I agree to fast from (some mind-habit or behavior that blocks your way—criticism, impatience, laziness, an addiction). I know that my efforts will be supported by your matching grant of grace and bring me into greater alignment with your wisdom and your love.

March 29

Seed Thought

Self-discipline is a way of life that requires patience, and patience is one of the least well understood virtues. A Swiss spiritual teacher by the name of Hugo clarified what patience is not. He said that what most people think of as patience is really impatience stretched to its limits.

Prayer/Practice

Take a few letting-go breaths and begin to quiet your mind. Place your attention in front of you, at the Eastern Gate of your body temple. Call upon Uriel and the angels of clarity to help you contemplate the true meaning of patience.

Throughout the day, whenever you feel impatient, take a letting-go breath and use the opportunity to practice mindful awareness.

March 30

Seed Thought

Patience is related to authentic spiritual courage. It is the deep faith
that the universe is unfolding as it should, even when things
are not happening according to our own plans or timetables. All
we can do is act with integrity, in accordance with our priorities
and the guidance of the still, small voice within. After that, we must
surrender all attachment to the results.

Prayer/Practice

Great Spirit, thank you for deepening my understanding of patience
and the faith on which it is based. It is easy to be patient when
I can see the fruits of my actions. It is harder to be patient when
no fruits have yet appeared. Help me find fulfillment in
performing my actions as a dedication to You and all beings rather
than judging them solely by their results.

*Today, pay attention to the attitude with which you do your work.
When you leave your body at the time of death, and the Being
of Light helps you review your life, you'll find that the attitude
you had—rather than the results you produced—was the
most important measure of your life.*

March 31

Seed Thought

The first line of the medieval poet Wolfram's grail legend states that
every action has both good and evil results. All we can do is
intend the good. This understanding bolsters faith, patience and
surrender. I remember being eight years old, with a bent baton.
When my older brother tried to straighten it for me, it snapped in
two. I began to cry, and he thought it was for my broken baton.
But the tears were for him. He had intended the good, although
the baton was ruined. Through its ruin a higher good was
achieved—the awakening of compassion within my heart. Life is
not always as it seems, but we can trust that a good intention
will always carry us through even if the immediate results are not
what we had in mind.

Prayer/Practice

*Place yourself in the egg of light and practice Metta meditation
as we learned February 11–15. Metta is a practice of love,
patience, faith and surrender. Metta is an intention for good. As
you go through the day, notice the intention behind your
actions. When the intention is motivated by love and service, you
can be assured of a good outcome on a higher level, even if
poor results are outwardly obtained.*

EASTERN GATE

Archangel Uriel

SPRING

APRIL

Freedom: Moving from the Ego to the Higher Self

April is a month of freedom and the redemption of innocence.
Passover, Easter and Ramadan—
the April Holy Days of Judaism, Christianity and Islam
are about being made new,
being born again out of the slavery of the ego
into the spaciousness of Divine Mind.
The Spring Equinox
is likewise the invitation of the Earth Mother and her angels
to become again as little children,
to be born anew in the wholeness of our potential.
This requires learning to be as wily as the fox and as gentle as the dove,
becoming aware of how the ego works and
practicing the mental martial art of sidestepping its fears.
In so doing we become more mindful,
more able to live in the spacious, nonjudgmental awareness
of the present that is the doorway through which
we will enter the Holy of Holies.
On that sacred ground we attain true humility,
the absolute security that we are children of the One Loving Source.
Listen to the call of the Ancient Ones
as winter dies away in the promise of spring:

> *New cubs emerge from the den*
> *as the sun climbs higher*
> *in the Eastern sky.*
> *Under the tutelage of the*
> *Archangel Uriel*
> *we are renewed.*
> *We claim our power*
> *through humility,*
> *the security that follows*
> *from understanding*
> *that we are*
> *Children of the Light.*

April 1: All Fools' Day

Seed Thought

All Fools' Day is a celebration of the rebirth of innocence revealed in the newness of spring. Many mystic traditions talk of being "a fool for God." Fools are often much wiser than scholars because they see through the eyes of a child and are not too "smart" to notice when the emperor has no clothes—even when the emperor is themselves!

Prayer/Practice

Great Spirit, thank you for the delights of a fresh spring morning and for the rebirth of innocence in my soul. May I let go of the jaded mind-habits of cynicism, conceit and pride that keep me a prisoner of the limitations of small mind.

Take a few letting-go breaths and find the place of inner stillness. Open your eyes if they have been closed, and look around as if for the first time. Find an object and inspect it minutely with eyes, nose, hands, even tongue if appropriate. Pretend that you just landed here from Mars and have never encountered such a marvelous thing before.

Today, whenever you feel bored or jaded, take a deep breath and look around with mindful curiosity.

April 2

Seed Thought

Most spiritual traditions teach through parables to reach beyond our "know-it-all" nature and connect directly with the innocence we had as children. In a famous Zen parable, a college professor visits a monk to see whether the monk has anything to teach him. The monk pours tea for the professor, but just keeps on pouring until the cup overflows. The professor jumps up in alarm, judging the monk a hopeless fool. The monk remarks calmly that the cup is like the professor's mind—already so full that nothing more can fit in.

Prayer/Practice

Great Spirit, let me fly to freedom on the wings of humility. Help me realize that the less I profess to know, the more I can actually absorb of life's teachings.

Spend a few minutes in the stillness and innocence of centering prayer. The mind has nowhere to go, so just be present without expectations.

April 3

Seed Thought

Truly, I say unto you, unless you turn and become like children,
you will never enter the kingdom of heaven. Whoever humbles
himself like this child, he is the greatest in the kingdom of heaven.

—Jesus (Matthew 18:3–5)

Prayer/Practice

*Practice humility by recognizing that most of what we think we
know is actually the hypnosis of consensual reality. Look
around you right now and focus on an object. Think to yourself,
"What if I have never really seen a (light, a sink, a hand)
before." Call upon Uriel and the angels of clarity to help you
see this object as it is rather than as you have decided it is.
Repeat this exercise two or three more times today.*

April 4

Seed Thought

Don Juan is an Indian "man of knowledge" made famous in the series of books by anthropologist Carlos Castaneda. Don Juan says that we fail to see the world as it is because our energy field gets locked in by our sense of self-importance, what some philosophies refer to as our ego. We are then like television sets that tune into only one channel, the channel most relevant to our own concerns and lifestory.

Prayer/Practice

Great Spirit, thank you for teaching me to see the world with new eyes. Help me to see beyond the relevance that people and things have for me, to their essence. Help me to extinguish the sense of self-importance that twists all my perceptions into a limited field of importance most relevant to the "I" and its selfish interests.

Take a few letting-go breaths and move into the place of inner stillness, the place beyond your usual definitions and concerns. With open eyes, scan the room and say to yourself, "Everything I see exists in relation to myself. I call upon Uriel and the angels of clarity to help me see without self-interest."

April 5: Feast of Kwan Yin, Chinese female Buddha of compassion

Seed Thought

We cannot give up our sense of self-importance and move beyond the limits of "I" and "mine" until we have a sense of self to begin with. A common pitfall in the search for identity and union with the Divine is taking a "spiritual bypass." In our hurry to give up the ego, we fail to go back and analyze our lifestory, heal our wounds and reap the wisdom of our pasts. Until this is done, we have not moved fully into our egos, so we cannot consciously move out of them.

Prayer/Practice

Great Spirit, my heart yearns for freedom and union with your Loving Presence. Please help me complete the work of self-reflection and self-acceptance so that I can surrender my self-importance to you and begin to see the world as it really is.

Take a few letting-go breaths and spend a few minutes in centering prayer or in the egg of light. Reflect on the healing of your lifestory that you have done to this point. Congratulate yourself for what has been accomplished so far and think about further steps you might need to take.

April 6

Seed Thought

To be a child again and to approach the world with innocence and humility, we must become aware of our dual nature. Our Higher Self, the Godseed within, has always been in conscious contact with the Divine Presence, has always seen the world as it is. Our ego, the mask of self-importance that we show to the world, is entirely conditional upon the story of our lives.

Prayer/Practice

The ego is a consummate teacher of spiritual martial arts. If we argue with it or engage it, it becomes stronger. If we see it and let it go, our Higher Self naturally emerges.

Today, when your ego shows up as judgment, fear, insecurity, pride, or the "know-it-all," don't bother analyzing your responses. Just notice and let them go. "Oh, there's my ego." Take a deep breath and move on.

April 7

Seed Thought

In *The Power of Silence,* author Carlos Castaneda wrote of a striking realization of the difference between his ego and his Higher Self. His Higher Self seemed "old, at ease, indifferent ... because it was equal to anything. It enjoyed things with no expectation. The other part was ... new ... nervous, fast. It cared about itself because it was insecure and did not enjoy anything, simply because it lacked the capacity to connect itself to anything." Castaneda realized that he saw the world exclusively through this lonely, vulnerable part of himself.

Prayer/Practice

The Tibetan Buddhist practice of shamatha/vipassana, the meditation of calm abiding and insight, is a basic practice for seeing with the Higher Self, rather than through the eyes of the ego.

Sit in your seat with great dignity, back straight and eyes open. Look directly in front of you, eyes down slightly, without particular focus. Become aware of your breathing—how breath comes in and fills you and how breath moves out into space. Keep about 25 percent of your attention on breathing and the other 75 percent on the feeling of spaciousness. When thoughts arise, just let them go by. Continue for five minutes.

April 8

Seed Thought

The ego is relentless in its thinking and judging. In fact I often call it the Judge. There is no way to outsmart or outreason the Judge; one can only leave it behind, the same way we learn to leave our thoughts behind in meditation. Sogyal Rinpoche, a Tibetan Buddhist lama, compares the thoughts that arise in meditation to waves that rise from the ocean. It is the ocean's nature to rise. We cannot stop it, but as Rinpoche says, we can "leave the risings in the risings."

Prayer/Practice

The practice of meditation teaches us the mental martial art necessary to sidestep the tricky ego and its constant judgments. Practice shamatha/vipassana for several minutes as in yesterday's practice. When thoughts arise, "leave the risings in the risings." Throughout the day, when your ego starts its tiresome judging, "leave the risings in the risings."

April 9

Seed Thought

We can recognize the ego as that part of ourself that lives in our
historical past, our story, rather than in the present moment.
When some one says something and we respond way out of proportion
to the comment, that's the ego responding from its insecure
place of self-importance. As we learn to sidestep the ego, we also
learn not to take the bait when some one else's ego challenges
us.

Prayer/Practice

Great Spirit, thank you for helping me on the road to freedom. It
is difficult to see the world with new eyes and to disregard the constant
criticisms of my noisy ego. I am so tired of the suffering that my
judging self causes. Please help me learn to approach life with
a more spacious spirit, a spirit that sees irritations coming and just
lets them go.

*Call upon Uriel to help you maintain a clear mind today, turning
down invitations to become hurt and irritated. Spend a few
minutes practicing shamatha/vipassana.*

April 10

Seed Thought

There is an old adage that says, "However fast you run you cannot run away from your own feet." Another adage puts the same thought slightly differently: "Wherever you go, there you are." You take your ego into every situation, creating the meaning of everything that happens and everything you see, out of the images of your past.

Prayer/Practice

Today, when your ego responds to situations with judgment or irritation, let the opportunity to feel hurt and self-important pass right by. Then think about what person from your past, or what incident from your past you were really reacting to. Affirm, "I am ready to be free of the past. I choose freedom."

Spend a few minutes in centering prayer, the egg of light or shamatha/vipassana meditation.

April 11

Seed Thought

Shamatha/vipassana is a practice of present-centered awareness that moves you out of your history into the present moment. This is the type of meditation that the Buddha was practicing when he awakened out of his ego underneath the Bodhi tree. Since your eyes are open when you are practicing this type of meditation, it carries over easily into the rest of the day.

Prayer/Practice

Spend at least five minutes in shamatha/vipassana meditation. If you wish to sit for longer than five minutes, stretch after each five-minute period so that your bodymind can stay fresh and in the moment. Remember that only 25 percent of your awareness is on the breath. The other 75 percent is on being spacious, letting thoughts and perceptions come and go through the skylike nature of your mind.

April 12

Seed Thought

We can extend the practice of mindful awareness and spaciousness beyond the period of sitting meditation into the rest of life. The Vietnamese Buddhist poet, peaceworker and meditation teacher, Thich Nhat Hanh, has written a beautiful book called the *Miracle of Mindfulness*. With true simplicity and beauty he reminds us that we can wake up in the ordinary activities of life by bringing our full attention to eating, washing the dishes, smelling the roses, walking, making love.

Prayer/Practice

Today, choose a piece of fruit and eat it mindfully. Be aware of its look, smell and feel. Notice the way that your mouth fills with saliva in anticipation of its flavor. Be aware of each bite moving down your throat into your stomach. To be mindful is to be present in your Higher Self rather than your ego.

April 13

Seed Thought

I once had a patient who consulted me about learning mind/body healing techniques to treat an ulcer. As we talked, she confided that she also had a problem enjoying sex. I asked her when she and her husband made love. "Saturday mornings," she said, "right before the trip to the grocery store, the dry cleaners and the car wash." "Where is your mind when you make love?" I asked. "At the supermarket, the dry cleaners and the car wash." No wonder lovemaking was mediocre, there was no one home to enjoy it.

Prayer/Practice

Practice five minutes of shamatha/vipassana and be firm in your intent to live mindfully today. Choose one activity, like taking a walk, washing the dishes or taking a shower, and commit to doing it as mindfully as possible. You will really enjoy yourself!

April 14

Seed Thought

The nature of the ego is to live in its constant thoughts, separating us from the reality of what is. The nature of the Higher Self is to live in the present, feeling its connectedness to all things. Since the present is the only time we can enjoy ourselves, the ego is always discontent and unhappy. The only remedy it has for this is to clutch greedily after things, believing that if only it had this or that, then it would be happy. It is happy in the instant of acquisition, because it stops seeking elsewhere for that moment. But that moment is always short-lived.

Prayer/Practice

Practice five or more minutes of shamatha/vipassana, and then review your mindfulness activity from yesterday. Did you do it? What was it like? Did your mind wander as it does in meditation? Did you remember to focus on your breathing to still your mind and come back to the present? Repeat yesterday's mindfulness exercise again.

April 15

Seed Thought

The Higher Self feels connected to all things. It is neither attracted
to people or situations nor repelled by them. It just is. Therefore
it pays attention with choiceless awareness. It has moved beyond
the attachments and aversions that cause so much suffering.
This Higher Self, the Godseed within, is your Christ self, your
Buddha nature. It is the part of you that has always been awake
and has never fallen into the hypnotic spell of self-importance
and separation.

Prayer/Practice

Great Spirit, thank you for the freshness of this spring morning.
May I see it with mindful awareness, ever wary of the ego and its
judgments. I call upon Uriel and the angels of clarity to help me
see the world with the choiceless awareness and innocence of a
child. This is the path to freedom and awakening.

Spend at least five minutes practicing shamatha/vipassana,
remembering to keep about 25 percent of your attention on
breathing and the rest on spacious, mindful awareness.
Throughout the day, when you get pulled into fear or worry,
remember to take a letting-go breath and come back to
mindfulness, to spaciousness.

April 16

Seed Thought

Every philosophy has its own way of describing the Higher Self. Jesus called it the kingdom of heaven. The Hindus call it the Self which is birthless and deathless, that part of us that cannot be burned by fire, cut by a knife or crushed by a rock because it is eternal and immortal. The Tibetan Buddhists call it our *Rigpa*, our own true nature. Rigpa reflects the drama of life like a mirror, without being tarnished. Our Higher Self has always been and will always be pure. It is the incorruptible mind of God.

Prayer/Practice

Great Spirit, please help me become more aware of my dual nature, the ego and the Higher Self. Help me take a deep breath whenever I'm caught in the ego and switch into an awareness of the present moment and the peace, joy, creativity and love of my own true nature, my Higher Self.

One day my husband and I were driving from New York City to a retreat center upstate, where we were going to provide a weekend spiritual retreat. Having been on the road for several days, I started to feel sorry for myself, thinking, "Other people from Colorado get to go skiing once in a while, and here I am working again!" Soon I was mired in self-pity—not even remotely spacious and present. But all it took was a flash of remembering that misery or spaciousness was my choice, and I was able to let go and enjoy the moment. Keep remembering your choices today.

April 17

Seed Thought

Every day we have glimpses of our Higher Self when we enter into what I call a "state of grace." We suddenly feel peaceful and contented, and see beauty around us. These states of grace may last for hours or for just a few seconds. By developing an awareness of them, we can extend the time that we stay in the Higher Self before we fall asleep again and get carried away in the insecure self-cherishing of the ego.

Prayer/Practice

Divine Beloved, thank you for the moments of grace when I spontaneously let go of small mind and am carried away in the spacious flow of Big Mind, Divine Mind. I call upon Uriel and the angels of clarity to help me be aware of these moments, to value these moments as opportunities to wake up more fully and stay in my Higher Self.

Be aware today of the moments of grace. Even fleeting moments of contentment are windows into the Higher Self. When you notice such a moment, revel in it. Stay with it as long as you can, sidestepping the pull of the ego's thinking and judging as you do in meditation. Spend a few minutes in shamatha/vipassana meditation, centering prayer or the egg of light.

April 18

Seed Thought

Yoga is a Sanskrit word meaning "union," the union of our mind with Divine Mind. Since our mind lives and breathes and has its being in Divine Mind, yoga is really more of a discovery that we have never been separated from God than a finding our way back. According to the *Yoga Sutras of Patanjali,* one of the earliest books on how to find union with God, yoga is the understanding of how to still the "modifications of the mind"—the chatter of the ego and its preoccupation with "me" and "mine."

Prayer/Practice

Great Spirit, how true is the wisdom "Be still and you shall know God." Please help me enter the still and silent flow of your love from which all life arises. Help me overcome the conditioned pull of my ego by repeatedly taking deep breaths and letting go to the present, the lifestream of the Divine Mind.

Spend five minutes in centering prayer or shamatha/vipassana meditation.

April 19

Seed Thought

Patanjali comments that everyone periodically falls into what I've called "states of grace" or holy moments when the beauty of life pulls us out of the small mind of ego into the Big Mind of God. Patanjali says that just tripping into a state of grace does not a yogi make. A yogi knows how to enter the state of grace consciously, and knows how to live in that state.

Prayer/Practice

Great Spirit, I am ready to wake up now. I realize that my deepest anxieties are nothing more than the cry of my Higher Self which has never given up its hope to awaken me from the deep sleep of ego. I give thanks to my Higher Self, to the Godseed within me. I pledge to pay attention to its promptings and to live my life like a meditation, to commit myself to union with God. I will be mindful in all my activities today.

April 20

Seed Thought

April is the month when we celebrate the freedom of overcoming the ego and entering the promised land of our Higher Self. This is the inner meaning of Passover, when the Jews escaped from enslavement by the Pharaoh in Egypt. Jesus acted out the same drama of awakening through the allegory of the crucifixion and the resurrection. Both holidays celebrate dying to our egos and being reborn into the light of our own true nature, our Godseed or Higher Self.

Prayer/Practice

Divine Beloved, thank you for the road maps you have left for us to find our way back to freedom, and the lives of those great beings like Moses and Jesus who symbolize overcoming our egos and finding the promised land, the kingdom of heaven within.

Practice a few minutes of shamatha/vipassana meditation. When you get up and go about your business, walk mindfully, walk with the dignity and grace of a free person.

April 21

Seed Thought

Freedom is an attitude rather than an external state. Etty Hillesum
was a Dutch Jew who died in the gas chambers of Auschwitz in her
late twenties. Her diaries, called *An Interrupted Life,* are a testament
to mindful awareness. Choiceless awareness. Her compassion
extended to the other *musselmen*, the inmates who were nothing
more than skin and bones, and the SS alike. The sun of Etty's
Higher Self shone with equal splendor upon all beings.

Prayer/Practice

Great Spirit, thank you for the gift of awakening this morning a
free person. Regardless of my outer circumstances, help me to
feel the inner freedom of choiceless awareness and compassion
toward all people.

*Practice Metta meditation, sending lovingkindness blessings to all
the people around the world who are imprisoned by bars, by
repressive political regimes, or by attachment to their past
histories and the self-importance of the ego. (See February 11–15
for instructions about Metta meditation.)*

April 22

Seed Thought

The ancient Jews spoke of finding the promised land. Jesus described that promised land as the kingdom of heaven. The Buddhists speak of *nirvana*, or rebirth into Pure Land. The great teaching stories of all cultures cast light upon the means for awakening from the sleep of the ego into the Light of our Higher Self and its connection to God and All That Is. For the promised land is within you, here and now.

Prayer/Practice

Spend a few minutes in centering prayer, the egg of light, shamatha/vipassana meditation or Metta. If you practice a particular religion or are familiar with different religious traditions, spend a few minutes in contemplation of the Great Stories of how we awaken and attain the promised land.

April 23

Seed Thought

The life of Jesus is one of the greatest teachings on freedom, humility and nonjudgmentalness. Jesus said,

Come to me, all who labor and are heavily laden, and I will give you rest. Take my yoke upon you, and learn from me; for I am gentle and lowly in heart, and you will find rest for your souls. For my yoke is easy and my burden is light.

—Matthew 11:28–30

Prayer/Practice

Divine Beloved, teach me of freedom. Help me put down the yoke of judgment and free myself from the chains of ego. In this Passover and Easter season, I call upon Jesus and Uriel to bring me forth into the promised land of clarity, mindfulness and choiceless awareness.

Spend a few minutes in the spacious awareness of shamatha/ vipassana meditation.

April 24

Seed Thought

A teaching story from the Zen tradition concerns two monks walking by a river swollen with spring rain. A woman in a long dress is stranded, unable to cross, so the first monk lifts her into the air and carries her across. Several hours later the second monk turns to his friend, filled with anger and judgment about how monks aren't even supposed to touch women, let alone carry them. The first monk smiles gently. "My brother, I put the woman down on the other side of the river early this morning. You are the one who has carried her all day."

Prayer/Practice

Great Spirit, let me go into this day with awareness and the intention to let go of the judgments my ego has about other people. Let me put my burdens down and not pick up the burdens of others. Let my mindful awareness expand into the spaciousness of true generosity of spirit.

Spend a few minutes in Metta meditation, focusing your lovingkindness blessings on anyone you are feeling judgmental about. (See February 11–15.)

April 25

Seed Thought

The Sufi teacher Janaid said, "If you seek a brother to share your
burden, brothers are in truth hard to find. But if you are in
search of someone whose own burden you will yourself share, there
is no scarcity of such brothers." Thinking of other people is a
time-honored way of extinguishing the ego's self-importance.

Prayer/Practice

Great Spirit, thank you for this April morning and for the urge in
my soul to fly free, to escape from the chains of self-cherishing
and to join You in the endless blue sky of clear mind. Today,
whenever I begin to look for sympathy or attention, help me
catch myself and seek to give attention and care to another instead.

April 26

Seed Thought

The Baal Shem Tov, or Master of the Good Name, was a Jewish mystic of the eighteenth century, Rabbi Israel Ben Eliezer. He taught that the humble person has "drawing power." As long as we cherish ourselves, placing ourself above others, we actually put limits on ourselves, and "God cannot pour his holiness" into us, for God is without limit. Only by relinquishing our self-importance do we become limitlessly capable of drawing the blessings of the universe through us.

Prayer/Practice

Divine Beloved, how I wish for the limitless freedom of humility so that your power, love and will can flow through me without obstruction. Help me to continue my watchful observation of the ways in which I put my interests first. Help me see the subtleties of the ego and the ways in which I use charity, helpfulness and other "good deeds" to enhance my self-importance rather than as compassionate ends in themselves.

Practice a few minutes of centering prayer, shamatha/vipassana or the egg of light.

April 27

Seed Thought

Baha'u'llah, the founder of the Bahai faith, pointed out that even
worship can be an exercise in self-cherishing. A woman had
invited him to dinner and planned an exquisite meal. In her intense
hope of pleasing him, she lost herself in prayer for the success
of the meal, meanwhile burning the dinner. Baha'u'llah laughed,
instructing her that while cooking, the proper prayer is to be
with what you're doing.

Prayer/Practice

*Consider every action a prayer. When you are eating, eat. Try
just eating one meal without talking, reading, or listening to
music, news or television. When you are walking, walk. As with
shamatha/vipassana meditation, anchor your attention by
remaining lightly aware of your breathing, placing the rest of
your attention on the sights, sounds, smells, feelings of whatever
you are doing. When your mind wanders, let go of thoughts and
return to mindfulness—the proper prayer.*

April 28

Seed Thought

While humility is an abandonment of self-cherishing, it is not to
be confused with putting ourselves down and disowning our power,
accomplishments and worth. Self-criticism is the voice of the ego,
not the unveiling of the Higher Self. The Baal Shem Tov taught
that every one of us is unique—no one like us ever existed before.
We must not forget, he said, that we are the sons and daughters
of a great king. That understanding is the basis of humility because
it gives us true security.

Prayer/Practice

Divine Beloved, Father/Mother God, let me remember with gratitude
that I am indeed Your child. Let me remember that life is an incredible
gift, an everlasting role in Your creation. Teach me that humility
is the natural expression of security and the realization that I
am always worthy of Your love. I have nothing to prove, for I am
proven because I am.

*Spend a few minutes in Metta, centering prayer, the egg of light
or shamatha/vipassana meditation.*

April 29

Seed Thought

Everything in the universe flows and moves. Nothing is static. Matter is slow-flowing energy. The negative pole of a battery is the receptive pole that draws the current to it. Humility is the negative pole of God's power that draws the energy of the universe into our sphere so that we can create, extending the works of the Divine architect through our ability to be receptive.

Prayer/Practice

Great Spirit, let me awaken to the power of a humble heart that draws your Divine energy into creation. Let me give up the insecurity that bolsters ego and take my rightful place as Your Divine Child, knowing that I am worthy of receiving the constant flow of your love. Let my heart be an empty cup, filled with your creative impulse.

Take a deep breath and close your eyes. Imagine yourself as a child of three or four, sitting in front of you. Can you remember the hopes and fears of your child-self? You, better than anyone, know the challenges, pains and pleasures that the child before you will experience in its growth toward wholeness. You are that child, worthy of complete respect and love. Sit for a few minutes and let that love fill your heart.

April 30

Seed Thought

As we put the capstone on the month of April, consider that freedom
can never be taught, only tasted. Intellectual understanding doesn't
amount to any more than yet another way to feed the sense of
specialness that is the nature of the insecure ego. Be simple,
like Nasrudin, the foolish wise man of many Sufi teaching stories.
Investigate freedom for yourself. One day, Nasrudin heard that
parrots live for 150 years. "Why should I believe such an outlandish
thing?" he wondered. So Nasrudin went out and bought himself a
parrot, determined to find the truth for himself.

Prayer/Practice

*It takes no more time to be mindful than mindless, and
mindfulness is the way that you will taste freedom. Commit to doing
one activity mindfully every day for the next month, in addition
to the other daily practices.*

MAY

Gratitude and the Divine Feminine

May is a month of gratitude and a celebration of the feminine aspect
of God
—God the Mother—
who creates and nurtures all things, including ourselves.
The beauty of May draws us out of hibernation into a
natural mindfulness of the blessing and abundance of nature.
Gratitude and mindfulness are intimately related, for
as we practice gratitude we come more aware, more present.
We wake up.
Spring calls us to simplify our lives so that we can
enjoy everything more thoroughly and graciously—
our relationships, our homes, our possessions.
In May our hearts remember what our minds sometimes forget—
life is a gift of inestimable value.
It is time to unwrap the gift.
Listen to the voices of the Ancient Ones as they speak
from within the heart of the quickening earth:

Bear cubs play in the sun,
grazing on the new growth
that the Earth Mother has provided.
The simple pleasures of spring rain,
opening buds and new moons
draw us out of worried mind
into a celebration of Divine Mind.
The Archangel Uriel and the
energies of the East
tutor us in the art
of mindfulness
and the sacrament
of gratitude.

May 1: Beltane

Seed Thought

May Day is the ancient festival of Beltane, the midway point between the vernal (spring) equinox and the summer solstice. The days are growing longer, coaxing the earth to open to the life-giving qualities of the sun and to bring forth every kind of fruit. Beltane is a celebration of the fertility of the earth and the fertility of our own souls. It is a call to gratitude that everything in the universe is continually being re-created, including ourselves.

Prayer/Practice

Great Spirit, I begin the month of May filled with gratitude for the increase in the light that brings forth life from my soul and from the earth. May my heart be fertile ground for the sprouting of your Godseed, that I may be of loving service to my family, my community and all beings.

Close your eyes and take a few letting-go breaths. Gradually, patiently, find your way into the inner stillness. Feel the surging of the lifeforce within that stillness. Meditate on the lifeforce within.

May 2

Seed Thought

In May the flowers are blossoming and the earth is greening. We can appreciate this miracle more deeply, having awakened out of the barrenness of winter. The beauty of God runs riot in colors, fragrances, warmth and a dizzying plenitude of forms and species. We get an inkling of the true splendor and fertility of our Cosmic Beloved. In the Jewish tradition it is God the Mother, or the Shekhinah, that brings all things into creation.

Prayer/Practice

Cosmic Beloved, Queen of Earth and Heaven, your abundance is truly awesome. You awaken us cyclically from our sleep and bring forth every fruit in its season, the fruits of the earth and the fruits of our souls. I give thanks to you and pray to realize the Divine Feminine within myself, the lifeforce that gives and nourishes life.

Spend a few minutes in the practice of Metta meditation (February 11–15), which is an expression of the love and blessing of the Divine Feminine within you.

May 3

Seed Thought

The Song of Songs is one of the most beautiful expressions of the joy and celebration of true spiritual love and its expression in the rebirth of spring. These famous verses from the Song of Solomon in the Old Testament date, in written form, to the fourth century before the birth of Christ. They celebrate the sacred union between the male and female within ourselves, between ourselves and God, and between the male and female aspects of the creator.

Prayer/Practice

Spend a few minutes in centering prayer or shamatha/vipassana meditation. Then recite the Song of Songs slowly, as a contemplation.

Rise up, my love, my fair one, and come away for lo, the winter is past, the rain is over and gone. The flowers appear on the earth, the time of the singing of birds is come, and the voice of the turtledove is heard in our land. The fig tree putteth forth her green figs, and the vines with the tender grape giveth a good smell. Arise, my love, my fair one and come away.

—Song of Solomon 2:10–13

May 4

Seed Thought

The Hasidim, a mystical sect of Jews that began in Europe in the mid-eighteenth century, celebrated their union with God in song, in dance, and in the ecstatic joy of waiting all week long for the coming of the Divine Feminine—the Shekhinah—whom they would welcome as a spiritual lover, the Sabbath Queen. During spring and summer, they would go out into the fertile, growing fields of corn on Friday evening and welcome the Sabbath Queen with the love song "Lechah Dodi," which thrills my soul when I hear or sing it.

Prayer/Practice

Great Spirit, Divine Mystery beyond the duality of male and female, mother and father, parent and child, help me to know you by understanding each of Your aspects. In this month of May, help me understand You as God the Mother, She who gives and nourishes life.

Spend a few minutes in centering prayer. Open yourself to the Divine Presence, being a receptive vessel for God's love.

May 5

Seed Thought

Each week is a cycle, a microcosm of the cycle of the year. Just as modern society has forgotten the larger cycles, the wisdom of the seasons and the earth energies that bring us into harmony with one another and the Sacred Mystery, so has the cycle of the week been largely forgotten. Attuning to the energy of the week, whose heart is the Sabbath, is one of the most easily forgotten of the Ten Commandments.

Prayer/Practice

Reflect on this ancient wisdom, given to Moses on Mount Sinai, as part of the formula by which we remember our unity with God.

Remember the Sabbath day, to keep it holy. Six days you shall labor, and do all your work; but the seventh day is a Sabbath to the Lord your God; in it you shall not do any work, you or your son, or your daughter, your manservant or your maidservant, or your cattle, or the sojourner who is within your gates; for in six days the Lord made heaven and earth, the sea, and all that is in them, and rested the seventh day; therefore the Lord blessed the Sabbath day and hallowed it.

—Exodus 20:8–11

May 6

Seed Thought

Every week has a Sabbath. Even if we cannot take an entire day to celebrate creation with family and friends—to feast, to sing, to dance, to pray, to make love and to give thanks—we can take a part of a day and consciously give ourselves over to a grateful celebration of the abundant blessings of our life.

Prayer/Practice

Think about how you could celebrate a Sabbath each week. Although the traditional Jewish Sabbath is Friday evening and Saturday, Sunday Sabbath gradually took over in the Christian tradition. If you don't attend a temple or church, is there a weekly ritual you could construct for yourself, family or friends? Prayer, spiritual reading, song, feasting and fellowship are a part of Sabbath tradition. Your celebration might last an hour or a whole day, but your intention is to stop the world for that window of time. To rest and recreate will have far-reaching effects on your life.

Spend a few minutes in meditation and contemplate the wisdom of the Sabbath and whether it feels right to add a Sabbath to your week.

May 7

Seed Thought

Just as we can rest in the womb of the Sabbath Queen weekly, so,
too, can we rest in a mini-Sabbath each day. A period of reflection,
prayer and spiritual practice restores a sacred rhythm to the day.
Time in the outer world is balanced with time in the inner
world. It is more important to be consistent with putting time aside
for prayer and meditation than it is to spend long periods of
time in spiritual pursuit. Even five minutes a day in prayer make
a difference, because this reminds us of our true life in the spirit.

Prayer/Practice

Divine Mother, let me seek the peace and stillness of your womb
in which I can re-create myself daily. The lifeforce flows through You
into the form of all things manifested on this planet. When I
immerse myself in Your peaceful Presence, my energy body will
take the shape of the Divine Will, and I will become more fully
who I am meant to be.

*Take a few deep breaths and allow your eyes to close. Focus on
your breathing, noticing the way that your body rises on the
inbreath and lets go, relaxing on the outbreath. Imagine that
you are relaxing into the arms of the Divine Mother with each
outbreath. Continue for two or three minutes.*

May 8

Seed Thought

The fifteenth-century Christian mystic Julian of Norwich is well known for her deep appreciation of God as mother. In the text of her divine visions, called *Showings*, she said, "This fair and lovely word 'mother' is so sweet and so kind in itself that it cannot truly be said of anyone or to anyone except of him and to him who is the true Mother of life and of all things. To the property of motherhood belong nature, love, wisdom and knowledge, and this is God."

Prayer/Practice

Divine Mother, thank you for bringing the world into being once again this morning. Let me feel your peace and stillness. Let me feel your arms wrapped around me as I let go to Your Divine Presence with each outbreath. As I walk in the world today, let me appreciate every aspect of nature as Your handiwork, pausing to feel Your pulse, your breath in all that lives.

Find a growing plant today—a houseplant, a tree, a flower or grasses. Sit down in front of it and center yourself through your breathing. Enter the place of inner stillness within yourself, and then gradually expand your mind to include the plant. Meditate on the lifeforce within the plant for a few minutes.

May 9

Seed Thought

Hildegard of Bingen is another of my favorite Christian mystics. She lived in the twelfth century, and her philosophy bridges science, art and religion. Hildegard was a great lover of nature, which she thought the truest mirror of divine creativity. She said, "The earth is at the same time mother, she is mother of all that is natural, mother of all that is human. She is the mother of all, for contained in her are the seeds of all. The earth of humankind contains all moistness, all verdancy, all germinating power. It is in so many ways fruitful. All creation comes from it."

Prayer/Practice

We can become aware of the force of nature, the Mother principle, through gratitude. Close your eyes and take a few letting-go breaths. Recall a holy moment in nature, a time when you were fully present to a sunrise, a mountain landscape, the magnificence of the ocean, a field of wildflowers, the germinating of beans in a paper cup in kindergarten. . . . Bring back the memory in every sense. What did you see? Were there any fragrances? Any sounds? What about physical feelings? The wind or sun? Movement? Feel your connection to the natural world and the gratitude that naturally arises in your heart.

May 10

Seed Thought

Gratitude is a natural outcome of mindfulness. It is also a way to become mindful. We often shut out natural beauty by becoming mindlessly absorbed in the chatter and worry of small mind with its endless self-absorbed attachments to past and future. Spring offers a compelling invitation to let go of our petty concerns and open ourselves to the Divine Mind through appreciation of the magnificence of nature.

Prayer/Practice

Divine Mother, you have clothed all of creation in the robes of spring. Even in the city there are trees in bloom, flowers budding and the sweet fragrance of blossoms blowing in the breeze. Today I call upon Uriel and the angels of clarity and mindfulness to help me truly see Your handiwork. Today I will practice gratitude. Whenever I see something of beauty I will stop and admire it. "Good work, Divine Mother."

May 11

Seed Thought

One of the most beautiful practices that I have retained from my Jewish roots is the recitation of blessings, called *brachot*, which are prayers of gratitude. Judaism is similar to Greek Orthodox Catholicism in being a tradition of gratitude. In Judaism there are over a hundred blessings which express our gratitude to God for every kind of natural wonder—things that grow, stars that shine, rainbows, food we eat, even the natural functions of elimination that keep our bodies healthy!

Prayer/Practice

The bracha is a blessing of God for all that has been created. You can say an impromptu blessing whenever you notice something of wonder or beauty:

Blessed art Thou, Creator of the Universe who has given us the first star of evening, or the light of the moon, or the smile of babies.

Today, recite at least five brachot upon seeing something of beauty. After each one, spend a minute or two in mindfulness. Be aware of the way in which the lifeforce awakens in your body through gratitude and mindful attention.

May 12

Seed Thought

David Steindl-Rast is a Benedictine monk who is one of a new breed of contemplative Christians with a deep understanding of mindfulness and the wisdom of the East. Steindl-Rast calls gratefulness the heart of prayer. He says that thinking of prayer as mindful attention frees us from religious jargon. "If we call it wholehearted living, it is easier to recognize prayer as an attitude that should characterize all our activities. The more we become alive and awake, the more everything we do becomes prayer."

Prayer/Practice

Divine Beloved, thank you for this spring morning and the recreation of the world in a new dawn. Today I call upon Uriel and the angels of clarity to help me live my life in mindfulness and gratitude. Let my attitude toward all I see and experience be a prayer of thanksgiving that glorifies all You have created.

Practice several minutes of centering prayer, flowing in the river of God's Divine love. When you feel still and in contact with the Divine, spend two or three minutes contemplating the things you are grateful for.

May 13

Seed Thought

Brother David Steindl-Rast practices gratitude as a way of learning mindfulness. Before turning out the light each night, he thinks of one thing for which he's never before been grateful. It's a wonderful practice. After doing it for several weeks, I began to use up the obvious sources of gratitude. Since I knew that I would be doing the practice at night, it reminded me to be mindful during the day and to notice and appreciate things that I might previously have missed.

Prayer/Practice

As you go about your day, remember to notice something that you've never thought of being grateful for. Just before going to sleep, review your day and give thanks for whatever it was that you appreciated newly today.

May 14

Seed Thought

My husband and I went to a healing service at a Roman Catholic Church. The priest, who was a beautifully humble and simple man, said something that we really took to heart. "Give thanks to God for everything in your life that doesn't need healing." At times when my restless ego begins the search for happiness in things outside myself, I experience boredom. Then I think of times in my life when I've been extremely agitated and anxious, and I give thanks for the peacefulness in my life which even allows my ego the room to feel bored!

Prayer/Practice

Divine Mother, thank you for this new day, this new mind and this new body. Thank you for all the things in my life that don't need healing.

Spend a few minutes contemplating these things and sincerely feeling thanksgiving. Finish with a few minutes of centering prayer or shamatha/vipassana meditation.

May 15

Seed Thought

One day my husband, Miron, and I returned to a hotel room after a long day's work in a distant city. We had two more weeks left on the road, and my ego began to indulge in self-pity. "Poor me; I work so hard." Then I stopped to think of what I had. A warm, comfortable room, meaningful work, a healthy family, a full belly, and the man I had shared over two decades with in the bed beside me. I looked into his eyes and was filled with gratitude just to be together, suddenly aware of the impermanence of all things, recognizing that a day would inevitably come when we must part ways at the gates of death.

Prayer/Practice

Divine Mother, I am so grateful for the many gifts of life, particularly the gift of love and caring for family and friends that I sometimes take for granted. Let me cherish the time we have together, remembering always the impermanence of life and the good fortune we have to be together now.

Next time you see a loved one or good friend, try this mindful hug that I learned from the Vietnamese Buddhist monk and teacher Thich Nhat Hanh. Embracing one another, on the first inbreath think, "I love you," and on the outbreath, "I am so glad to be here with you." On the next inbreath, "I really appreciate you," and on the next outbreath, "Knowing that someday we must part."

May 16

Seed Thought

Our bodies are generally unappreciated until we get sick, and then they are often criticized for letting us down. Before getting out of bed in the morning, I sometimes practice a short version of a Chinese Taoist meditation of gratitude toward one's body. It's fun because you get to smile at all your organs!

Prayer/Practice

Take a few letting-go breaths and gradually, patiently enter the place of inner silence. Direct your attention to your eyes and smile inwardly at them, thanking them for their service to you. Repeat this with your ears, your nose, your tongue, your vocal chords, your stomach and intestines, your heart, your immune system and as many organs as your time and anatomical knowledge allow!

May 17

Seed Thought

I received a greeting card that was inscribed, "The difference between an optimist and a pessimist is droll. The optimist sees the donut and the pessimist sees the hole." There are people whose lives are filled with blessings, yet they perceive only lack. There are others who have very little in a material way, people who may have suffered great tragedy, and yet they see the bounty of life. They have learned the secret of happiness.

Prayer/Practice

Great Spirit, I welcome You on this beautiful day. I reach out to You with a grateful heart and give thanks for all the blessings of my life. I pray for awareness today. When my ego starts in with its judgments about what is wrong, what is not good enough, let me notice this pessimistic thinking and instead, see my blessings.

Spend a few minutes practicing the mindfulness of shamatha/ vipassana meditation.

May 18

Seed Thought

How often I have taken pride in a well-stocked cupboard. After all, no one likes to run out of toilet paper when they live 9,000 feet up on a mountain, half an hour's drive to the market. But it's deeper than that. I survey our stores of soups and flours, tins of fruits and neat rows of spices. I feel secure until I recognize the humor of thinking that security resides in a cupboard. Life is always flowing, always changing and there is no security other than cultivating our sense of Oneness with God.

Prayer/Practice

Divine Mother, let me come to Oneness with you through the gates of mindfulness and gratitude. When my mind seeks security in the outer world, let me turn instead to my faith by reflecting on this beautiful teaching of Jesus:

Therefore I tell you, do not be anxious about your life, what you shall eat, nor about your body, what you shall put on. For life is more than food and the body more than clothing. Consider the ravens, they neither sow nor reap, they have neither storehouses nor barn, and yet God feeds them.... Consider the lilies, how they grow; they neither toil nor spin; yet I tell you even Solomon in all his glory was not arrayed like one of these.

—Luke 12:22

May 19

Seed Thought

We know that the Godseed within us is growing when we feel the
joy, the gratitude and the optimism of true humility. Humility
is the freedom of having nothing to prove because we are completely
secure in our identity as children of the Divine. Whenever the
weed of arrogance begins to sprout in our gardens, some insecurity
has taken root and caused us to forget our own true worth, our
own true nature of creativity, love and wisdom.

Prayer/Practice

Divine Mother, thank you for the lifeforce that surges through the
earth and pulses within me on this May morning. Help me tend
the garden of my mind which is like a fertile field in which Your
Consciousness grows. Help me weed out the sprouts of arrogance, the
"know-it-all" thoughts and actions based on the insecurity of the
ego, that prevent the Godseed within from coming fully to flower.

*Be aware today of the thoughts that come to your mind. Arrogance
is the bane of humility and therefore the antithesis of gratitude.
When an arrogant thought occurs, notice it and let it go by
appealing to the Archangel Uriel to restore your clarity of
mind.*

May 20

Seed Thought

Paying bills is a great spiritual teaching and even a cause for gratitude when seen rightly. We are alive, we are doing a co-creative dance with those people from whom we've bought services, and we are learning to make choices about how we allocate our resources and what is most important to us. Paying the bills tells us a lot about our world-view as optimists or pessimists. The optimist feels grateful for what has been given and received. The pessimist is more likely to indulge in a poverty of spirit that blames others for overcharging or cheating or having more than their share.

Prayer/Practice

Divine Mother, thank you for extending mindfulness of attitude into every corner of my life, particularly my view of money, which is a sensitive indicator of the richness or poverty of my spirit. Help me see how the choices I make in spending reflect the values by which I live my life.

Spend a few minutes in centering prayer, and then get your checkbook and last month's credit card bills if you have any. What is your attitude toward your expenses? Does your spending reflect your basic values? If not, what changes can you make?

May 21

Seed Thought

Complaining is a way of reinforcing the mindset of scarcity and lack. If something is wrong, take action to set it right rather than complaining. Pessimists complain and blame themselves and other people for what is wrong. They even blame God. Optimists have risen above blame. Even in threatening or difficult situations, they are thankful for the challenges that help them overcome their limitations.

Prayer/Practice

Be mindful today of the way your ego constricts your ability to be happy and mindful by blaming and complaining. Even when things are just fine, the ego can spin endless fantasies about what could go wrong. Resist them by practicing mental martial arts. Notice what your mind is doing and say to yourself, "Complaining, or blaming." Then just take a breath and let complaints go as you do thoughts in meditation.

Spend a few minutes in centering prayer or shamatha/vipassana meditation, skillfully letting the ego and its complaints move past you without engaging and giving them life.

May 22

Seed Thought

Human life is a great opportunity that is too often maligned or unappreciated. A woman I know tried to kill herself as an adolescent because her parents abused her. When she got to the Other Side, a loving Being of Light told her that life was a very great gift and that she had no right to terminate hers. When she complained that no one loved her, the Being of Light told her that this lifetime was a chance for her to learn that she must love herself. She returned with a sense of gratitude for life, and an understanding that she could even be grateful for the hardships through which she was learning life's most important lessons.

Prayer/Practice

Gratitude for hardships does not mean that we need to stay in abusive or unhealthy situations. There are times to take action and times to surrender. Both strategies are occasions for learning and reasons for gratitude. Spend a few minutes in meditation and then contemplate the difficulties in your life. Apply the serenity prayer.

God give me the courage to change the things I can, the serenity to accept the things I can't, and the wisdom to know the difference.

And I might add, God give me the understanding of life that allows me to be grateful for all circumstances.

May 23

Seed Thought

Many people who return from near-death experiences have a renewed appreciation for how precious a human lifetime is. They echo the teaching of Eastern philosophies, which say that human life is the greatest gift because it is the gateway to enlightenment. The Tibetan Buddhists say that if the Universe were as big as the ocean, and if there were a single wooden ring floating on the surface of that ocean, and a single turtle swimming around, the chance of getting a human birth would be the same as the turtle surfacing with his head in the wooden ring.

Prayer/Practice

Great Spirit, please awaken deep thanksgiving in my heart for the gift of my life. I am an eternal, immortal aspect of Your Mind, a growing edge of Divine Consciousness. My soul is being continually enriched by the experiences of life. Yet sometimes I forget this extraordinary situation. I am alive! I am alive! Thank you, Divine Beloved, for this amazing gift.

Spend a few minutes in centering prayer or shamatha/vipassana meditation. Then contemplate the absolutely awesome fact that you exist.

May 24

Seed Thought

Greek Orthodoxy is a wonderful tradition of gratitude. The human being is considered an intermediary between the creation and the Creator, a mirror that reflects back to God the beauty of what has been created. The Greek Orthodox position reminds me of the riddle from quantum physics concerning whether or not a tree actually falls in the woods if there's no one to witness it. If it is true that the observer and the observed are inextricably linked in creating reality, then our gratitude actually does help bring the world into being.

Prayer/Practice

Divine Beloved, let me be your eyes and ears, your tender touch, your emotions. By seeing clearly, by feeling deeply, by mindfully immersing myself in life I feel grateful and happy. I also help bring the world into being through my careful appreciation of Your Handiwork.

Center yourself in your breathing until you feel yourself slipping into the quiet, patient attitude of mindfulness. There is nowhere to go, nothing to do except to mirror the beauty of creation back to God. Look out at the sky and appreciate all its nuances, all its elegant beauty. Take your time and continue until you sense that you've felt the sky.

May 25

Seed Thought

Saint Leontius of Cyprus was a sixth-century Greek Orthodox priest.
He said that creation can't worship God directly, but only through us:
"It is through me that the heavens declare the glory of God, through
me the moon worships God, through me the stars glorify Him, through
me the waters and showers of rain, the dews and all creation venerate
God and give him glory."

Prayer/Practice

*Today, contemplate the thought that you make God's creation
visible, that you encourage the earth to bloom through your
appreciation. Practice Metta this morning, sending your
lovingkindness blessings to all the things that grow in your
home, your yard, your neighborhood, your city.*

May 26

Seed Thought

The Buddhist monk Thich Nhat Hanh teaches a wonderful grace before meals: Are you eating green beans for supper? Think of the people who plowed the fields and planted the seeds. Think of the wind and rain, the sun and moon, whose energies brought forth the beans from the seeds. Think of the people who harvested the beans, who shipped the beans and drove the delivery truck. Think of the people who unloaded the beans and displayed them in the store. Think of the person who bought the beans, who cooked them and placed them on the table. Think of the Great Mystery of life, the Creator, from which this entire drama sprang forth. Be grateful to them all.

Prayer/Practice

Great Spirit, thank you for the rich web of life in which I am a strand. Help me appreciate how all the strands of the web are connected with such elegance, such grace. Whenever I go to use something today—whether it's a plastic bag, the clothes I wear, my car, my computer, help me appreciate how many forces of nature, how many human hands, what Divine Wisdom, has gone into its creation.

Before you eat today, say a mindful, appreciative grace that really brings you into a connection with the forces of nature.

May 27

Seed Thought

Thich Nhat Hanh teaches mindful walking as a form of meditation. How many times have you gone out walking in a beautiful place and hardly looked around you? Have you ever spent an entire walk preoccupied with doing your income taxes, worrying about your relationships or making plans? Walking mindfully in nature is one of the most delightful activities. It brings us into the moment where we can appreciate nature, appreciate the bodies that move us from place to place, appreciate the air we breathe, the warmth of the sun or the wetness of the rain.

Prayer/Practice

Today, go for a mindful walk. Even if you can't go outside, walk mindfully in your home. Place your attention lightly on the flow of your breathing. At the same time, notice how your body moves, how the weight shifts from one foot to the other. Perhaps you can coordinate your footsteps with your breathing, two or so steps to each inbreath and outbreath. The sensation of breathing and walking is like the anchor for your attention. When you feel focused in breathing and walking, open your senses to everything around you. The breath is like a bridge between you and everything you see, touch, smell and sense. If your mind wanders, return to the sensation of breathing and walking. Enjoy!

May 28

Seed Thought

The more mindful we become, the more we appreciate beauty and order. Just as seeds germinate best in a garden where any excess has been cleared away, our life purpose comes to fruition most easily when we clear out unnecessary clutter from our lives. A spiritual teacher of mine once made the analogy that the state of one's drawers is a good mirror of the state of one's unconscious. I went home and cleaned my drawers. That was easy. Cleaning out my unconscious has been a much more long-term project!

Prayer/Practice

Divine Mother, you who are the cosmic gardener, thank you for planting the seeds of love and service in my heart. Help me weed my garden so that the seeds you have planted in my life can flourish.

Refresh your bodymind and soul with a few minutes of centering prayer or shamatha/vipassana meditation. Then think of a spring cleaning project—sorting your drawers and giving old clothes to charity, cleaning out a window box or flower bed, going through a room and getting rid of some of the inevitable clutter that mounts up over the years—returning the room to a simpler beauty. Make a plan to complete the project.

May 29

Seed Thought

An old adage states that less is more. Many years ago, our minister gave a sermon on how we become slaves to our possessions. A friend approached us after the service, saying, "When Reverend Chris asked what one thing we could do to simplify our lives I thought of the week Bruce and I spent house-sitting for you and Miron. Watering all your plants was so time-consuming that I couldn't help wonder if they're as much of a drain on you as they were on us." I love plants, but Linda's words helped me look at our collection in a new light. We kept the ones that we felt closest to and found new homes for about twenty others. We could appreciate the plants that were left in a whole new way. Before, in our hurry to water so many, we had hardly appreciated how beautiful each plant was.

Prayer/Practice

Divine Mother, you have given so many gifts to me that sometimes I forget to appreciate them. Help me simplify my life so that I can truly appreciate what I have. And help me spread your bounty by giving things away to others who can truly appreciate them.

Spend a few minutes in shamatha/vipassana meditation and then contemplate what you have too much of, and who you could give it away to.

May 30

Seed Thought

Every five years or so my husband, Miron, and I go on a diet. We
eliminate all but the essentials for our health, cutting out fat
and sugar and taking extra care to prepare lots of vegetables and
whole grains. We are always amazed at how much more we
appreciate our food when we've taken the time to prepare it with
care and then to savor every bite. We think of diets as times of
tremendous gratitude for the daily gift of food which, at other times,
we tend to take for granted. Once again, less turns out to be
more.

Prayer/Practice

Divine Beloved, I am so grateful for all that I have in my life. Food
to eat, shelter, and most of all, a growing love for You. Today, when
I sit to eat, help me to do so mindfully, savoring each bite. Let me
eat as if I have never eaten before and as if I might never eat
again, with complete absorption and great joy.

*Eat mindfully today, aware of each bite that you chew and each
bite that you swallow. Eat only if you're hungry.*

May 31

Seed Thought

True simplicity consists not in the use of particular forms, but in foregoing overindulgence, in maintaining humility of spirit, and in keeping the material surroundings of our lives directly serviceable to necessary ends, even though these surroundings may properly be characterized by grace, symmetry, and beauty.

—*Book of Discipline* of the Religious Society of Friends

Prayer/Practice

Divine Mother, thank you for helping me weed the garden of my life on this beautiful spring morning. I call upon Uriel and the angels of clarity to help me awaken to the understanding that discipline is not a giving up of things I need in order to be happy, but a deeper appreciation of what I have—which in itself is happiness. Humility of spirit is not false modesty, but the sheer joy of a mindful heart that has found its security in You.

Spend a few minutes in centering prayer or shamatha/vipassana meditation. Then place your attention directly in front of you, at the Eastern Gate of your body temple. Invoke the presence of Uriel and ask for clarity about simplifying your life. Sit quietly and wait for a response.

JUNE

Miracles of Light: Prayer and Spiritual Healing

June is a month of abundance during which the Godseed
within us continues its unfolding according to the blueprint of our souls.
Everything necessary for our growth has already been given,
and through the application of "scientific prayer" and spiritual healing
we lay claim to what is already ours and give aid to others
in unfolding the Divine blueprint within.
We become the agents of miracles.
The outer light and the Inner Light are bright in June,
and we can use this increased energy to
attune to the presence of the Archangel Gabriel
and our guardian angel,
who has accompanied us from before the
foundation of the world
in the evolution of our soul's will to love.
Listen to the voices of the Ancient Ones as they rise
on the warm winds of summer and shimmer on the lighted
grasses that wave gently in the summer sun:

*The lifeforce is surging
through the Earth Mother
and all manner of things are well.
The bear cubs play
in an enchanted forest
in which there is a doorway
where two worlds touch.
The Archangel Gabriel
and our guardian angels
instruct us in prayer.
In our dedication to service
we become the openings
through which miracles
of lovingkindness and healing
can manifest for the good
of all beings.*

Seed Thought

The days are growing ever longer in June, and the Medicine Wheel of the seasons will open fully to the South on the summer solstice, June 21. The illumination of the sun is bringing forth fruits from the earth, and encouraging clarity in our perception. This is the time when the energies of the Light can bring forth true spiritual healing, the realization of our Oneness with God that alleviates all suffering and ideas of limitation.

Prayer/Practice

Divine Beloved, may I see clearly, may I know in the depths of my soul that I and all beings are One with You. May I realize that You are manifesting right here, right now as me, as family, friends, enemies and all beings. In that perception I am healed.

Practice Metta meditation (February 11–15), sending blessings of lovingkindness to all beings.

As you go through your day, bring Metta into your relationships. If you sense someone's pain, send a blessing. You can do this with eyes open, mentally extending light and caring to this person, and simultaneously receiving it yourself.

June 2

Seed Thought

The Apostle Paul wrote:

For now we see through a glass darkly; but then face to face: now I know in part; but then shall I know even as also I am known.

—First Corinthians 13:12

Paul defines spiritual healing by contrasting the difference between living in relative reality, where we see "through a glass darkly," and awakening into the perception of absolute reality, the Mind of God that is beyond all the pairs of opposites in which we usually live, the state where "I know even as also I am known," the state of conscious union with God.

Prayer/Practice

Divine Beloved, thank You for the growing Light of correct perception through which I am awakening to Who I really am, a Divine Child, an indivisible aspect of Your Consciousness.

Practice a few minutes of centering prayer or shamatha/vipassana meditation. Now look around you and recognize that everything exists as part of the Mind of God. That chair is made of God's mind, that window is made of God's mind. You are made of God's mind. There is nowhere that God is not.

As you go through the day looking at people, places and things, remind yourself of the miracle of existence by affirming: "This person, or this tree, is the mind of God made manifest." Do this three or four times today.

June 3

Seed Thought

Jesus stated repeatedly that "my Father and I are One." God manifests as a multiplicity of apparently individual beings, yet each of us has our identity in union with the Divine. When we pray it isn't a matter of us down here talking to someone up there. "My father and I are one." Not two. If our perception was clear, as the perception of Jesus, or Buddha or any of the other Awakened Ones, we would instantly rise out of the duality of God and humankind, me and them, good and bad, life and death. We would know that the eternal Kingdom of Heaven exists here and now within every one of us.

Prayer/Practice

One of the oldest spiritual adages states, "See God in each other." As you go about your business today, see every person that you meet as an aspect of God in form. When we see another person as completely worthy of our respect and love, the perfection of Divine Mind manifests in and through them, and we become channels of true spiritual healing.

June 4

Seed Thought

Praying to God as a cosmic Santa Claus who exists to fill our special requests keeps us bound to the concept of scarcity. There is an abundant supply of everything in the Universe. God has already provided entirely for our needs. We need only open to the grace that is already present. The spiritual healer and mystic Joel Goldsmith wrote, "You begin to see that God cannot give and God cannot withold. You can shut yourself off from the grace of God, but through prayer, you can be reunited with your Source. Your prayer will not be a seeking for any thing; it will be an asking and a knocking for more light, greater spiritual wisdom, greater discernment."

Prayer/Practice

Divine Beloved, thank you for the gift of light which is awakening me to a new realization of who I am and how it is truly Your pleasure to give me the Kingdom. I call upon Uriel and the angels of clarity to help me seek right understanding and discernment and right relationship to You. You are not here to fulfill my needs, for You have done that already. I am here to reflect back the magnificence of creation to You. As I learn to do that, all my needs will be filled, for I will have undammed the flow of Your grace.

June 5

Seed Thought

A Course in Miracles has defined a miracle as a change in perception.
Spiritual healing is truly a miracle because it enables us to let
go of our limited concepts and realize that whatever is happening
on an outer level cannot disturb our inner peace and harmony
when we have made the realization of our Oneness with God our
first priority.

Prayer/Practice

Divine Beloved, thank you for light and clarity which are awakening
me to my true nature, Your Divine Mind and the infinite peace, wisdom
and love that I am. I call upon Uriel and the angels of clarity to
help me view the happenings of this day with right perception.
No matter what the outer appearance of things may be, let me think
of the "bookmark prayer" of Saint Teresa of Avila:

Let nothing upset you,
Let nothing afright you.
Everything is changing;
God alone is changeless.
Patience attains the goal.
Who has God lacks nothing;
God alone fills all her needs.

June 6

Seed Thought

Ian Gawler was a twenty-five-year-old veterinarian and decathlon athlete when his leg was amputated at the hip because of bone cancer. Within a few months, the cancer had metastasized throughout his body, and he was given two weeks to live. Instead of accepting the limitation of his prognosis, he married Grace, his veterinary nurse, and the two of them set about receiving healing on every level. They consulted energy healers and psychic healers. Ian changed his diet and spent hours each day in a form of deep, silent meditation similar to centering prayer. Over a period of four years the cancer gradually disappeared. Twenty years later, my husband and I asked Ian to what he attributed his remarkable healing. He answered, "Peace of mind."

Prayer/Practice

Great Spirit, help me awaken to the peace of mind that is my own true nature, my birthright in You.

Spend a few minutes in centering prayer or shamatha/vipassana meditation. Finish with Metta meditation, since lovingkindness is the very essence of the Divine Presence and the true expression of spiritual healing.

June 7

Seed Thought

Peace of mind creates the most conducive conditions for physical healing. The great behaviorist Ivan Pavlov lay dying of a widespread infection years before the discovery of antibiotics. He sent an assistant to the river with the odd task of bringing back a bucket of warm mud. That done, Pavlov stuck his hands in the bucket and began to play in the mud like a child. A few hours later his fever broke. He reasoned that if he could re-create the most peaceful, wonderful moment of his life, his body would have the maximal chance to heal. Remembering that his mother used to do her laundry in the river when he was a child, telling him stories as he played contentedly in the mud, he re-created that scene, and, sure enough, his body returned to homeostasis—inner balance.

Prayer/Practice

After you have shut your eyes and found the inner stillness, bring to mind a memory of a time when you felt peaceful and contented. A day in the sun, a time with a pet, a moment from childhood. Once a memory comes back, relive it with all your senses. Recall the sights and colors, the fragrances, the sense of movement, the perception of touch and the felt sense of peace. How does peace feel in your body?

Two or three times today, remind yourself that you know how to be peaceful. Take a deep breath and remember how peace feels in your body. If you need a little help, bring back this morning's memory.

June 8

Seed Thought

Peace of mind is the key to healing. The experience we call peace is the physical/emotional perception of being in God's Presence, feeling at One with the Source of our being. Cardiologist Herbert Benson has described the physiology of peace, which he calls the "relaxation response." This is a "wakeful, hypometabolic state" that is deeply restorative. It lowers blood pressure and heart rate, brings the immune system to balance and quiets the rational mind, allowing a deeper wisdom to emerge.

Prayer/Practice

Great Spirit, my heart is filled with gratitude for the continual awakening into the Light that I am experiencing as the newness of spring ripens into the lushness of summer. Help me give up the idea that I need to constantly be "doing" in order to heal. Letting go into your peaceful Presence, let me experience the being that is my own true nature.

Practice several minutes of centering prayer. Remember that meditation is a not-doing. It is just letting go of small mind and merging with the stream of Divine Mind.

June 9

Seed Thought

There is no illness or life condition that cannot be cured. But if we insist on cure, we may miss out on real spiritual healing, especially if our attachment to cure creates a battle inside of us. If recovery from an illness is in the service of our own growth or the growth of another, a physical cure—even a so-called miraculous cure—can happen in the twinkling of an eye. If being ill is in the service of our own growth or the growth of another, cure is unlikely, but spiritual healing is very likely if we make peace of mind our most important priority.

Prayer/Practice

Divine Beloved, may the Light of your Being shine into every recess of my mind, dispelling the clouds of illusion and negativity that prevent healing in my life. I accept complete and total healing from You now, knowing that my spiritual sight is not great enough to know what form that healing will take, other than a peaceful mind and a compassionate heart.

Allow yourself a few minutes of centering prayer to sink into the Mind of God, and feel the peace that passeth understanding.

Two or three times today, practice peacefulness. Take a deep breath and remember how peace feels in your body.

June 10

Seed Thought

A woman who had been in a serious car crash had a near-death experience. The Being of Light who guided her explained that she had three choices: She could stay on the Other Side, she could return with minor injuries or she could return in a vegetative state. The Being of Light then showed her a life review of all her loved ones, run from the perspective of her returning in relatively good shape or in a vegetative condition. When she was satisfied that no one would receive particular benefit from her choosing to return in a permanent coma, she came back with minor injuries. Consider that one person's illness or injury may, in fact, be a gift of service for others.

Prayer/Practice

Great Spirit, I pray for the strength to accept the role I have chosen in this lifetime and to allow others to do what they have chosen to do, or what is karmically appropriate for them. When I pray for my own healing or that of another, let me pray only that the highest good be done, whatever that may be. Let me strive to have no thoughts, no images, no expectations of what healing is in any situation but only to hold the one being prayed for in the highest love and esteem, in the knowledge that they are One with You.

Pray for the healing of someone you know.

June 11

Seed Thought

Pediatrician Melvin Morse, who is an expert in near-death and Light
experiences, tells this amazing story: A woman with a non-serious skin
cancer, scheduled for surgery in the morning, went to bed terrified.
Suddenly a ball of loving Light appeared in her room. She was
awestruck and began to pray. The Being of Light told her that what
most people consider prayer is actually more like complaining.
He instructed her to send all the love and light she was experiencing
to her worst enemy. When she did, she felt as if her blessing had
bounced off a mirror and returned to her manyfold, filling every
cell of her body with Light and healing. The Being of Light then
told her that she had prayed for the very first time. When she went
to the doctor in the morning, the cancer was gone.

Prayer/Practice

*There is wisdom in the saying that whatever we give comes back
again. When we pray for others, healing returns to us—
whether physically, emotionally or spiritually. Today, do several
minutes of Metta meditation, which is a wonderful way to
practice spiritual healing. It is quite similar to how the Being of
Light told the woman in today's story how to pray.*

June 12

Seed Thought

There is an old saying that nothing is certain except for death and taxes. Nonetheless, a sad misunderstanding of healing views death and illness as a psychological or spiritual failure. This mistaken belief holds that if we only thought right or had awakened to our union with God, we would live to a ripe old age in perfect health. Perhaps we might even ascend directly to another dimension, leaving behind a little pile of hair and fingernails. There certainly are accounts of a few saints doing just that, but most of them die in a very conventional way. Saint Bernadette, whose vision of the Virgin at Lourdes led to an awesome healing shrine, died in her thirties of bone cancer, as did the great Indian saint Ramana Maharshi. The Buddha died at eighty-one of food poisoning, but not before assuring the cook that he was grateful for the meal that gave him a way to end a lifetime that had been completed.

Prayer/Practice

Divine Beloved, thank you for this spring morning. All around me the earth is in bloom, and your lifeforce blesses and increases all things. I call upon Uriel and the angels of clarity to help me understand that your lifeforce also blesses me perfectly, that everything I need to heal has already been given. Let me be open to all possibilities, living the full circle of my life in gratitude no matter when that circle is complete.

June 13

Seed Thought

Mental healing and spiritual healing are two entirely different methods. Mental healing relies on the connection between body and mind. Affirmations and images, when engaged in with enough concentration, can certainly affect physical function. This type of goal-directed healing is frequently useful, but can block spiritual healing which views the mind not as a creative force, but as an instrument of awareness. The receptive nature of mind can tune in to the creative force of the Divine Mind, the Godseed within which operates on a much higher level than goal-directed thinking.

Prayer/Practice

Divine Beloved, grant me the faith that if I let go of trying to change things with my own mind, I can become receptive to the healing power of Your Divine Mind.

Spend a few minutes in centering prayer, and then contemplate the idea that everything in your life is perfect and harmonious, unfolding in God's infinite wisdom and love.

June 14

Seed Thought

Physician Larry Dossey has written several books on medicine, the Infinite, prayer and healing. In *Meaning and Medicine*, he quotes one of his colleagues, Brad Lemley: "We tend to think that the purpose of prayer is to terminate sickness, but we forget that the purpose of sickness may be to initiate prayer, or, more generally, a consciousness of the Infinite."

Prayer/Practice

Close your eyes and take a few letting-go breaths, patiently entering the silent, mindful place within you. Contemplate the nature of God, the nature of the Infinite, for a few minutes.

When you go outside today, look up in the sky (but not at the sun) and contemplate its infinite spaciousness for a minute or two.

June 15

Seed Thought

The sixteenth-century mystic and saint Teresa of Avila practiced and taught "mental prayer" despite the fact that the Dominicans who led the Spanish Inquisition thought that it bordered on the heretical. Why? Such prayer brought about conscious contact with God without the necessity of a priest or the sacrament of communion. Saint Teresa defined this heretical act as "nothing else than an intimate sharing between friends; it means taking time frequently to be alone with Him who we know loves us."

Prayer/Practice

Close your eyes and take a few letting-go breaths, following your outbreath slowly and patiently into the center of mindful stillness deep within. Speak to God as you would your most intimate friend. Then let go of all thought and enter the sweet silence of centering prayer for a few minutes.

June 16

Seed Thought

Rabbi Nachman was a nineteenth-century Jewish mystic. He taught that it was the passion and intention of our prayer—our will to make conscious contact with God—that was of much greater import than what we actually said. He used this metaphor: "As the smoke ascends from burning wood, but the heavy part cleaves to the ground and becomes ashes, so from prayer only the will and the fervor ascend, but the external words crumble to ashes."

Prayer/Practice

Great Spirit, I welcome You this June morning and fervently wish for a closer relationship with You. Let me tell you of my life, my hopes, my dreams, asking for nothing and humbly accepting the flow of Your Divine grace.

Enter the stillness of meditation and invoke the presence of the Archangel Uriel in the space in front of you. Speak to Uriel from your heart, asking for help in any area where you need more clarity. You can also ask Uriel to help you be more aware of your relationship with God. Next, speak to God as you would your dearest friend. Then meditate in quiet receptivity, without an agenda for what you may hear in reply and when it might come.

June 17

Seed Thought

Mother Meera is a contemporary Hindu saint who teaches that if
we want anything we have to ask for it with our whole heart
in a way that "your heart can be empty and God can fill it." To
pray in this way it is necessary to remember that God has already given
you the kingdom. The Divine One has created all that you could
possibly need. Your fervent prayer with a receptive heart does
not cajole God into doing personal favors, it just opens you up to
receive what has already been given.

Prayer/Practice

Great Spirit, I am filled with the awesome beauty of Your creation
on this beautiful spring morning. The earth and sky, the trees
and flowers are alive with your being. Just as I can receive their
beauty only when I am mindful and grateful, so let me receive
your abundance by thanking you with great gratitude for all those
things I need that I know you have already supplied.

*Spend a few minutes in centering prayer, and open your heart
to the Divine Presence. Then thank God for all you need, as
if you have already received it.*

June 18

Seed Thought

Agnes Sanford was a well-known spiritual healer who taught a very specific and directed method for prayer and healing that is quite different from the more nondirected approaches that we studied earlier this month. Physician and researcher Larry Dossey reviewed all the scientific studies of prayer and concluded that both directed (specifying an outcome) and nondirected (praying for the highest good) were effective. He discovered that extroverts tend to prefer more directed approaches like Agnes Sanford's, while introverts are more comfortable with nondirected prayer. The best way to decide what type of prayer fits you best is to try both approaches. The three steps for the "scientific application of healing prayer," the directed approach of Agnes Sanford, are these: Contact the power of God; turn on the power; believe that the power is flowing and accept it by faith, since "no matter how much we ask for something it becomes ours only as we accept it and give thanks for it."

Prayer/Practice

Step 1: Relax into your breathing and contemplate how God's lifeforce permeates the Universe. This connects you with God.

Step 2: Turn on the power with a prayer such as "Thank you for the tremendous energy and vitality that is now pouring through my body, mind and soul."

Step 3: Direct the flow of God's power to a specific end: "I am grateful to be restored to perfect health" . . . or whatever you need.

June 19

Seed Thought

One of the most common blocks to effective directed prayer is the
fear of failure. What if the prayer isn't answered? Does that mean that
God doesn't exist or doesn't care? Agnes Sanford has a helpful
metaphor for overcoming that fear. If you went to turn on a
lamp and nothing happened, you wouldn't doubt the existence of
electricity. You would probably conclude that something was
wrong with the lamp and set about repairing the wiring—the way
you connect to the limitless abundance of God's power. She
urges you to have the open-minded attitude of a scientist, to choose
something specific to pray for and to observe the results, using
failed experiments to learn from.

Prayer/Practice

If you choose to try a scientific experiment in prayer, settle on a
small objective which you can readily judge as having been
accomplished or not. Agnes Sanford makes a good point about
some people's hesitation to choose some small goal like a phone
call from an estranged friend. She says, "How strange it is that
people who fear to do this do not hesitate to pray for the most
difficult objectives of all, such as the peace of the world. . . . If
everyone who prayed for the peace of the world had enough prayer-
power to accomplish the healing of a head cold, this would be a
different world within twenty-four hours."

June 20

Seed Thought

An important consideration in the application of prayer, and whether or not one's objectives are met, concerns God's will. Agnes Sanford suggests that trying to accomplish something contrary to God's will is like trying to make water run uphill. It just won't happen. Personally, I find that a great relief. If every person who thought they knew what was best were able to actualize their prayers, we'd have a big mess! When I pray for a specific outcome, for example a physical or emotional healing or right livelihood for a friend, I pray according to Sanford's method, adding at the end a thank-you which specifies that I accept the deed as accomplished "if it is according to Your will."

Prayer/Practice

Pray according to the technique that we have learned over the last three days, accepting with gratitude the expected outcome if it is in accordance with the Divine Plan. Today, if you wish, ask a friend if there is any way you can help them through prayer. Make a commitment to pray for that person in a scientific manner for one week.

June 21: Summer Solstice

Seed Thought

Today is one of the four cardinal points of the year, Summer Solstice, the day of greatest light. The Medicine Wheel has completed its spring turning and is fully open to the Southern Gate, the gate of summer. Summer is a season for appreciating the abundance of life, the reality of both the physical light and the spiritual Light, and of recognizing the unique gifts we have to share with the world. The Archangel Gabriel, a Hebrew name meaning "the strength of God," is the guardian of summer and the protector of the birth of all living things.

Prayer/Practice

Go outside and sit down upon the earth. If it's raining, sit on a plastic sheet and hold an umbrella. If that's not possible, do the exercise indoors. Feel the light of the sun shining down on you. You can do this regardless of whether or not clouds or a roof may partially obscure the light. Welcome the light with a prayer like, "Great Spirit, I give thanks for the light of the sun which provides life and I give thanks for the increase in the lifeforce that I feel within me now, increasing my energy and vitality. I feel myself awakening to the Light within, gaining the will and wisdom to be of service." As you breathe in, feel the light entering the top of your head, and as you breathe out pass it into the earth. Continue this meditation for a few minutes.

June 22

Seed Thought

The archangels are thought to be genderless, a blend of masculine and feminine. Gabriel, however, has a more feminine aspect and is the archangel who is present at births—the birth of small beings and the birth of ideas. Gabriel has shown up throughout history as a messenger about our creative role in the cosmos. It was Gabriel who appeared to Mary to tell her that she would bear Jesus and to Elizabeth to tell her that she would bear the son who was to become John the Baptist. It was also Gabriel who revealed the Koran to Mohammed and who instructed Joan of Arc to aid the Dauphin. Gabriel awakens us to our creative role in the cosmos.

Prayer/Practice

Close your eyes and take several letting-go breaths, patiently and slowly entering the Holy of Holies, the inner sanctum within you. Invoke the presence of Gabriel to your right, the Southern Gate of your body temple. Give thanks to this Awakening Spirit for helping you come into greater awareness of your creative potential so that you can bloom abundantly, unfolding like the blessing of summer for the benefit of all beings. Sit quietly and receptively, aware of the Presence of Archangel Gabriel.

Two or three times today, place your awareness on your right side and invoke the presence of Gabriel.

June 23

Seed Thought

Each of us is truly a bridge between heaven and earth. Just as the physical light of the sun is transformed by plants into all the organic matter on the earth, we are the transformers of the Divine Light that accomplish God's creation on the earth plane. Summer is a time for drawing down the Light.

Prayer/Practice

One of the ways that we draw down the Light is by opening our hearts compassionately to others. Continue your prayers for whatever specific objective you have chosen, and for the friend you are praying for this week.

As you meet and think of people today, remember that every thought is a prayer. Mentally wish people well. Imagine them as happy.

June 24

Seed Thought

The twelfth-century mystic and Benedictine nun Hildegard of Bingen spoke with great eloquence about the creative power of God and the drawing down of the Light into creation. "God was and is without beginning before the creation of the world. God was and is light and radiance and life. And God said, 'Let there be light,' and so were the light and the radiant angels created."

Prayer/Practice

The long, light-filled days of summer are an excellent time to deepen your receptivity to the radiant angels who are ever present, ready to help us step into our co-creative partnership with God. Take a few letting-go breaths and patiently, mindfully slide into the inner stillness. Place your awareness to your right and ask for the presence of Gabriel. Continue as if you have already felt the angelic presence. "Beloved Gabriel, my guide and strength, thank you for your presence. I am happy to know you better so that I can call upon you for help in my creative purpose." Sit quietly, expecting nothing, and deepen your appreciation of Gabriel's presence.

Two or three times today, become aware of the space to your right and invoke the presence of Gabriel.

June 25

Seed Thought

I was being helped by a particularly kind agent at an airline ticket counter one day. What a surprise I had when she told me that she would hear from her spirit guides—what we may think of as guardian angels—if she was not kind. When I asked her how she talked to them, she said that she had been able to see and hear them from childhood. She added that my guardian angel had been trying very hard to get my attention. I have to admit that I didn't know whether or not to take her seriously. But when she told me the graphic details of a head-on collision I'd recently been involved in—details that were being supplied to her by my angel—she got my attention. I decided to listen to what my angel had to say.

Prayer/Practice

The practice of listening to one's guardian angel—which I think of as an agent of awareness—takes patience and faith. And it is imperative to let go of any expectations. It took months for me to tune in to angelic guidance because I was waiting for "fireworks." I wanted lights and music and physical apparitions. Instead, I got comforting presences and strong hunches. They have served me very well. Today, enter the stillness of centering prayer or shamatha/vipassana meditation. Ask your guardian angel to help you listen to it. Wait patiently throughout the day for hunches, or a heightened sense of awareness that seems to call your attention to something. You may also feel the presence of your guardian angel.

June 26

Seed Thought

I am writing this book in a room that feels sacred to me, and I wonder where you are reading it. My writing studio is filled with plants that I know individually and have a special relationship with. Heart-shaped stones, containing the light of the summer beaches on which I found them, and the love of my friend Celia who taught me to look for such things, are all around. Paintings and books enclose me in a kind of cosmic womb. These harmonious and beautiful surroundings are simple and uncluttered. I feel at home here. Are you reading this in a place that feels sacred to you?

Prayer/Practice

Clarity of mind and bringing down the Light of God are enhanced by studying and practicing in a place that feels sacred. Do you have such a space in your home? If so, does it continue to change as you change or has it lost some of the life it once had? Spend a few minutes in centering prayer and invoke the presence of Gabriel. Ask for help in creating a living, sacred space, even if it's just the top of your dresser. Now invoke the presence of your guardian angel and continue to familiarize yourself with its energy.

June 27

Seed Thought

Nature is a sacred space that has the power to draw us out of our small mind into the Big Mind of God. During warm weather, praying and meditating outside in nature can naturally enhance your practice. You can pray anywhere, even on the subway, but whenever you find yourself in a place that feels sacred, you have already made the connection with God. Why not deepen the connections that are spontaneously presented by the beauty of long summer days and the balmy fragrance of moonlit nights?

Prayer/Practice

Meditate outside today if you can. With eyes open, begin by relaxing into the feeling of the light shining down from above. Next, feel the energy of Mother Earth beneath your feet. Now breathe in the light from above and the earth energies from below and let them meet in your heart. Breathe out the creative, loving energies of earth and sky that have been blessed by your heart. Let each outbreath expand to caress all creation. This is a meditation on bridging earth and heaven. It helps to put you in the window between the worlds where you can most easily commune with your guardian angel.

June 28

Seed Thought

The beauty of nature clears our mind because it draws us into the present moment. Kallistos Ware, a Greek Orthodox priest, said that the present is the place where time touches eternity. In Greek, *chronos* means "clock time." *Kairos* means "the eternal present." *Now* is where chronos and kairos meet, creating a space of limitless possibility. This is the space in which miracles occur that defy the rules of time and space as we know them. This is also the space in which mystics have visions and angels appear.

Prayer/Practice

Practice mindful walking outside today. Center your attention in the same "bridging earth and heaven" meditation that we practiced yesterday. When you breathe out from your heart, follow your breath into a mindful appreciation of the beauty all around you. Ask Gabriel to walk with you and help you stay in the now. Talk to your guardian angel and ask for whatever help or guidance you need.

June 29

Seed Thought

As a scientist I am particularly fascinated by miracles that defy the laws of nature. There is an international healing commission that investigates medical miracles that have occurred at the shrine of the Virgin Mary at Lourdes. Over sixty such miracles have been meticulously documented, and thousands of others have no doubt taken place, according to the testimony of people whose prior medical condition lacked sufficient documentation. These miracles occur in the twinkling of an eye, outside of time.

Prayer/Practice

We have to get inside of time before we can move outside of time. Our ability to focus the mind and stay present allows the deep connection with the Divine Presence that is the basis of miracles. Today, review basic concentration meditation. Close your eyes and notice that your belly expands on the inbreath and flattens on the outbreath. As you breathe out, mentally count four, on the next outbreath three, then two and one. Continue counting back from four to one for about five minutes, allowing thoughts to move past without getting involved in them. When you feel focused, talk to your guardian angel, then listen receptively.

June 30

Seed Thought

Miracles and excursions into *kairos* tend to happen at two times: moments of present-centered awareness in which we become one with the Mind of God, and moments of terror when our mind stops because it cannot comprehend what is happening. These states of mind create a window between the world of relative reality in which we live and the kingdom of heaven in which all things are always possible.

Prayer/Practice

Great Spirit, I give thanks that my faith and understanding are flowering in the light of summer. With Gabriel on my right side, I am learning to be mindfully present to life so that I can stop the world and step through the window of time into Your kingdom where all things are possible. With my guardian angel always by my side, I dedicate all my study, prayer and practice to the awakening of all beings. May these long days of light hasten our awakening into your kingdom.

Practice a few minutes of centering prayer, and then approach your guardian angel with the innocence and expectancy of a child who can easily enter the place of "magic" where the two worlds touch.

SOUTHERN GATE

Archangel Gabriel

SUMMER

JULY

Creativity, Vision and Purpose

July is a month of extraordinary creativity.
Fruits and flowers take an abundance of forms.
The eggs of bluebirds hatch, leaving tiny shells the color of sky
beneath nests noisy with the cry of hungry young.
This cycle of hatching and maturation brings us into
heightened awareness of our own life purpose,
the gifts we have been given to share with the Sacred Circle of Life.
In exploring our life purpose this month,
we will also explore the attitude with which we work,
for when our activities are dedicated to the good of all,
creativity flourishes, the energy of mind and body flow freely,
and we share the joy of our essence as a
blessing to this world.
By following our intuition this month, we will learn to tune in to
the messages from the Higher Self
and from the angelic realm
that help us find our way with the joy, delight and levity that
make life worthwhile.
Listen to the voices of the Ancient Ones singing from the trees:

*The Godseed within
is coming to flower in the
radiant light of summer.
Listening to the voice of intuition
we realize our life's purpose,
using our gifts with joy
in the service of
all beings.*

Seed Thought

The energy of July builds on the clarity of June. As we become more aware both of the creative fire within ourselves, and of the promptings toward greater awareness that come both from the Archangels and our personal guardian angels, we become more attuned to the pulse of the Universe and to our own part in bringing about heaven on earth, the awakening of all beings to our true potential as co-creators with the Divine One.

Prayer/Practice

Great Spirit, I enter July filled with gratitude for the warm light of the summer and the flowering of nature and my own creative potential. I am grateful for my growing awareness of the continuous messages from the Universe that guide me in how I might best develop and use the unique potential that I have been given.

Spend a few minutes in centering prayer or shamatha/vipassana meditation. Pray for guidance as to how you may best be of service.

July 2

Seed Thought

The Cherokee teacher and healer Dhyani Ywahoo reminds us that in order to actualize our life purpose we must maintain a continual awareness that life is a gift of inestimable value and that we are caretakers of that gift. In her luminous book, *Voices of Our Ancestors*, she says, "To bring our will into harmony with the sacred law is to understand our life purpose. Why am I here, what are my gifts? Human life is a great opportunity. Each one has particular gifts, a unique role in the circle. Conscious will becomes manifest as one dedicates one's gifts for the benefit of family, clan, nation, all beings."

Prayer/Practice

Sit for a few minutes in the meditation of bridging earth and heaven (June 27). Now consider what gifts you are currently bringing to the world, and offer a prayer of thanksgiving to the Great Spirit for allowing you to be of service in this way. Dedicate all the activities of your day to your family, your clan, your nation and all beings. In this way, the obstructions to the flow of grace through you are gradually eroded.

As you do your work today, think of how each action is helpful to others, and dedicate it to the service of all. I find this particularly helpful when doing something for which I'm just not in the mood. It often transforms a difficult task into a creative, joyful one.

July 3

Seed Thought

Joseph Campbell answered the question of how to know where our
life purpose lay with the simple instruction "Follow your bliss."
Saint Teresa of Avila put the same sentiment a little bit differently:
"The important thing is not to think much, but to love much;
and so do that which best stirs you to love." After all, it is in loving
that we find our bliss and accomplish the greatest service toward others.

Prayer/Practice

Divine Beloved, thank you for the guidance that continually comes
from my Higher Self and the angels of light who are my guides and
awakeners.

*Spend a few minutes in centering prayer and then contemplate
the different things you have done in your life. Which of them
brought you the most bliss, the greatest opportunity to love? Are
you continuing to use those gifts?*

July 4: Independence Day

Seed Thought

Today we celebrate both outer freedom and inner freedom. Inner freedom manifests itself when we no longer march to the beat of any drum but to that which calls from within, the still, small voice of our own Higher Self. That inner voice leads us to forgiveness, gratitude, peace and an understanding of our life purpose. It is the active intelligence of Divine Mind within, which can alone ignite our will and intention to serve all beings.

Prayer/Practice

Practice Metta meditation this morning (February 11–15), sending out the blessing "May all beings be free, May all beings know the love and beauty of their own true nature, May all beings find happiness in service to all."

July 5

Seed Thought

The modern proverb "Use it or lose it" is very wise. If we don't exercise our muscles, they waste away. If we don't exercise our minds, they begin to close. If we don't use our God-given gifts, we become depressed and dam up the flow of life energy, which is meant to fill our lives and bring us into full creative bloom.

Prayer/Practice

Let he or she who has ears hear. Take a few letting-go breaths and slowly, patiently, slide into the place of inner stillness. Now consider this well-known parable of Jesus: The lord of a manor gave three of his servants a sum of money, greater or less according to their ability, and asked them to invest it for him. When he returned from a trip the two servants who had been given the larger amounts had doubled them. The lord then gave both men a place of responsibility in his kingdom, since the person who can be trusted with small things can also be trusted with greater things. But the servant who had been given the least amount had buried it out of fear of losing it and angering his lord. From him the money was taken away, since he had no trust either in his lord or in himself.

Reflect once again on what your unique talents are. How can you use them? (Using them does not mean that you have to make a living with them.)

July 6

Seed Thought

The Lord Krishna, who gives spiritual instruction to the Prince
Arjuna in the classic Hindu text, the Bhagavad Gita, says, "It is better
to do your own duty, however imperfectly, than to assume the duties
of another person, however successfully. Prefer to die doing your
own duty; the duty of another will bring you into great spiritual
danger."

Prayer/Practice

*Today is a day of reflection. How and why did you decide to
perform the work that you do? I got a wonderful lesson on
doing your own duty when I was a seven- or eight-year-old child.
Our family doctor's son dropped out of Harvard Medical
School in his junior year because he felt completely miserable;
he wanted to be an artist rather than a doctor. My parents
couldn't believe that he would give up a career in medicine and
disappoint his parents. I applauded the courage of that young
man and resolved to be just like him—to march to the beat of
my own inner drummer. Whose drum do you march to?*

July 7

Seed Thought

Our life purpose has both a general and a specific aspect. The first
has nothing to do with our work in the world and everything
to do with learning how to give and receive love. About a third of
people who have near-death experiences review their lives in the
presence of a Great Being of Light that exudes perfect love and
understanding. Most return saying that they are aware that the
general purpose of life concerns learning how to love. Most also say
that they become aware of a particular purpose for their lifetime,
and many choose to return to earth to complete that purpose.

Prayer/Practice

*Contemplate this thought: When people talk about their life review,
they say that they see every event through the eyes of the people
with whom they interacted. If they brought love, joy or
encouragement to another, they felt that. If they caused fear,
anger, hurt or helplessness in another, they felt that. The life
review can be very painful when we recognize that we are
responsible for every action. It is also very uplifting when we
realize that we can learn from our mistakes. People often say
that without the unqualified love and support of the Being of
Light who leads the review, it would be far too painful to endure.
As you interact with other people today, keep this in mind: Can
you bring a consciousness of love into every interaction?*

July 8

Seed Thought

Regardless of whether our life purpose is to nurture children, to discover quantum theory or to help others awaken through some difficulty we voluntarily take upon ourselves, it is good to keep the words of Mother Teresa in mind: "We cannot do great things in this world, we can only do little things with great love."

Prayer/Practice

Spend a few minutes in Metta meditation (February 11–15), generating the attitude of lovingkindness toward all beings. As you go through your day today, perform every act with kind attention and patience. You can wash the dishes with love, give directions with love, talk to your family with love, write your reports with loving attention to detail and thoughtfulness for the one you are communicating with.

July 9

Seed Thought

Every person, every situation, every blade of grass has a role in the Divine Plan. We have been given exactly the circumstances required to develop our unique gifts. We have the freewill to wake up and use our life circumstances as educators that bring forth our potential or to remain asleep. The question we must ask consciously about every decision is: "Is it my will or Thy will?"

Prayer/Practice

Divine Beloved, I begin my day centered in Your peace, love and wisdom. The long days of summer are bringing forth a great abundance from the earth and an abundance of love and willingness to serve from my soul. Thank you for the great gift of life. I will be a good steward, ever trying to increase what you have given me by seeking your will and dedicating every action to the benefit of all beings.

Today, whenever you are faced with a decision, take a minute to tune in and pray, "What would you have me do, Divine Beloved?" Pay attention to the physical sensations that occur as you consider whether or not to make a certain choice. Spirit often speaks through our bodies.

July 10

Seed Thought

Spirit speaks to us continuously, revealing the paths which will be most harmonious for us to follow. The art of intuition is in learning to listen to the voice of spirit so that we can make our way more easily through the world, in accordance with the Divine Plan.

Prayer/Practice

Practice a few minutes of centering prayer or shamatha/vipassana meditation. Both types of meditation are lessons in listening that enable us to hear the voice of spirit throughout the day. As you go about your business today, be mindful of the clues that the Universe leaves for you about what direction to follow in your life—sometimes the chance comments of friends and strangers, book titles, magazine articles, billboards, even scraps of paper that we pick up from the ground may have messages for us.

July 11

Seed Thought

A friend of mine who has been a lifelong student of Eastern philosophy taught me an important lesson. When you have a plan in mind and have tried honestly and diligently to make it happen, pay attention when nothing happens or when roadblocks constantly pop up. Obstructions in the flow, according to Steve, mean that "there is no shakti" in the plan. *Shakti* is the Sanskrit word for the feminine creative energy. So, if your plan isn't working, consider the wisdom of not pushing the river and working against the flow.

Prayer/Practice

Divine Beloved, Your creation is so awesomely magnificent that it is nearly incomprehensible. Your creative energy is always flowing and moving. Please help me attune to that flow and pay attention to when I'm in it and when I'm not. I call upon Gabriel and my guardian angel to help raise my awareness of what it is to go with the flow.

Practice a few minutes of centering prayer, the egg of light or shamatha/vipassana meditation. Talk to your guardian angel about any questions you might have concerning the direction of your life.

July 12

Seed Thought

Discerning the wisdom of intuition—communications from your
Higher Self—from the insistent wants and fears of the ego
requires patient observation. Intuition speaks gently and without
fireworks. It doesn't get involved in the twin trap of ego:
attachments and aversions. When ego masquerades as intuition, the
communication is more likely to feel scary or to ignite desires
or to puff you up so that you feel full of yourself.

Prayer/Practice

*Spend a few minutes in centering prayer or shamatha/vipassana
meditation. Pray for awareness of the Divine Will and for the
discernment to tell whether messages are coming from your ego
or your Higher Self. Keep aware today, as you did yesterday,
of any messages arising from the external world, as well as of
hunches from within. When you feel like a message is coming
through, call upon your guardian angel and ask a simple yes
or no question: "Am I supposed to pay attention to this
message?" Notice any changes in physical sensation. A sense of
peace, love or warmth is generally a yes. No response, or
mounting anxiety is likely to be a no. Keep track of the messages,
the physical responses and the outcome of situations to which
the messages pertained. In time, you will be reliably aware of
the difference between ego and intuition.*

July 13

Seed Thought

As we develop the ability to listen to our Higher Self, we need to pay close attention to our motives. The motive of the Higher Self is always love and service. The ego's motives are more separatist and often concern security, self-aggrandizement or paranoia. Generally, the ego speaks the language of fear. Writer and mystic Ken Carey puts this very nicely: "Those who are motivated by fear, no matter how they justify such motivation to themselves, are working to keep the world in darkness."

Prayer/Practice

Tonight, before you go to bed, review all the actions of your day beginning with the last thing you did and ending with the first. For each activity, ask yourself whether you were motivated by love or by fear. Don't be hasty in deciding. Instead, tune in to your body and the energy field around you that reflects communication from your guardian angel. Pray for help in overcoming fear.

July 14

Seed Thought

Gabriel means "the strength of God." Whenever I feel that I have been sidetracked by fear, and that I cannot do my work or live my life as an act of love and service, I place my attention to the Southern side of my body—the right side—and I call upon the help of Gabriel to overcome my fears so that I can truly bring forth the abundant blessings of God in my life.

Prayer/Practice

Great Spirit, Archangel Gabriel, guardian angel and all the Beings of Light whose radiant presence lights our way, thank you for my growing awareness on this beautiful July morning.

Quiet yourself with a few letting-go breaths. Gradually and patiently enter the place of inner stillness. Place your awareness on your right side—the Southern Gate of your body temple— and invoke the presence of Gabriel. Offer Gabriel the fears which you reflected on last night and any others that come to mind this morning. Pray that your fears be removed so that you can bring forth your life purpose for the benefit of family, clan, nation and all beings.

July 15

Seed Thought

The twelfth-century mystic and abbess Hildegard of Bingen said that "at birth our divine potential is folded up in us like a tent. It is life's purpose to unfold that tent."

Prayer/Practice

Divine Beloved, I am grateful that before I was even created there was a role for me in helping you to unfold the Universe. I have been moving more and more consciously into that role for eons and am ready to awaken here and now to my greatest purpose.

Today, as you move through your activities, be aware of the energy of your guardian angel. Whenever there is something of particular import that I am supposed to pay attention to, something that will help me unfold the tent of my life purpose, I feel a strong, loving presence on my left side that broadcasts the message "Listen, love, serve."

July 16

Seed Thought

The Nag Hammadi library of Gnostic Gospels is a compendium of early Christian thought that dates back to the second century. The fifty-three Gnostic manuscripts had been buried in the Egyptian desert for seventeen hundred years until their discovery in 1945. One of the manuscripts, called the Gospel of Thomas, is full of the words of Jesus. Some of his sayings are similar to those in the New Testament. Many others, like this one, sound surprisingly like the modern depth psychology of Carl Jung: "If you bring forth what is within you, what you bring forth will save you. If you do not bring forth what is within you, what you do not bring forth will destroy you."

Prayer/Practice

The creative impulse is like an electric current. If you use it, it will bring great benefit to life. If you obstruct it, it will burn out your circuits and cause depression, malaise and illness. This morning, contemplate your creative urges. Do you act on them or are they burning out your circuits?

Spend a few minutes in centering prayer, the egg of light or shamatha/vipassana meditation.

July 17

Seed Thought

In the Gnostic Gospel of Thomas that we discussed yesterday, Jesus' disciples ask him how they can realize the kingdom within: "Do you want us to fast? How shall we pray? Shall we give alms? What diet shall we observe?" Jesus replies, "Do not tell lies and do not do what you hate."

Prayer/Practice

Shakespeare gave us a practice through which to actualize the teaching of Jesus. "To thine own self be true and it follows as the night follows the day that thou cannot be false to any man."

Continue the practice of retrospecting your day before you go to bed tonight. You will be asking yourself specifically if the things you did today were in accord with your deepest beliefs and with what you feel your life purpose is. If you ask these questions of yourself throughout the day, the answer during tonight's retrospection is more likely to be yes.

July 18

Seed Thought

In Native American tradition, there is an affliction called two-heartedness. A person is two-hearted when they know they have a certain gift and want to use it, but don't bring forth their creativity because they get in their own way by making excuses, thinking that they really don't have the talent, procrastinating, giving in to fear or otherwise failing to follow their heart. A person is also two-hearted when they lie to themselves about their true motivation.

Prayer/Practice

Continue yesterday's practice of retrospecting your day before you go to sleep. Were you one- or two-hearted? If you made excuses about why you couldn't accomplish the things you really believe are important, what were they? Pray to God and Gabriel, the angel of creativity and strength, to help you bring forth your purpose with a single mind and heart.

July 19

Seed Thought

In the sermon on the mount, Jesus speaks very eloquently about
the dangers of being two-hearted and of serving the ego rather
than the Higher Self and the Will of God:

For where your treasure is, there will your heart be also. The light
of the body is the eye, if therefore thine eye be single thy whole
body shall be full of light. But if thine eye be evil, thy whole body
shall be full of darkness. If therefore the light that is in thee be darkness,
how great *is* that darkness!

—Matthew 6:21–23

Prayer/Practice

*Continue the practice of retrospecting your day before bed.
Motivations for actions that benefit you or your loved ones
are not necessarily two-hearted. If you are serving the God within,
you will tend to create win-win situations wherein your own
life improves as you are serving others. Motivations for activities
that benefit others are not necessarily one-hearted if they are
based on guilt or the need to look good. Finish your retrospection
with prayers of thanksgiving.*

July 20

Seed Thought

Once we have lightened the hold of the ego over us, the intention to fulfill our life's purpose becomes less a matter of personal identity and more a strong commitment to make the world a better place. Viktor Frankl, a psychiatrist who survived four Nazi death camps, wrote that "man should not, indeed cannot, struggle for identity in a direct way; he rather finds identity in the extent to which he commits himself to something beyond himself, to a cause greater than himself."

Prayer/Practice

Take a few letting-go breaths and slowly, patiently, slide into the place of inner stillness and wisdom. What is the cause with which you most identify, that "something beyond yourself" about which you feel most passionate? What are you doing with that passion?

July 21

Seed Thought

Where there is no vision, the people perish.

—Proverbs 29:18

Everyone lives according to some vision, whether it is conscious or not. That vision becomes the hidden force that energizes our motivations. It is important to articulate a vision by which we can live, so that we can hold ourselves accountable to those values that are most important, and in so doing, prosper and flourish.

Prayer/Practice

Spend a few minutes in centering prayer or shamatha/vipassana meditation. Now think back to yesterday's contemplation on that "something beyond yourself" to which you are committed. Build on that, considering it in the context of a guiding philosophy of life.

July 22

Seed Thought

In our desire to bring forth the fruitfulness of our souls, sometimes we end up wearing ourselves out and taking on so many things that we feel overwhelmed. Being overwhelmed makes it very difficult to listen to the still, small voice within, or pick up on the messages that the Universe leaves for us to follow. Try this advice of the guiding spirit, White Eagle: "When your tasks seem a little heavy and overwhelming remember to do one thing at a time quietly, and leave the rest because the rest is not your job. What you cannot get through you must hand back to God and He will work it out for you."

Prayer/Practice

Great Spirit, thank you for the dawning of another summer morning. I dedicate all my activities today to you and to the benefit of my family, my clan, my nation and all beings. I will work diligently, mindfully and joyfully with the awareness that any tasks remaining undone are Yours, not mine. I will offer them to You in faith that You will work them out in accord with the highest good.

Meditate outside today if you can, sitting on the earth. Do the meditation on bridging heaven on earth that we learned on June 27.

July 23

Seed Thought

You are a bridge between earth and heaven through which the creative power of God flows. God does not desire to overwhelm your circuits—so any overload is your own responsibility! It is also your responsibility to keep the circuits open through rest, recreation, time in nature and activities that are fun and therefore increase the flow of the lifeforce through you.

Prayer/Practice

Go for a mindful walk outside today if you can. When you finish, sit down and think about balance in your life. Are you spending sufficient time recreating yourself or are you in perpetual overload? Do you know how to have fun or have you forgotten the meaning of the word? Make a firm plan to do something restorative and enjoyable.

July 24

Seed Thought

What one person finds invigorating another may find overwhelming. The difference is in the attitude. People sometimes look at my schedule and shake their heads in dismay, commenting that I must be exhausted. In truth, sometimes I am, but only when my attitude needs adjustment! We plan my schedule intuitively, accepting the jobs that the Universe seems to have sent. We also leave ample time for spiritual retreat, vacation and the large number of friends and relatives who love to visit our Rocky Mountain home. If I felt that I was responsible for doing all my work personally, I would be exhausted. When I recognize that God is working through me, I am refreshed, even at the end of a long day.

Prayer/Practice

Great Spirit, thank you for the incredible gift of life that is manifesting so abundantly in the green of summer. The plants flower through your grace and your lifeforce rather than through personal effort. Help me develop that same attitude toward all I do, becoming a channel for your energy rather than being the "doer."

Meditate outside if you can, near something that is growing. Keep your eyes open, and center your attention on your breathing, slipping slowly and patiently into the inner stillness. Contemplate the plants that grow, how the lifeforce of God fills them and brings forth their innate potential. Go through this day receptive to God's energy, and let it move through you in all you do.

July 25

Seed Thought

There is an old story about three masons who are laying bricks. A man walks up to them and asks them each the same question: "What are you doing?" The first mason spits on the ground and looks up. "I'm laying bricks. What in hell does it look like I'm doing?" The second mason groans and mops his brow. "I'm earning a living." The third mason looks up with light in his eyes and says, "I'm building a cathedral." Who do you think feels most refreshed at the end of the day?

Prayer/Practice

Repeat yesterday's meditation, ending by opening yourself up to the flow of God's energy through you. Be particularly mindful today of your attitude toward everything you do, from washing the dishes to greeting the change handler at the toll booth. Which of the three mason's attitudes are you in? How does your attitude affect your energy level?

July 26

Seed Thought

Our good friend, spiritual teacher and humorist Loretta LaRoche, gives side-splitting workshops on how to prevent "hardening of the attitude." At one point she asks the group to think of a work issue that bothers them. Then she whips on a Groucho Marx–type pair of glasses with a rubber nose and mustache, puts her hands on her hips and asks them to consider, "Now just how serious is this anyway?" Most of us do have the tendency to take ourselves way too seriously, which instantly blocks the flow of God's creative energy through us and leads to terminal hardening of the attitude.

Prayer/Practice

I learned this elevated spiritual practice from Loretta, and it's been quite effective in adjusting my attitude: Get a pair of outrageous nose and glasses, and keep them handy in your desk drawer. Loretta recommends a spare for the car, in case of traffic jams. When you have totally lost your perspective and things seem way too serious, put on the glasses in front of a mirror and ask yourself, "Just how serious is this anyway?" Repeat until you lighten up.

July 27

Seed Thought

There is an old adage that angels can fly because they take themselves lightly. Steve Bhaerman is a humorist who often performs under the alias of Swami Beyonananda, the Yogi from Muskogy. Levity, he says, is the very best way of overcoming gravity. Have you heard the story about the guy who actually left his body permanently during a course on death and dying? He got an A.

Prayer/Practice

A joke a day may not keep the doctor away, but there is good scientific evidence that laughter actually brings forth the relaxation response. Why not? A good joke instantly breaks you out of everyday trance and the attachment to past and future and delivers you into the present moment where joy, harmony and peace are as natural as breathing. Your spiritual practice today is to learn, and then tell, one joke. Notice the increase of the lifeforce energy when you laugh.

July 28

Seed Thought

Every time you see the Dalai Lama, whether in person or in a video, it's impossible not to be touched, delighted and disarmed by his robust gales of laughter. Like many Tibetan monks, His Holiness has an amazing sense of humor and a laugh that seems to shake his body down to the single cells and then move into the bodies of his listeners, awakening the joy and lifeforce latent within each one. This is not a man who laughs because he has avoided suffering. After all, his country was destroyed in the Chinese holocaust of the 1950s. Rather, he seems to laugh from an inner, unperturbable place that always exudes peace and vitality.

Prayer/Practice

According to the Dalai Lama, the most important spiritual practice is kindness. His ability to bless the very people who tortured the Tibetans and destroyed their temples and their land, certainly has prevented any hardening of his attitude.

Today, practice Metta meditation (February 11–15), one of the best ways of opening your heart and letting the sun of your own true nature shine. When the heart is open, good humor flows and the ego's rigidity melts like snow in the sun.

July 29

Seed Thought

Another way to let go of the serious self-importance of the ego that stifles the easy flow of creativity is to spend some time helping other people. Over ninety million Americans do some type of volunteer work, and studies show that those who do are less anxious and depressed, and actually live longer, than those who don't. Rather than increasing stress by decreasing the time available for other work, volunteering is a proven way to reduce stress because it reduces the tendency to self-absorption.

Prayer/Practice

Great Spirit, I give thanks for a new day rich with the fragrances of sister wind and mother earth. My life is so full of abundance. Please inspire me to share this abundance with others in small and large ways so that I may be a channel of your love, and in so doing, enlarge the opening in me through which that love flows.

Spend a few minutes in Metta meditation (February 11–15), sending lovingkindness blessings to yourself, loved ones, any neighborhood or national situation that needs healing, and to all beings. Then reflect on how you could give some of your time and energy to help others.

July 30

Seed Thought

Sometimes we complicate things too much. There is great wisdom in keeping things simple. When the Dalai Lama was asked to explain his religion and philosophy of life, he answered very simply that his religion is kindness. Can you envision a world in which kindness was everyone's primary motivation? We would be living in heaven on earth.

Prayer/Practice

Make kindness your vision today, and let it be the primary motivation behind every interaction. If you are out and about in the world, smile and say hello to at least three people who you generally would not have talked to.

July 31

Seed Thought

Richard Bolles's books, *What Color Is Your Parachute* and *How to Find Your Mission in Life*, are marvelous guides to right livelihood and purposeful living. In the latter book, Bolles summarizes all the work we've done this month as the three stages of Mission. The first two are shared by every human being, and the third is unique to each of us.

1. "To seek to stand hour by hour in the presence of God, the One from whom your mission is derived."

2. "To do what you can, moment by moment, day by day, step by step, to make this world a better place, following the leading and guidance of God's spirit within you and around you."

3. "To find your unique gift, the talent which is your birthright and which brings you joy, and to use it how and where spirit leads you."

Prayer/Practice

Great Spirit, I give thanks for the greatest of all gifts, my life. I trust that everyone has been created with a purpose in life, and that as long as I commit myself to listening to Your guidance, You will lead me in the paths of right livelihood and right use of my time. Today, and all days, I dedicate all my activities to the benefit of my family, clan, nation and all beings.

Spend a few minutes in centering prayer, the egg of light or shamatha/vipassana meditation.

AUGUST

Spiritual Maturity

August is the month during which nature celebrates her maturity.
The hatchlings in the nest have found the wings to fly,
and the boughs of the old apple tree are heavy with fruit.
The Godseed within our hearts is also ripening
so that we become more flexible, more tolerant of the shades of gray
that characterize life on planet earth.
Every interaction becomes an opportunity to encourage,
to be kind as we acknowledge the Godseed within all.
As the pumpkins ripen on the vine, mellowing in the shortening days
and colder nights, the vine itself begins the dying time.
Its purpose is complete.
August reminds us of the impermanence of all things.
All that seems so dependable will someday pass away.
In that poignant knowledge we mature into a
deeper appreciation of all we have,
of all we love.
Listen to the voices of the Ancient Ones that call from
the roots of the oaks and willows:

Nature is setting seed,
storing the energy of the light
for future generations.
Likewise, our souls are coming
to spiritual maturity—
a flexible, gracious attitude
that finds intense joy
in the very impermanence
of life.

August 1: Lammas, or Teltane

Seed Thought

Lammas, or Teltane, is a cross-quarter day midway between summer solstice and fall equinox. Although the days are still long, the sun rises later and sets earlier. The rhythm of the earth is shifting, and energies are beginning to draw inward. To ensure the balance between sun and earth energies necessary for a successful harvest, the ancient Celts celebrated a ritual marriage between earth and sun, male and female, each Teltane. Likewise, August is a time for us to bring about balance between our male and female aspects so that we can harvest the fruitfulness of our souls.

Prayer/Practice

Great Spirit, I give thanks for the celestial harmony which turns the cosmic wheel this cross-quarter day. My energy, like Mother Earth's, is beginning to draw inward. Yet I am aware that it is still a season of outward activity. May I find balance by aligning with the energies of earth and sky, sun and moon, male and female, through whose dance all creation comes into being.

Take a few letting-go breaths and mindfully feel your way into the place of inner stillness. Sense the energy of Mother Earth. Sense the energy of Father Sun. Weave them together in the meditation of bridging earth and heaven, simultaneously inhaling both energies into your heart, then exhaling their union back out into creation.

August 2

Seed Thought

As the outer harvest begins, it is time to harvest the work we have done in growing to spiritual maturity. Saint Paul spoke of this work in his letters to the Corinthians:

Though I speak with the tongues of men and angels and have not charity, I become as sounding brass or a tinkling cymbal. And though I have the gift of prophecy, and understand all mysteries, and all knowledge: and though I have all faith so that I could remove mountains, and I have not charity, I am nothing. And though I bestow all my goods to feed the poor, and though I give my body to be burned, and have not charity, it profiteth me nothing.

—1 Corinthians 13:1–3

Prayer/Practice

Divine Beloved, I am thankful for my gradual awakening to a mature spirituality. May the blessings of charity—humility, encouragement, forgiveness, non-judgment, generosity of spirit, innocence, kindness, compassion, flexibility and the ability to see God in all people—flow from me as the soul's true harvest.

Spend a few minutes in centering prayer or shamatha/vipassana meditation. Contemplate a life of charity, beyond the usual meaning of giving material support to the needy.

Approach all your relationships today with a charitable heart.

August 3

Seed Thought

Buddist teacher and therapist Jack Kornfield writes of spiritual maturity in his excellent book, *A Path With Heart*: "As one matures in spiritual life, one becomes more comfortable with paradox, more appreciative of life's ambiguities, its many levels and inherent conflicts. One develops a sense of life's irony, metaphor and humor and a capacity to embrace the whole, with its beauty and outrageousness, in the graciousness of the heart."

Prayer/Practice

If possible, center yourself with a few minutes of mindful walking in the beauty of nature. Allow your senses to take in as much as they can—the beautiful and the not so beautiful, that which is growing and that which is dying—be spacious enough to welcome everything. Practice this generosity of spirit, what Kornfield calls "graciousness of the heart," throughout the day.

August 4

Seed Thought

Graciousness of the heart shows up as flexibility, spaciousness and a "live and let live" attitude. One may prefer certain foods, for example, and find that the friends who are hosting dinner eat very differently. The gracious spirit manages to find something to eat, encouraging and acknowledging the efforts of the host. The more rigid spirit gives a lecture on the virtues of healthy eating, all the while believing that it is doing the friends a favor.

Prayer/Practice

Divine Beloved, thank you for the flowering of the Godseed within me that acknowledges and encourages other people and myself. Guide me in maintaining the basic disciplines of a healthy mind and body without falling prey to the rigidity and fanaticism of the ego and its constant efforts to prove itself worthy by being "right."

Practice a few minutes of centering prayer or shamatha/vipassana meditation, and then contemplate the ways in which discipline and flexibility can work together.

August 5

Seed Thought

In the early 1970s, I was doing cancer research and teaching at
Tufts Medical School. Several students and staff members used to gather
twice a week for meditation and discussion during the lunch hour.
In my mind, the most august member of our group was a
medical student who already had a degree from Harvard Divinity
School and had actually been a member of Ram Dass's Guru
Blanket Band. He opened up his brown bag one day and took out
a salami sandwich. When my jaw dropped, he laughed, wondering
if I really believed that spirituality meant one had to be a vegetarian.

Prayer/Practice

Great Spirit, thank you for granting me a sense of humor when I
go back through my life and recall the unfolding of spiritual
understanding. May I never lose sight of the fact that every intolerant
attitude I have ever entertained has been, or could be, the scaffolding
from which real tolerance and humility are reached.

*Today, as you go about business, be aware of any judgments
you have about another person's spirituality, values, behaviors
or attitudes. Take a deep breath and realize that you are actually
judging yourself. If it is helpful to you, use Ram Dass's method
of owning the projection by saying, "And I am that, too."*

August 6

Seed Thought

Chogyam Trungpa was one of the first Tibetan Buddhist monks to teach in the West. One of his many books, *Cutting Through Spiritual Materialism*, was a real eye-opener for me in the 1970s. At that time, we were members of a mystical Christian group to which we tithed 10 percent of our income. I felt pretty charitable. On the other hand, I was often disappointed with my spiritual life, because I couldn't seem to have any "big experiences." It was a relief to understand that my desire for "fireworks" (I'd hoped for at least an out-of-body experience) was a kind of greed, a spiritual materialism no different from the secular materialism I had hoped to transcend through tithing.

Prayer/Practice

Today is a time for contemplation. Place your energy on the right side of your body temple and invoke the presence of Gabriel whose role it is to help you come to full flower. Move peacefully and slowly into Gabriel's energy and then contemplate this question. In what ways do your spiritual expectations and judgments get in your way?

During the day, when you find yourself becoming judgmental, ask for Gabriel's help in letting go.

August 7

Seed Thought

One of the most insidious forms of spiritual materialism is attachment to intellectual attainment. When we have experienced spiritual truths personally, we have wisdom. When we have only read about them, we have knowledge. Knowledge can be an important steppingstone to wisdom when it is viewed with humility, or it can be a block to our growth when it is accumulated out of the insecurity of the ego or used to put us above others.

Prayer/Practice

Great Spirit, let me approach you this morning through my heart rather than my mind. May the grasses and flowers be my teachers, the wind and rain my allies, the sun and moon my awakeners.

If possible, go for a mindful walk today and let your mindfulness of God's creation bring you into the wisdom of the heart.

August 8

Seed Thought

In spiritual maturity we become able to hold the paradox of "both/and" rather than being bound to the rigidity of "either/or." While the intellect can at times be a trap, it is also one of God's greatest gifts. And although prayer and meditation have a very important role in leading us to the wisdom of the heart, sometimes the intellect is the more skillful means to awakening. When the Dalai Lama was asked what the main method of fostering inner awareness was, he replied, "Introspection and reasoning is more efficient for this purpose than meditation and prayer."

Prayer/Practice

Try this exercise of introspection. Relax into your breathing and let go into the still place within. Consider these thoughts, adapted by the psychiatrist Pierro Ferrucci from ancient methods of self-inquiry:

I have a body, but I am not my body
I have feelings, but I am not my feelings
I have desires, but I am not my desires
I have a mind, but I am not my mind

Then contemplate who it is who has been watching your sensations, feelings, desires and thoughts—your Higher Self. Meditate on this Self that is pure consciousness.

August 9

Seed Thought

As soon as we start to hunger for "experiences" in meditation, we give free reign to the ego and shut the door to the emergence of our own true nature, our Higher Self. Meditation is a complete letting go to what is. If nothing in particular is happening, the goal is to have equanimity toward that experience. If we have a vision of the Christ, or the Virgin Mary or the Buddha, the goal is to have equanimity toward that experience. In spiritual maturity we begin to transcend the incessant attractions and aversions of the ego.

Prayer/Practice

Practice shamatha/vipassana meditation this morning. Maintain an attitude of non-attachment. Remember the words of Saint Francis, who said that if one's heart wanders for the entire hour of meditation, it is still an hour well spent.

August 10

Seed Thought

Non-attachment, or the transcendence of attraction and aversion, is easily misunderstood as apathy. We can and must care passionately about our lives and actions without letting the trap of attachment drain us of the energy needed to do our work in the world. If our actions stem from honesty, kindness, caring and vision, then, no matter what the result of our efforts, we have added something of value to our souls and to the world.

Prayer/Practice

Great Spirit, thank you for making me new this morning in body and in mind. I willingly and gratefully accept all guidance in my deepening understanding of non-attachment and surrender. Since I cannot surrender that which I do not have, grant me the healing in mind and spirit that is necessary for me to go through life honestly, sanely and deliberately with the attitude "What is is. I can do my part to make things better, but if things don't get better I can accept that, too."

Spend a few minutes in the sweet surrender of centering prayer or shamatha/vipassana meditation. During the day, when despite your best efforts, things are not going the way you had hoped, affirm, "What is is. I can do my part to make things better, but if they don't get better I can accept that, too."

August 11

Seed Thought

The further we go on the spiritual path, the more we realize what beginners we really are. In my mid-twenties I studied for several years with the Self-Realization Fellowship, founded by the twentieth-century mystic Paramahansa Yogananda. His mission and his gift was to reveal the unity of Christianity and Eastern thought. I was so excited with the daily meditations and spiritual practices we were learning that, with the enthusiasm of youth, I assumed that I would be enlightened any minute. Hearing that there was a local study group, I called. The seventy-year-old leader, who had been studying both Christianity and Eastern religions for forty years, referred to herself as being in "spiritual kindergarten." After another twenty or so years of study, I finally understood what she meant.

Prayer/Practice

Divine Beloved, I arise with a grateful heart on this beautiful summer morning. May all the study, practice and prayer that I do be an offering to the enlightenment of all beings. May I be content to leave the Great Mystery of the Universe as a mystery, without thinking that I can figure it all out. Let the honesty, humility and lovingkindness that are growing daily in my life be the measure of my spirituality.

Spend a few minutes in centering prayer, the egg of light or shamatha/vipassana meditation. During the day, if you are invited to share your spiritual practice with anyone, remember that humility, non-judgment and respect for other's points of view are the best measure of spiritual attainment.

August 12

Seed Thought

The unfolding soul thinks less and less about "me" and more and more about "us." Many Buddhists take the vow of the Bodhisattva, agreeing to forgo their own evolution into a Pure Land (a heaven realm) in order to continue being reborn on this earth or in any realm where they can be of service to those who are still suffering from the illusions of unworthiness and separation.

Prayer/Practice

Practice Metta meditation (February 11–15) today, sending blessings of lovingkindness to all beings in all realms of existence. As you watch television, read the newspaper or magazines, or encounter suffering in any form, send lovingkindness blessings. The world doesn't need any more anger or indignation, but it could certainly use more love.

August 13

Seed Thought

My husband and I happened to be in Germany on All Souls' Day,
the day of visiting and remembering the dead. We decided to visit the
Holocaust memorial at Dachau, where many political prisoners as
well as Jews were tortured and killed during the Nazi regime.
One whole barracks housed priests and other clergy who were involved
in rescuing Jews and speaking out against oppression. The courage
to speak one's truth, particularly in the face of such horror, takes
tremendous faith and spiritual maturity.

Prayer/Practice

*Quiet your bodymind with a few minutes of centering prayer or
shamatha/vipassana meditation. Contemplate what it means
to you personally to speak your truth. If there are areas in which
you don't yet have the courage to speak out, seek the guidance
and help of Gabriel—the Archangel who is not only "the strength
of God," but the angel who awakens us to our creative purpose
and our unique role in the Divine Plan.*

August 14

Seed Thought

One plaque at the Holocaust museum at Dachau commemorated Titus Brandsma, a Dutch Catholic priest. The SS subjected Brandsma to hideous medical experiments, the last of which resulted in his death. As the nurse administered the fatal injection of phenol, his last act was to forgive and bless her. The ability to forgive those who have ignored us, wounded us or even killed us, comes only after long practice, and leads to the deepest personal freedom.

Prayer/Practice

Quiet yourself with a few moments of deep breathing. Now contemplate whether or not there are people in your life whom you need to forgive. Real forgiveness can be a slow and painstaking process, requiring us to honestly face our hurt and anger in the search for healing and humanity. Titus Brandsma is being sainted, so be gentle with yourself if you're just at the beginning of a forgiveness process! Practice a few minutes of Metta meditation (February 11–15), paying special attention to the step in which you send blessings to your enemies.

August 15

Seed Thought

The commentator and writer Charles Kuralt once hosted a television special about everyday heroes. One woman whom he featured lived in a small town in the Midwest that was a major railroad crossroads. All the young men who were being shipped out to fight in World War Two passed through there. Kuralt's everyday heroine cooked up a storm, handing out plates of food at the depot so that every boy would have a last home-cooked meal. She saw everyone's son as her own son. Regardless of what her religious beliefs may have been, this was a spiritual woman.

Prayer/Practice

Great Spirit, may the eyes of my heart open this morning so that I see every person I meet today as deserving the greatest respect and love. You see every person as Your own dearest child. May I see every person as my brother or sister.

Spend a few minutes in the quiet of centering prayer or shamatha/ vipassana meditation. Contemplate how you would behave if you saw each person as completely worthy of your love.

August 16

Seed Thought

My father died when I was a young woman in my late twenties. He was an agnostic, which I realized many years later was, for him, a point of great spiritual maturity. He didn't pretend to know what God was, only that there was something of great grandeur and mystery in a universe as beautiful and orderly as this one. His agnosticism was a kind of innocence, an empty cup, which was filled with wonder. We went to the zoo and he saw the glory of creation in the soft eyes of a deer. I will always remember him wiping tears from his eyes as he contemplated how anyone, other than a starving person, could ever shoot such a gentle creature. My father's childlike wonder and lovingkindness have lighted my heart and my way for all the years of my life.

Prayer/Practice

Spend a few minutes in the quiet of meditation. Think about someone that you've known who has been a model of lovingkindness, wonder, joy or any aspect of spirituality. As you go about your day today, try to apply the quality that you admire in that person to all your interactions.

August 17

Seed Thought

In seeking role models for the spiritual life we need to be aware of
the tendency to idealize people and then become disappointed
when we discover that they are human. Most people are a mixture
of qualities—they are exemplary in some ways and still have
much to learn in others. The tendency to judge people in an either/
or way—enlightened or not, saint or sinner—makes it difficult
to learn from the people we meet, whether or not we consider them
"teachers." If we broaden our point of view to consider every
person a potential teacher, every encounter will prompt the question
"What can I learn from this person?"

Prayer/Practice

Great Spirit, thank you for the gift of life and the continual
enrichment of my soul that brings such joy, gratitude, peace
and delight. May I learn to consider every circumstance of my day,
and every person that I meet, as a teacher. Free me from the
pitfall of idealization and disappointment, receiving every teaching
as a gift—especially those that are not pleasing.

*Practice a few minutes of centering prayer, the egg of light or
shamatha/vipassana meditation.*

August 18

Seed Thought

Spiritual attainment is not ascending a ladder into heaven and hobnobbing with the angels. It's being able to function with clarity and love right here on earth. When you can make that uncomfortable phone call, rather than avoiding it, then you are making spiritual progress. When you can give money to charity without needing the applause of others for your generosity, then you are making spiritual progress. When you can own your projections and let go of the ingrained habit of judging others, then you are making spiritual progress.

Prayer/Practice

Practice a few minutes of centering prayer or shamatha/vipassana meditation. Contemplate the simple acts you could perform that would help you feel freer or more loving. Is there an overdue thank-you note? A phone call you've put off? A letter that you really need to write? Do it as soon as you can.

August 19

Seed Thought

The foundation for spirituality is ethical conduct. In Eastern traditions people don't begin to meditate, to engage in exercises of introspection or study learned texts, until they have shown the virtues of honesty, discipline, humility, charity and right conduct. Judeo-Christian tradition is similar in stressing observance of the Ten Commandments as the cornerstone of spiritual life. What is the point of meditation and prayer if we aren't honest in our relationships and with ourselves?

Prayer/Practice

Practice a few minutes of centering prayer or shamatha/vipassana meditation. Contemplate ethical conduct and be honest with yourself as you review your actions. Awareness of the little ways that we tend to be dishonest with ourselves leads to great strides in applying honesty and integrity to all our interactions.

August 20

Seed Thought

In Judaism, ethical conduct involves more than refraining from harmful activities. One must also perform beneficial activities, or *mitzvot*. Mitzvot are good deeds that are a blessing on the person they are done for, a blessing on the person who does them, and a blessing on God. Visiting the sick is a mitzvah, as are such things as feeding the hungry, welcoming strangers into one's home on holidays, and taking good care of one's body.

Prayer/Practice

Spend a few minutes in centering prayer or shamatha/vipassana meditation. Contemplate a good deed that you could do for your own body or for another person today. When you begin to derive great joy from mitzvot, the Godseed within you is well on its way to blooming.

August 21

Seed Thought

Right speech is just as important as right conduct. The Buddha pointed out that one's speech is a direct reflection of what is in one's mind. Telling stories at the expense of another person, revealing details of conversations that would best remain private, exaggerating or distorting facts and speaking with authority when the expertise is not ours are ways in which the ego seeks self-importance. As the Godseed within us begins to mature, our speech becomes simpler, humbler and more truthful.

Prayer/Practice

Great Spirit, thank you for the growing maturity in my soul and the awareness of right speech. I call upon Gabriel today, and upon my guardian angel, to keep me aware of what I say, and to whom. May my words be truthful, encouraging and humble. May my words be kind and filled with care.

August 22

Seed Thought

Our speech stems directly from our thoughts, and in addition to right action and right speech, a maturing spirituality cultivates awareness of right thinking. When we catch ourselves thinking belittling, judging, cynical or snide thoughts, we are on the way to surrendering old habits of mind and planting the seeds of kind, encouraging thinking. Awareness of our thought habits and the intention to change them is an important aspect of cultivating kindness.

Prayer/Practice

Take a few letting-go breaths and place your awareness on the right side of your body temple, the Southern Gate of your energy field. Invoke the Presence of the Archangel Gabriel and ask this cosmic agent of awareness for help in observing your thoughts today so that you can develop the virtue of right thinking. When you catch yourself thinking uncharitable thoughts, mentally resolve to stop and send out more kind, encouraging thoughts.

August 23

Seed Thought

According to the Kabbalah of mystical Judaism, the world was created
out of ten emanations, or thought-forms, that arose from the
Mind of God. Union with God can be attained by attuning to any
one of these emanations. As our spirituality matures, we begin
to feel what the right path or emanation is for us. These paths are
archetypes, or energy patterns, that help guide the unfolding of
our soul according to its own predilection. They include beauty,
mercy, splendor, wisdom, understanding, victory over the ego,
discipline, ethics, nature and the mystical path.

Prayer/Practice

Great Spirit, You have created Yourself as the mystical tree of life
that encompasses many different paths home to You, each
requiring the soul to grow in a slightly different way. I accept with
gratitude Your guidance in helping me focus on the right path that
will encourage my soul to grow into the specific splendor you
intended when you first planted it as a seed in Your garden.

*Spend a few minutes in centering prayer, the egg of light or
shamatha/vipassana meditation.*

August 24

Seed Thought

Each person has capacities for spiritual awakening that are unique to them. Not all of us can meditate and not all can employ the intellect for introspection. We once took a series of classes at our church. One of the group members, a man by the name of James, was mildly retarded. He didn't read or write but took a very active part in the classes. The minister remarked that when one's first thought every morning was a prayer of gratitude to God, then you were making a little spiritual progress. James's face lit up. "Really, really? You mean you can really remember to do that? That's great!" The next week most of us had finished our assigned reading, but only James had mastered the practice of making gratitude to God his first priority of the day.

Prayer/Practice

Divine Beloved, when I remember You with gratitude when I awaken and when I go to sleep, Your Presence is with me throughout the day. Dear Gabriel, please continue to awaken me to a day-by-day, hour-by-hour, minute-by-minute remembering of the Divine Beloved. When I remember God, then true charity flows effortlessly from my heart.

Begin your day with a prayer of thanksgiving to God. Tonight, end your day with a prayer of gratitude to God. Throughout the day, remember the June practice of brachot—prayers of thanksgiving to God—whenever you see something of beauty that opens your heart.

August 25

Seed Thought

We live in unprecedented times during which the secret or esoteric teachings of many traditions have become available for the price of a paperback book. There is both danger and opportunity in the easy availability of detailed spiritual practices. The danger is that we can easily become dilettantes, digging a thousand shallow wells without ever hitting water. On the other hand, having a chance to taste a variety of practices enables us to get a feeling for what attracts us the most, so that we can find the best fit.

Prayer/Practice

Practice centering prayer or shamatha/vipassana meditation and then contemplate the matter of depth in spiritual practice. For the past eight months, we have been focusing on a few basic practices in order to develop concentration skills. For many people, this is more than enough. But we have also tasted a variety of more specialized and esoteric approaches to Divine Union. If any of these attracted you, how might you pursue that attraction in more depth? If you already have a spiritual tradition, are you comfortable with your level of involvement? Are there any groups, temples or churches in your area that you might find spiritual community with?

August 26

Seed Thought

Ralph Waldo Emerson was a mystic who allowed his life to unfold through the guidance he found in opening himself to the beauty of nature in times of solitude. He said, "A wise man will never impawn his future being and action, and decide beforehand what he shall do in a given extreme event. Nature and God will instruct him in that hour."

Prayer/Practice

If possible, meditate outside today. Look around you and appreciate the beauty of the earth and sky. With eyes open, do the meditation of bridging earth and heaven (August 1). Now place your awareness on your right side—the Southern Gate of your body temple—and invoke the presence of the Archangel Gabriel. Pray that you will remain open to the guidance of God and nature in all aspects of your life.

August 27

Seed Thought

The nineteenth-century English poet Edward Carpenter writes of spirituality as a patient waiting for our souls to flower. We must have faith that they will do so at the appointed hour, regardless of how much we may implore God to move up the timetable! Carpenter describes a patient waiting of the spirit that is an excellent suggestion for our late summer's meditations: "Let your mind be quiet, realising the beauty of the world, and the immense, the boundless treasures that it holds in store."

Prayer/Practice

If possible, go for a mindful walk in nature this morning. Seek nothing but the awareness of the beauty around you, and allow that beauty to bring forth the wisdom in your heart.

August 28

Seed Thought

As I walk, as I walk
The universe is walking with me
In beauty it walks before me
In beauty it walks behind me
In beauty it walks below me
In beauty it walks above me
Beauty is on every side
As I walk, I walk with Beauty.

—Traditional Navajo Prayer

Prayer/Practice

If possible, go for a mindful walk this morning, seeing everything as the beauty of God unfolding all around you. Practice seeing beauty all around you as you go through your day.

August 29

Seed Thought

The beauty of nature is a gift of God that brings forth peace of mind, heals our ragged emotions and uplifts our souls. When I was going through a particularly dark night of the soul in my early twenties, I could find no consolation from people, books or distraction. Reasoning didn't help, and I'd not yet heard of meditation. Even if I had, I was probably too agitated to practice. I was attracted to some little plants that I found in the supermarket, so I brought them home. Every day I sat with them, felt the soil to see if water was needed and watched the unfolding of new leaves. My soul grew more and more peaceful. When people in nursing homes are given plants to care for, they live a year longer than the average expectation.

Prayer/Practice

Identify a plant that is already in your home, or purchase one to form a relationship with. Plants tutor us in the ability to nurture life and reward us by creating more beauty and peace in our environment. It is a wonderful spiritual practice to care for, and be cared for in return by, plants.

August 30

Seed Thought

As our spirituality matures, we begin to take greater delight in beauty and in life's simple pleasures, like having our loved ones with us. I recall one winter's evening when our son Andrei, who was twenty at the time, arrived home from college with the flu. He was so grateful for the simple pleasures of a warm house, his childhood blanket to wrap up in, and a mother to stroke his head and talk with him. Sitting with this manchild, I was poignantly aware that we might not have many more evenings like this as he grew to adulthood and I grew to old age. I don't think I've ever been happier than in that moment, made almost unbearably sweet by the realization that all things are impermanent and that nothing we love can ever be taken for granted.

Prayer/Practice

Great Spirit, how incredibly rich is the experience of life. Please awaken me to its beauty and help me open my mind to the very impermanence of life—to the reality that everything I love will someday pass away—that I may open my heart in wild thanksgiving to the gifts and joys of the present moment.

Spend a few minutes in centering prayer or shamatha/vipassana meditation. Contemplate the blessing of impermanence as it awakens us to the joy of the present moment.

August 31

Seed Thought

The Twenty-third Psalm has inspired and intrigued people for thousands of years:

The lord is my shepherd, I shall not want. He maketh me to lie down in green pastures: he leadeth me beside the still waters. He restoreth my soul; he leadeth me in the paths of righteousness for his name's sake. Yea, though I walk through the valley of the shadow of death I will fear no evil; for thou art with me; thy rod and thy staff they comfort me. Thou preparest a table in the presence of my enemies; thou annointest my head with oil; my cup runneth over. Surely goodness and mercy shall follow me all the days of my life; and I will dwell in the house of the lord forever.

Prayer/Practice

If possible, go out into nature and read the Twenty-third Psalm slowly. Seek to realize that it is a song of thanksgiving to God for what has been attained, rather than a prayer of hope. Such is the joy and promise of spiritual maturity.

SEPTEMBER

Dreams, Intuition and the Inner Life

September is a pivotal month during which the outward-directed
energy of summer begins to shift inward in preparation
for the six months spent in the darkness of the Earth Mother's womb.
This month we will review our lives in the form of
spiritual autobiography.
We will open our sixth sense by noticing synchronicity, and
we will enter the world of dreams.
September is the gateway to Mystery,
and as the Medicine Wheel turns from summer to fall,
we are greeted by the Archangel Raphael
—the Healer of God—
who remedies the sickness of belief in perfection
by administering the great medicine of wholeness.
Listen to the voices of the Ancient Ones
who call from the mycelial mat that grows beneath the forest floor:

The inner and outer
harvests are complete
and the storehouse of the unconscious
is swept clean.
We enter the Gates of Mystery
through the Dreamworld
descending into the
fertile darkness in which our souls
are made new again.

September 1

Seed Thought

September is the culmination of the harvest and the storing of earth's abundance. The produce we put by sustains us through the winter, when, like Mother Earth, we withdraw our energies from the outer world and focus them on the mysterious inner darkness. In preparation for storing the fruits of recent growth in the deep caverns of our unconscious, the universal energies sweep its depths and stir up old ideas, old business and old wisdom so that we will know what to preserve and what to jettison as we move more consciously into the Great Archetypal Story of our life.

Prayer/Practice

Great Spirit, I give thanks for this late summer morning and the hint of fall that is already present in the lingering coolness of night and the gradual waning of daylight hours. As I prepare myself for the turning of the cosmic wheel, I call upon Gabriel to awaken me to the reality of my inner life so that I can be exquisitely attuned to the grace that comes in the fall housecleaning of my unconscious, and so that I can store the fruits of spirit with greater skill.

If possible, take a mindful walk in nature today. Cultivate an awareness of the silent place within and its connection to all that grows. Find a plant or a tree and sit by it. Extend your awareness into the plant and notice whatever you can about its flow of energy and the cycle of its growth.

September 2

Seed Thought

Psychiatrist and mystic Carl Jung described a personal and a collective unconscious. The personal unconscious teems with repressed and forgotten feelings, images and memories from our past, both light and dark. This boiling pot of psychic energy is the hidden guide and motivator of most actions. The collective unconscious is inherent in every person, regardless of past experience. Populated by demons and angels, heroes and Hitlers, this well of archetypal stories is like a factory-installed direction finder for the way back home to God. The mythology, religious literature and folktales of all cultures emerge from these collective archetypes, as do many of our dreams, calling us to an awareness of our roles in the Great Cosmic Drama.

Prayer/Practice

Today marks the beginning of an eight-day exercise in retrospection during which you will write a spiritual autobiography and begin looking into your personal and the collective unconscious. Some of the exercises were adapted from Dan Wakefield's book *Writing Your Spiritual Autobiography*. Others were inspired by the work of theologian James Fowler, who wrote *Stages of Faith*.

Spend a few minutes in the quiet of centering prayer or shamatha/ vipassana meditation. Now go back in your imagination and recall whatever you can about your childhood room. Draw a picture of that room. What were your thoughts about God when you lived in that room? Make a few notes for use later in the week.

September 3

Seed Thought

In 1937, Carl Jung gave a famous lecture at Yale University in which he challenged his audience to move beyond the concepts and confines of organized religion into a direct encounter with religious experience. My first day of Hebrew school was such an encounter. While I remember nothing of the teacher's words, I clearly remember being gripped by the shape of the Hebrew alphabet and carried beyond my conscious knowing into a meeting with Mystery that revealed the numinous Presence of God and the promise that life was filled with unspeakable wonder.

Prayer/Practice

Once again, take a mindful walk if possible, letting your conscious mind take a back seat to the immediate experience of nature. When you are through, contemplate this question. "What was your first spiritual experience, your first direct encounter with the numinous?" Make a few notes for future reference.

September 4

Seed Thought

When I was a little girl, my bed was under a big bay window. At night I would lie still and watch the moon. One day my father brought home a record about a princess who was very ill. The court physicians could find no cure, but finally the Lord High Chamberlain, whose deep voice was filled with magic, found a solution. The Princess must have the moon. But although the moon seemed very close, no ladder was tall enough to reach it. Finally, the Lord High Chamberlain made a silver moon for the princess, and she became well. He tried to keep her away from the window at night, so that she would not discover that it wasn't the real moon on a chain around her neck. But one night, she chanced to see the moon in the sky and was delighted that God had grown a new one for all to enjoy.

Prayer/Practice

Spend a few minutes in the peace of centering prayer or in shamatha/vipassana meditation. Can you remember what your favorite story was when you were a child? Did it relate in any way that you can appreciate now to your spiritual life? Make a few notes for use later in the week.

September 5

Seed Thought

Children live in a world of fairies and demons, good guys and bad guys—a world that is painted in black and white rather than in shades of gray. As children we are easily frightened and just as easily soothed. The ideas we have about the Universe tend to be vibrant and filled not only with the things we experience firsthand, but with a population of characters that have inhabited the mythology, folktales and religious literature of the world from the beginning of time. They are part of the collective unconscious that all people share, the ground of soul memories from which our personal stories spring.

Prayer/Practice

Relax into your breathing, and let go into the peace of centering prayer or shamatha/vipassana meditation. What were your childhood beliefs about how the world came to be? Did you think about heaven and hell? If so, who got to go to which place and why? What did your parents believe? Make a few notes to use later in the week.

September 6

Seed Thought

Adolescence brings a flowering of spiritual belief, based on personal experience woven together with collective archetypes. We transcend the black-and-white beliefs of early childhood that cast God as a powerful, sometimes malevolent Santa Claus. If our parents are punitive and authoritarian, however, we may not make this adolescent leap until much later in life, when we finally heal the early wounds to self-esteem. But if all goes well, and we have developed a confident sense of self that is ready to be independent from our parents, the spiritual task of adolescence is to find role models that confirm and extend the numinous experiences we have had.

Prayer/Practice

If possible, go for a mindful walk today. When you are finished, find a place to sit outside or look out a window. This is a time for reflection. Who were the role models who were most important to you as an adolescent? What were the values they espoused? Were these similar to the values of your parents, or were they different? Make a few notes for future reference.

September 7

Seed Thought

One of my adolescent heroes was Aldous Huxley, whose book *The Doors of Perception* opened me to the Universe within. Another was the roguish Errol Flynn. His autobiography was one of high adventure, ranging from the farthest outposts of romantic fantasy to rugged and often rude individualism. I remember being particularly enthralled by a passage revealing the graphic details of how he castrated sheep on an Australian ranch. Errol Flynn may not seem like a very spiritual role model, yet we first come in contact with the archetype of the Higher Self through stories involving heroes, wise women and men, kings and queens, prophets and saviors and people who stretch the limits of what we consider "normal."

Prayer/Practice

Quiet your conscious mind and open to the wisdom of the unconscious by taking a mindful walk or by practicing a few minutes of meditation. What were your favorite movies or books as a teenager? Who were your idols? What aspect of your growing awareness do you think they represented? Take a few minutes to make some notes for later reference.

September 8

Seed Thought

As a young adult, if we have successfully made the psychic separation from our parents into our own sense of self, we have articulated an opinion about the big questions: "Who am I? What is the meaning of life? Is there a God?" But it isn't until midlife that spiritual understanding really ripens, following the experience of what theologian James Fowler calls the "sacrament of defeat." Our youthful idealism crumbles, and we face the fact that there are no ready answers to life's great paradoxes and no way to escape impermanence and suffering. Bad things routinely happen to good people. At this point the scaffolding of outer religious belief often topples, and, if we successfully negotiate the ensuing dark night of the soul, a deeper spiritual understanding can emerge.

Prayer/Practice

If possible, take a mindful walk again today. When you return, contemplate the religious or spiritual beliefs of your young adulthood. Did you undergo a "sacrament of defeat" at some point when your suffering was so intense that all your previous ideas about the universe crumbled? If so, did any new spiritual beliefs begin to emerge? Make a few notes for later in the week.

September 9

Seed Thought

During the past week you were invited to dip into the images, feelings, beliefs, stories and myths that mingle in your personal and the collective unconscious. It's time now to put all these "memories, dreams and reflections" (this is also the title of Jung's autobiography) into your own cohesive spiritual autobiography. There is no better way to figure out where you are than to reconstruct where you've been! Very often we've been traveling an interesting road, only dimly aware of the evolutionary journey that our soul is taking.

Prayer/Practice

You will need a clean sheet of paper for today's practice—the bigger the better. You will also need more time than usual, at least an hour and more likely several. Starting with the time of your birth, draw a road map of your life, marking the highlights (both good and bad) every five years or so. Looking over your notes from the past week, superimpose the evolution of your spiritual understanding on the events of your life. Write a brief summary of your spiritual autobiography.

September 10

Seed Thought

My husband, Miron, and I were sitting under a tree one summer, deep in discussion with our friend Rick. At that time, Miron had a full beard and fierce demeanor. Rick looked him in the eye and said, "Miron, you're a strong archetype of something. Do you have any idea what?" We all laughed, but Rick's question was very incisive. Our archetype is the story our soul is mastering at any given time. One archetype is no better than another, since ancient wisdom suggests that each of us must eventually live through every archetype.

Prayer/Practice

Spend a few minutes in meditation. Consider whether you have experienced these or other archetypes that come to mind.

- *The Grand Inquisitor, "protector of the faith"*
- *The victim*
- *The martyr*
- *The rescuer*
- *The healer*
- *The wise woman/man*
- *The fool*
- *The mystic*
- *The hero*

September 11

Seed Thought

There are times in our life when we have completed the soulstory
associated with one archetype and are moving into another aspect
of our ongoing spiritual autobiography. The transition time is a
harvesting and a clearing. If we fail to recognize these transitions,
we keep playing the same role over and over, which can lead to a
sense of futility, boredom, "stuckness," depression or stress. As
the cosmic wheel turns from summer to fall and our energy begins
its annual descent into the dark realms of the deep unconscious,
it is time to contemplate whether our sojourn in our current archetype
is complete, and if so, into which new one we are progressing.

Prayer/Practice

*Practice a few minutes of centering prayer or shamatha/vipassana
meditation. Contemplate the questions, "Who are the people
you respect the most? Of these people, who would you most like
to emulate? What archetype do they represent?"*

September 12

Seed Thought

In moving from one house to another, we take stock of our possessions and carefully consider what we want to bring with us. Similarly, in moving to a new place on the journey of our soul, we need to carefully consider what to bring along and what to leave behind. In recent years, I moved out of the archetype of healer and into the archetype of mystic. In the transition I left behind much of my orientation to pain and found that I focused more naturally on joy, gratitude and peace. My dominant role model switched from psychiatrist Alice Miller to the Dalai Lama. In the wake of that enormous shift, I naturally changed the work I did and the way that I related to people and to life.

Prayer/Practice

Take a few letting-go breaths and slowly, patiently enter the temple of inner silence. Place your awareness to your right side, the Southern Gate of your body temple. Call upon the Archangel Gabriel, whose strength and guidance can help bring you through the different stages of your soul's journey. Ask for help in considering what archetype you are currently expressing, and if you are ready to move on, which archetype you are moving into. Consider which qualities you will leave behind and which you'll take along.

September 13

Seed Thought

When we are making a shift from one archetype to another, the Universe often engineers synchronicities that help us along. For example, perhaps you have worked through enough anger toward your long-estranged father that you are thinking of making contact. At just that moment, he calls on the phone, hoping to make amends. Jungian psychiatrist Harry Wilmer defines synchronicity as "the simultaneous occurrence of two meaningfully but not causally connected events in which an inner psychic subjective state or event parallels an outer event in the objective world. Not only is the cause unknown, but the cause is not even thinkable." Synchronicities transcend time and space, revealing the unified field, the Mind of God in which we live and move and have our being. Coincidences, on the other hand, lack the dimension of inner meaning that defines synchronicity.

Prayer/Practice

Divine Beloved, how remarkable is the Mystery of Your Creation and the interconnectedness of all things. May I be alert to the synchronicities that help boost my awareness of the unfolding story of my life, that I may live that story with love, humor, compassion, wisdom and kindness.

Center yourself with a few minutes of centering prayer or shamatha/vipassana meditation. Place your awareness of the right side of your body and invoke the Presence of Gabriel. Ask for help in perceiving the messages that are always being left by the Universe.

September 14

Seed Thought

Carl Jung once created a mandala that he called "Window on Eternity." About a year later, he painted another mandala with a gold castle in the center. As he contemplated the mandala, he was puzzled by its distinctly Chinese feeling. At just this time, a package arrived from a friend. It contained a manuscript describing an ancient Chinese Taoist alchemical treatise with the request that Jung write a commentary on it. When Jung read the manuscript, the meaning of the mandala was revealed. Now that's synchronicity!

Prayer/Practice

If possible, go for a mindful walk today. Invoke the presence of your guardian angel to walk with you. When you're done walking, sit quietly and thank your guardian angel, who is the agent of many of the synchronicities you have experienced—the book that practically falls off the shelf when you need it, the stranger whose conversation you overhear that heals an old wound.... Think of a synchronicity that you've recently experienced and give thanks for it. Does it apply to an archetypal situation in your life?

September 15

Seed Thought

It's humbling to recognize that our minds are quite like icebergs. Most of their substance is hidden beneath the surface. We typically look for wisdom or God or solutions to our problems in the visible, logical level of life, missing the real sphere of action. Perhaps you remember the story of the drunk who was searching for his keys under a streetlamp. A good samaritan stopped to help and asked, "Where, exactly did you drop the keys?" The drunk pointed to the vacant lot across the street. When the incredulous passerby asked why he was looking for them under the lamp, the drunk replied with perfect logic, "Because the light is better."

Prayer/Practice

Great Spirit, thank you for this late summer morning and for my gradual awakening to the worlds below the surface, to the inner realms of my psyche and their mysterious connection to the outer world of form. Today, I will continue to be a patient observer of the world beyond the senses, the world of dreams, archetypes and imagination.

Tonight before bed, establish a firm intention to remember at least one dream. Put a journal and a pen on the bedstand. Upon awakening, and before moving, immediately think, "What was I dreaming?" Rehearse the dream in your mind and give it a snappy title before writing it down in the first person, present tense. Be patient if you don't remember a dream tonight. It may take several nights before the power of your intention is sufficiently set that you will have easier access to the dreamworld.

September 16

Seed Thought

Dreams are the naked truth-tellers of the unconscious. The mental censors that continually distort our thoughts and feelings in waking life (so that we'll look good and feel acceptable) are suspended in dreamtime. The dreamself is brutally honest, but also has a great sense of humor, which makes its revelations more tolerable. I once dreamed about a problematic colleague. He was in the hospital for tests, sitting on a pedestal. When he got up, he left a large Buddha-shaped mound of feces behind. I said with great relief, "Thank goodness he wasn't sick after all; he was just full of shit." I journaled the dream without much understanding, and only later, when my waking mind had fully taken over, did I get the pun! Since every dream character represents a part of ourselves, I had to face my own spiritual bullshit and do some serious thinking about humility. It was easier to do so while laughing than if my hubris had been pointed out some other way.

Prayer/Practice

Practice a few minutes of shamatha/vipassana meditation or centering prayer. Did you remember any of your dreams last night? If so, while you are still in the state of meditation— a state in which the conscious and unconscious minds mix and mingle—review the dream. If you think about your dream as a wake-up call from your Higher Self, what do you think it is trying to tell you?

September 17

Seed Thought

We all have five periods of rapid-eye-movement sleep each night,
during which we dream. Dreams are generally as evanescent as
smoke unless they are particularly gripping or disturbing. But even
if you don't generally remember your dreams, you can train
yourself to do so. Fall and winter, when our conscious minds are
closest to the unconscious, is the perfect time to begin or to
reinstate a dream practice.

Prayer/Practice

*Write down these five rules of thumb for dream practice and
apply them to either a recent or an old dream:*

• *All dreams come in service of your Higher Self.*

• *Some dreams are clearer than others. Some seem to be rehearsals
on a theme that will be more obvious in later dreams.*

• *Treat every dream as a jewel. Do not judge it as a mature
dream or as a rehearsal before you have carefully journaled
and reread it. When you first awaken, even amazing dreams
often seem pedestrian.*

• *Symbols in a dream can be both personal and archetypal.
Because you might have a personal slant on an archetypal
symbol like a cross, you can't rely on interpretations found
in dream books or those offered by friends unless you get
the sensation of an inner "aha."*

September 18

Seed Thought

Jeremy Taylor, a Unitarian minister, has written several books on dreams, including *Dreamwork*, which is a guide to leaderless dream groups. For several years, our "group" was whoever showed up for breakfast. The guidelines for group work are simple:

- The presenter of a dream narrates it as if it is happening—in the first person, present tense. "I am walking down a dark road and a bear with luminous eyes steps out of the brush."

- No one interrupts the narration. When the dreamer is finished, then the others ask for any points of clarification.

- When everyone is as clear as possible on the dream, they offer their thoughts for exactly what they are—projections—by saying, "If that were my dream...."

- The only reliable indicator that a person has hit upon some truth is an "aha" on the part of the dreamer.

- Because the sharing of dreams is very intimate, it is important to agree to some rules of confidentiality so that the group is a safe place.

Prayer/Practice

If possible, walk mindfully outside today. As you look around you, consider the possibility that everything you see is of the nature of a dream. Continue to consider this possibility throughout the day. Think about getting a dreamgroup together.

September 19

Seed Thought

How do you know that you are not dreaming right now? No, pinching yourself won't work. If you pinch yourself in a dream, you'll just feel pain. *Stop and think about this* before reading on. There are two or three reliable indicators. First, you can fly or float in a dream. If you try to rise up out of your seat and float right now, what happens? Are you dreaming? Second, if you read something in a dream and then look away, it will not remain the same. Look away and read this paragraph again—carefully—because sometimes the changes are very small. Are you dreaming? Third, you can generally walk through walls in dreams. Do you want to give that one a try? Are you dreaming?

Prayer/Practice

Put a little ink spot on the back of your hand. Every time you look at it ask yourself, "Am I dreaming?" Then try one of the three tests. It's easy to fool yourself in a dream, so you have to be very mindful of how carefully you perform the tests. If you remember to test whether or not you're dreaming with any frequency, one of two things will happen. You will remember to test your state while you are dreaming, and you will then "awaken" in the dream (this is called a lucid dream) or you will wake up out of the dream of daily life, which is called enlightenment. (The latter is hearsay on my part. I've woken up in my night dreams, but not in the daydream of life!) The practice of asking whether or not you are dreaming is one of the most ancient spiritual practices of awakening, best developed as Tibetan Dream Yoga.

September 20

Seed Thought

Stephen LaBerge is the director of the dream laboratory at Stanford University and one of the leading authorities on lucid dreaming. His books *Lucid Dreaming* and *Exploring the World of Lucid Dreaming* are classics on the mind, the unconscious and the spiritual life. Lucid dreaming may or may not be a practice that you feel ready to try at this point, but it is worth understanding since most people have occasional lucid dreams whether or not they remember them. The most typical way that beginners become lucid is in nightmares. Perhaps you are trying to run and cannot. Suddenly you think, "Wait a minute, I must be dreaming." You then awaken into the dream, rather than into your bed, and you may find that you have some control over the action and can end your nightmare in a way that transforms fear into wisdom.

Prayer/Practice

Our usual critical faculties are suspended while dreaming. It doesn't seem at all unusual to be "at home" in a totally strange place when a sixty-pound red duck flies in the window and eats the dog's food although you have no dog. Today, pay attention to such "anomalies" in everyday life. Is something out of place? Does someone appear strangely dressed? Do you have an odd feeling? Ask yourself, "Am I dreaming?" and then do one of the three tests we learned yesterday. Since what you do during the day tends to show up in your dreams at night, if you regularly look for anomalies, sooner or later you will do so in a dream and become lucid.

September 21

Seed Thought

The value of lucid dreaming is remarkable. First, you can overcome fears and develop confidence in a heightened state of awareness that carries over beautifully into daily life. In fact, the lucid state feels much "realer" than real life. What I've mastered "there" has transferred "here" very easily. Second, it's great fun. You can fly to the moon, explore the galaxy and have great adventures. You can practice being any archetype you like! Third, the lucid state favors numinous experience—*numinous* meaning a "meeting with Mystery." I have had several light experiences in the lucid state that were among the greatest blessings of my life.

Prayer/Practice

Go for a mindful walk on this early fall day if you can. Be present to the changes in the earth, the different colors and smells, the feel of the breeze and the temperature. Summer is over. Everything keeps changing, moving, flowing on. Consider once again that this life is of the nature of a dream. Today, continue the practice of looking for anomalies and asking, "Am I dreaming?" Record any dreams you have tonight.

September 22: Autumnal Equinox

Seed Thought

Today the cosmic wheel turns and opens fully to the West. The hours of light and dark are exactly equal on this first day of fall. By tomorrow we will be beginning our descent through the Western Gate into the darkness of the underworld. The light is fading and the call of dreams, archetypes and synchronicities grows stronger. We have prepared ourselves to listen to their messages so that the wisdom of our unconscious can mature in the growing darkness. We can look forward to emerging from the underworld transformed in six months, on the spring equinox.

Prayer/Practice

If possible, go out into nature and do the meditation of bridging earth and heaven. Center yourself in your breathing and become aware of the energy of the sun. Now open to the energy of the earth. Breathe in the sun from above and the earth from below, letting their energies mingle and balance in your heart. Breathe out the marriage of earth and sun, conscious and unconscious, to all beings. You are the bridge between the realms. You are the cosmic awakener!

September 23

Seed Thought

With the passage through equinox, the gates of the underworld are
open and the great cosmic cellar cleaning can begin. In the Jewish
tradition, the high holy days of Rosh Hashanah (New Year) and
Yom Kippur (the Day of Atonement) fall at about this time.
During the ten days between the two holidays, it is said that the
gates of heaven are open. These days of deep, unflinching soul-
searching are the holiest days of the Jewish year. Unfinished issues
are unearthed and resolved. One admits one's wrongs to self,
others and God, making amends where necessary and giving
forgiveness where appropriate. One's conscience is cleared and
the soul is freed to ascend through heaven's gates.

Prayer/Practice

Divine Beloved, I arise with a grateful heart on this fall morning.
I am ready to let go of the regrets, resentments and unconscious acts
and attitudes that separate me from You and others. I open the
door of my heart and invite You in. Sweep me clean that I may
wake up to the love and joy that are my own true nature. Sweep
me clean so that my life can be a blessing to others and to You.

*Spend a few minutes in the stillness of centering prayer, the egg
of light or shamatha/vipassana meditation. Did you remember any
dreams last night? Are you dreaming now? Keep up the dream
practices if you can.*

September 24

Seed Thought

With the turning of the cosmic wheel from South to West, from summer to fall, the Archangel Gabriel passes the torch to Raphael. In Hebrew, *Raphael* means "healer of God." Associated with the winged serpent of the Caduceus, Raphael is also the guardian of science and knowledge. As a healer, Raphael possesses the power to purge us of the illusions that keep us separate from God and from realizing the deepest potential within our souls. Raphael is the agency or power that brings the unconscious to consciousness, the darkness to light.

Prayer/Practice

Take a few letting-go breaths and slowly, patiently slip into the place of stillness, the Holy of Holies. Thank God for your gradual awakening. Now place your attention in back of you, at the Western Gate of your body temple. Invoke Raphael, the Healer of God, guardian of the Western Gate. Sit with that powerful presence and ask for help in exploring whatever elements of your unconscious are ripe for discovery. Continue the dream practice and your awareness of synchronicity.

September 25

Seed Thought

We become whole, healed, by making the invisible visible and
bringing the darkness to light. From the time we were children,
we have been conditioned to put our best foot and face forward. We
have been shamed when our behavior was less than perfect or
we seemed greedy, arrogant, or otherwise naughty. Everything "not
good" got shoved into the cellar of the personal unconscious.
Jung called it the shadow. It is the alter ego that plays Hyde to our
Jekyll. Hedge all you want, but it's in there, stuffed with everything that
you deny, hate and disavow. The shadow is your evil twin.

Prayer/Practice

*We have done some shadow work already in noticing that when
we particularly dislike another person, or judge someone we
hardly know, we are actually projecting our own shadow. If we
are particularly offended by some one else's anger, our own
unseen anger has found a screen to play upon. What can we
do about it? Owning its truth is a big step, since what we
cannot see has power over us. Other clues about our shadow
show up in dreams. Look for your shadow today, and continue
your dream work.*

*Spend a few minutes in centering prayer, the egg of light or
shamatha/vipassana meditation.*

September 26

Seed Thought

While working on this book I had a dream about facilitating a
healing group in a cellar. Several people are sitting in a circle, and I
am talking. Three howler monkeys suddenly jump down at me from
an open window and begin to attack. I hit them hard, causing
serious injuries. I am filled both with true remorse and also with
fear that the group will see my violent nature and consider me
a spiritual misfit. I wrap the seemingly dead monkeys, oddly shrunken
to the size of mice, in toilet paper and put them gently in a plastic
bag, hoping to nurse them back to health. They begin to breathe.
I open the bag, and they leap out of the cellar window into a
sunlit field, where they happily eat clover. I feel very relieved.

Prayer/Practice

Spend a few minutes in the quiet of meditation.

*If that were your dream, what would it say about your shadow?
Remember the dreamgroup guidelines from September 18. Your
interpretation of my dream is in itself a projection that can give
you valuable information about yourself. If I could hear your
"If that were my dream" comments, I'm sure I'd also learn a
lot more about myself. How are your dreams going? Is there
someone you can share dreams with? Are you dreaming now?*

September 27

Seed Thought

What to do with your shadow? The long and short of it is to be
aware of it, own it, withdraw its projections, and learn to live
with it. It ain't going away because we need it. We live in a world
of opposites. Without evil there's no good. Without your shadow
you wouldn't long so for the light. Without greed there'd be no
movement toward generosity. At some point, when we awaken
from this dream of us and them, up and down, black and white,
male and female, we won't need our shadows because we will
live in wholeness. But for now, the shadow has its place. So give
the devil its due and toss out any illusions of being perfect. At
least while you're on earth.

Prayer/Practice

*If possible, go out for a mindful walk today. Enjoy the turn of
the seasons and rest in Mother Nature's womb. Tonight,
continue the dream practices.*

September 28

Seed Thought

Nathaniel Hawthorne reached down into the world of archetypes
and pulled out a splendid short story called "The Scarlet Hand." In
this tale, a young chemist marries a woman who is so incredibly
beautiful that people stop in the streets to stare at her. She is
as near as a human being can come to perfection, her beauty
marred only by a tiny birthmark on her face in the form of a
scarlet hand. Her husband becomes obsessed, or should I say
possessed, by the need to find a cure for her birthmark, a cream
that will fade it. Working day and night, he finally finds the formula
for a vanishing cream. But as the birthmark fades, life slips out
of his beautiful young wife, and he is left with a perfect corpse.

Prayer/Practice

Spend a few minutes in the meditation practice of your choice.

*Give thanks to God for such a rich landscape of unconscious
wonders! If that story were your dream, what would it tell
you about your shadow? Remember that every character in a
dream is part of yourself. Have you ever felt possessed by
something? Don't tell me the devil made you do it, unless you
can own the devil as part of your shadow. Keep up your
dream work by day and by night. Do you think you could be
dreaming now?*

September 29

Seed Thought

Hawthorne's chemist was possessed by the archetype of perfection. Since he couldn't own his own need for perfection, he projected it onto his wife, with disastrous consequences. Perfection is a cunning little devil, but if we engage it head to head, it will awaken the thirst for true wholeness. And what is wholeness?

- The dignity with which we keep on keeping on, acknowledging our mistakes and inquiring where they are trying to lead us.

- The graciousness with which we accept our shadow—not in complacency, but with the humility to engage our evil twin consciously, so that we can withdraw from the battles it will otherwise create.

Prayer/Practice

Settle into a few minutes of centering prayer or shamatha/ vipassana meditation. Now contemplate the matter of perfection as opposed to wholeness.

September 30

Seed Thought

In periods of sudden change, when the bottom drops out of things, most of us are prone to move into perfectionistic thinking. We really blew it, so we must be bad, very bad. And far from perfect. Take a few letting-go breaths and read this excerpt from a letter of Carl Jung: "If you are now in the dumps and up to your ears in the mire, you must tell yourself that you were flying too high and that a dose of undiluted hellish blackness was indicated. The pickle you are in is certainly something you couldn't have brought on yourself. This shows that someone 'out there' is surrounding you with provident thoughts and doing you the necessary wrong."

Prayer/Practice

Great Spirit, I enter this season with gratitude for the things I will learn from the cosmic agents of awareness, those "someones out there" who sweep the unconscious and create the dramas that bring me to wholeness. I call upon Raphael to stay by my side this fall, providing the courage to face myself anew that I might embrace that wholeness and be of greater service to God and all beings.

Take a few letting-go breaths and slowly, patiently, enter the inner stillness, the Holy of Holies. Put your awareness in back of you and invoke the Presence of Raphael. Ask the Archangel of healing for help in becoming whole.

WESTERN GATE
Archangel Raphael

FALL

OCTOBER

Taking Stock

October is a month of introspection and retrospection,
of taking stock.
The leaves are falling. The light is fading. Death is a reminder
that this life is limited and precious.
Are you using it well? Are you happy? Have you discovered
the means to develop a heart of lovingkindness?
We will consider several moral conundrums together this month,
when it's not so easy to see who wears the white hats
and who wears the black hats.
We will think deeply about our values, our relationships,
our motivation and our mind-habits.
We will take responsibility for living our lives with
awareness and love.
Listen to the voices of the Ancient Ones as they blow on the wind
that whistles through the naked branches:

*In the fading light of fall
we begin the annual journey
to the underworld.
The Medicine Wheel is fully open
to the Western Gate.
Realizing that our time on earth
is limited,
we make death our ally and teacher,
bringing us face to face with
the results of our choices
and kindling the intention
to make lovingkindness
our primary virtue.*

October 1

Seed Thought

When I was a child growing up in a suburb of Boston, fall was my favorite season. The trees were at their most elegant in shades of red, orange and gold. Their transformation by the chill air and the growing darkness awakened a feeling of mystery, which was deepened by the physical delights of jumping, rolling and burying myself in the fallen leaves. The most beautiful specimens were tucked between sheets of waxed paper and pressed in the pages of a big dictionary. It was their burial crypt. Although the death of summer was at hand, the stirrings of new life already seemed palpable deep beneath the ground.

Prayer/Practice

If possible, take a mindful walk out in nature today. What can you sense about the energy of nature and the cycles of death and rebirth? Contemplate this cycle as it pertains to you. What is dying in your life now? As to what will be born, have patience. That will emerge like new leaves at winter's end. Everything needs time to gestate.

October 2

Seed Thought

Death fascinates us in the abstract and repels us in the particular. We're riveted by the untimely demise of all those unfortunate others who die in the fires, wars and drive-by shootings featured on the evening news. But for the most part, we can observe the reality of death day in and day out without really considering that the angel of death will one day knock upon our own door. More's the pity. Without the recognition that our time here is limited, it's so easy to overlook the many gifts and opportunities of life, falling into complacency or the tiresome indulgence of self-pity.

Prayer/Practice

Spend a few minutes in centering prayer or shamatha/vipassana meditation. Now contemplate the fact that you could die tomorrow or even today. What do you think your obituary would say? What would you really like it to say? What can you give birth to in your life that will enable you to leave this earth with a sense of completion?

October 3

Seed Thought

I have always enjoyed being with people who are facing death, because many of them are far more alive than the average person. Having cancer or AIDS can give you permission to speak your mind. Hidden strengths may emerge. Life seems more precious and immediate when there is an end in sight. When you may never see another spring, the blooms of an azalea are almost painfully magnificent. When you may not see your child's next birthday, every minute you have with him is a gift. These things were always gifts, but when we live life without an awareness of death, it is harder to perceive the beauty and love around us. Death is a great eye-opener.

Prayer/Practice

Take a few deep breaths and slowly, patiently enter the silent place within, the Holy of Holies. Imagine that you just received the news that the world was going to end in six months. What would be most important to you? What do you think you would miss the most?

Endless variations of your fantasy can and will come true. Can you live your life today as if you might never see another tomorrow?

October 4

Seed Thought

In the late 1980s, I was facilitating a group for people with AIDS.
I read them the passage below from *A Separate Reality*, by anthropologist
Carlos Castaneda. His mentor, Don Juan, is teaching him to become
a warrior, a person who lives with awareness, impeccability and
power. He says that "to be a warrior a man has to be, first of all,
and rightfully so, keenly aware of his death." I finished reading
Don Juan's words, feeling somewhat sheepish since I didn't have
AIDS and wasn't facing death in such a head-on way. So I added
rather lamely that the time of anyone's death is uncertain. After
all, I could have a car crash on my way home. Which I did.

Prayer/Practice

Great Spirit, I awaken this morning with a renewed appreciation
for the gift of life. May I walk through this day mindfully, gratefully,
with the knowledge that I could awaken from the dream of life at
any moment. I call upon the Archangel Raphael to help me
awaken to life through embracing the reality of death.

*Take a few letting-go breaths and slowly, patiently enter the silent
place within, the Holy of Holies. Place your attention behind
you, on the Western side of your body temple, and invoke the
presence of Raphael. Ask for assistance in using the awareness
of death as your ally in life.*

October 5

Seed Thought

The last thought I had before careening into a head-on collision after the AIDS group we discussed yesterday was "Maybe I'll at least have a near-death experience." I didn't in the literal sense, but I did in the sense that I died to my old life right then and there. One nose-reattachment surgery and several days in the hospital later, I woke up to the fact that I didn't like some of the choices I was living. When any moment may be your last moment, why wait to make changes? Within a few months I had left my position at the hospital and given up a faculty appointment at Harvard Medical School.

Prayer/Practice

Practice a few minutes of centering prayer or shamatha/vipassana meditation. If my talk with the AIDS group and the subsequent head-on collision had been a dream, what projections would you have on it? Reread the practice of September 18 if you need to, and then contemplate "If that were my dream . . ." One of my friends made the astute observation that if it had been her dream, she would have been struck by the fact that since my nose had nearly been severed, I had "lost face." This had great relevance to my life situation at the time.

By the way, are you continuing your dream practice?

October 6

Seed Thought

An awareness of death necessarily puts us face to face with our
beliefs about the soul. Carl Jung wrote in his autobiography that "we
must have a myth about death. A man should be able to say that
he has done his best to form a conception of life after death,
or to create some image of it—even if he must confess his failure.
Not to have done so is a vital loss." Although Jung had a number
of stunning visions and dreams about the continuity of the soul,
he was always careful to note that we can never really know
what happens at death. Our ideas about it, however, are vitally
important to how we live our life.

Prayer/Practice

*Practice a few minutes of centering prayer, the egg of light or
shamatha/vipassana meditation. Contemplate your beliefs
about death and what happens to the soul at that time. If you
have let go of your dream practice consider picking it up
again. The archetypal content of our contemplations is more than
likely to be elucidated by your Higher Self in dreamtime.*

October 7

Seed Thought

In the spiritual classic *The Bhagavad Gita*, Arjuna is a warrior involved in a civil war. Faced with fighting friends, cousins and teachers, he finds himself in a painful moral dilemma. His charioteer, who is none other than the Lord Krishna, says to him, "The truly wise mourn neither for the living nor the dead. There was never a time when I did not exist, nor you, nor any of these kings. Nor is there any future in which we shall cease to be. Just as the dweller in this body passes through childhood, youth and old age, so at death he merely passes into another kind of body. The wise are not deceived by that.... Worn-out garments are shed by the body; worn-out bodies are shed by the dweller within the body. New bodies are donned by the dweller, like garments."

Prayer/Practice

Take a few deep breaths and slowly, patiently let go into the place of inner stillness. Move into the wisdom self beyond judgment and concept. What do you think about Krishna's speech and Arjuna's dilemma? Think of it as if it were a dream. Consider, "If that were my dream ..." What does the story bring up for you?

October 8

Seed Thought

There is an ancient saying that the relative and the absolute are like two wings of a bird representing how things appear and how things are. The two must stay in balance, or the bird will fall out of the sky. Death has confronted Arjuna with a moral dilemma. It may be that in absolute reality we are birthless and deathless, but in relative reality our wounds bleed, we die and our loved ones mourn. So what is a warrior to do?

Prayer/Practice

If possible, take a mindful walk today. Feel the forces of the earth all around you. When you are finished, contemplate the two wings of death—the absolute and the relative. What would you do if there was a civil war? Would you kill to abolish slavery? Would you kill to protect your family? Would you need to wait until the moment had arrived to make that choice? October is a time to take stock of our deepest held beliefs.

October 9

Seed Thought

Sometimes a patient in an unusual predicament would ask me what I would do in their position. My answer was generally the same: "I don't know." Until we are in a particular situation it is sometimes hard to know what we might do. But we do need to have guidelines by which to live our lives in ordinary circumstances that might help inform our actions in extraordinary circumstances. The Buddha suggested three guidelines that we have been exploring in different ways throughout the year. He said to cultivate virtue, do no harm and tame your mind.

Prayer/Practice

Spend a few minutes in the quiet of centering prayer or shamatha/ vipassana meditation. Contemplate the question "What does it mean to cultivate virtue?"

October 10

Seed Thought

One aspect of cultivating virtue is to make lovingkindness the primary goal of every interaction. To do this, we must first be able to distinguish kindness from people-pleasing. Until we have developed self-respect and the humility that arises from authentic inner security, we are likely to feel guilty if we fail to please people, even if pleasing them would be harmful in some way. Lovingkindness is the attitude that a psychologically healthy mother has toward her child, resulting from her selfless desire to encourage his or her best potential. Such a mother naturally sets limits and speaks her mind, but always with the greatest respect and love.

Prayer/Practice

Spend a few minutes in shamatha/vipassana meditation or centering prayer. Now retrospect your interactions yesterday, beginning with the last one of the day and going back to morning. Were there any episodes of people-pleasing? Consider the potential harm of this behavior. Were there times when you encouraged another's potential with lovingkindness? Set a strong intention to practice lovingkindness today, and to let go of people-pleasing.

October 11

Seed Thought

Authors Hugh and Gayle Prather wrote something in their book for couples, *Notes to Each Other*, that Miron and I have adopted as a guideline for cultivating virtue in our marriage: "Will the time come when we won't have to work so hard on our relationship? No, the time will come when there will be no lapse in our efforts. The time will come when it will be unthinkable for us to take a break from kindness."

Prayer/Practice

Spend a few minutes in the silence of centering prayer, the egg of light or shamatha/vipassana meditation. Bring to mind a person that you have a relationship with. How are you doing in practicing lovingkindness? Read today's entry to that person at a time when you think they might be receptive to a discussion (not when either you or they are feeling closed down, hurt or angry).

October 12

Seed Thought

Religious institutions might well consider the cultivation of virtue as a measure of their success. Author Karen Armstrong, who wrote the excellent book *A History of God*, critiqued the failures of some modern religious institutions in an interview published in *Time* magazine. She said, "Only Western Christianity makes a song and dance about creeds and beliefs. The authentic test of a religion is not what you believe. It's what you do, and unless your religion expresses itself in compassion for all living things, it is not authentic."

Prayer/Practice

Spend a few minutes in the silence of centering prayer or shamatha/vipassana meditation. Contemplate Karen Armstrong's statement both in general and with particular reference to whatever religion you were brought up in (if any), and whatever religion you subscribe to now (if any).

October 13

Seed Thought

The cultivation of virtue through lovingkindness is both a selfless act and one that the Dalai Lama calls "wise selfish." The reason for that is simple. Every action calls forth a reaction, so that we must respect the potential effects of all our deeds. In Eastern thought this is called *karma*. In Hebrew it is called *sekhar ve-onesh*. The immediate reaction to a kind act is that we feel happy doing it. The long-term benefits of kindness are as far-reaching as the ripples of time, since they are handed down from generation to generation.

Prayer/Practice

Spend a few minutes in centering prayer or in shamatha/ vipassana meditation. Contemplate the effects that your parents' lovingkindness or lack of the same had on your life. Think of one person who has shown lovingkindness to you and contemplate the effects of this on your life. Practice lovingkindness today.

October 14

Seed Thought

Now that we have contemplated the cultivation of virtue, we are
ready for its corollary, acting in ways that "do no harm." Although
abstention from harm may seem a self-evident extension of
lovingkindness, life abounds with conflictual situations. It is
precisely by being placed in such situations and reconciling good
and evil as best we can that the soul grows. For example, what
about the well-meaning person who, in a fanatical opposition to
abortion, inflicts emotional or even physical harm on women
or abortion clinic workers? Although they may rationalize that
hurting a few people now will save potential babies later, they
cannot pursue their course and "do no harm."

Prayer/Practice

*Practice a few minutes of shamatha/vipassana meditation.
Imagine that you are a forty-year-old single mother, pregnant by
a rapist. You are trying to enter an abortion clinic for counseling,
and picketers close in, calling you a child-killer. Next, imagine
being a picketer who sincerely believes you are saving women
from hell while also saving the lives of the unborn. Next,
imagine that you are a soul who would choose to incarnate if
the pregnancy came to term. Finally, imagine a respectful
dialogue between all the characters.*

October 15

Seed Thought

"Do no harm." A raccoon coat sits in my front hall closet. The
harm is done. The raccoons are dead. I rejected a suggestion to
bury the coat because it did not honor the sacrifice of the animals
and make the best use of their gift. So the coat sat in the closet for
several years, which was a copout. I finally decided to wear it. On
our very first outing, the raccoons and I were approached by a friend.
She pointed out that wearing fur gives other people the message
that it's okay. More animals will then have to chew their legs
off escaping from traps. The salvation of this dilemma was my
relatives in the Ukraine. A nice fur coat can purchase an
apartment. The raccoons are moving to Kiev.

Prayer/Practice

*Practice a few minutes of centering prayer or shamatha/vipassana
meditation. If there was a fur coat hanging in your hall
closet—if this was your dream—what would you do about it?
And don't get all self-righteous and tell me that there wouldn't
be a fur in there. This is a dream and all things are possible.
Without infinite possibilities and many different conflicts there
would be no growth.*

October 16

Seed Thought

"Do no harm." What about experimenting on animals? It seems a terrible cruelty if we're discussing the testing of a new hairspray. It seems a necessary evil if we're discussing a vaccine for AIDS. The Universe rarely draws straight lines with the white hats on one side and the black hats on the other. Once we don either hat, we're committed to battle. How can we do no harm?

Prayer/Practice

Practice a few minutes of centering prayer or shamatha/vipassana meditation. Contemplate this fantasy: You are the father of twin two-year-old boys with hemophilia. They live in constant fear of falling and experience terrible pain from bleeds into their joints. Experiments with gene replacement therapy are likely to produce a cure in five to ten years. Unfortunately, this research can only be done with rhesus monkeys. Now, put yourself in the position of a monkey . . . of the little boys with hemophilia . . . of a person so sensitive to the imprisonment and pain of animals that you are willing to bomb the laboratory. Finally, have a conversation between all the characters.

October 17

Seed Thought

Tolerance is a virtue that is as misunderstood as patience. We previously discussed the fact that most people's concept of patience is actually impatience stretched to its limit. In a similar vein, the prevalent notion of tolerance is a polite holding back from telling those ignorant unfortunates the truth that might enlighten them. Real tolerance is more akin to the Native American notion that we need to walk in another person's moccasins for a thousand miles before we judge them. At that point we're too tired to judge anyway. And if we still have a mind to comment on their life, we're likely to do so with more lovingkindness than a cursory examination would bring forth.

Prayer/Practice

Spend a few minutes in shamatha/vipassana meditation, the egg of light or centering prayer. Bring a person to mind that you have felt intolerance toward. Fantasize being this person. What was your childhood like? What are your fears? What are your hopes? What are your greatest regrets? What are the accomplishments that make you feel best about being human?

October 18

Seed Thought

Honesty, like patience and tolerance, is a misunderstood virtue. We speak of being "honest about our feelings." I could imagine Woody Allen producing and starring in a movie about honestly expressing our feelings. In his mind he might go up to a woman on the street whose scowl reminded him of his critical mother and say, "Wipe that stupid scowl off your face, you miserable old hag! Don't you know that you're ruining my day!" That's being "honest about your feelings" in pop culture. The notion that our feelings are some kind of sacred cow that merits special honor is one of the greatest embarrassments of the self-help movement.

Prayer/Practice

Spend a few minutes in the peacefulness of shamatha/vipassana meditation, the egg of light or centering prayer. Contemplate being "honest about your feelings." When you express feelings do you expect someone else to fix them or not? When you express feelings, are you stating what is or are you blaming someone? If expressing your feelings generally makes you or other people feel worse—doing harm—try thinking about feelings as teachers, rather than as judges about how the world is treating you.

October 19

Seed Thought

There is a myth abroad about good and bad emotions. "Good" emotions like love, joy and peace are considered virtues. "Bad" emotions like anger, jealousy and sadness are considered vices. This is another example of thinking that the good guys always wear white hats. If we never experienced anger, we would have little sense that our boundaries had been violated and that we needed to pay attention and possibly make new choices. If we didn't experience the pain of jealousy, we would have little motivation to cultivate happiness at another's good fortune. If we didn't feel the sadness that arises when we encounter impermanence, we wouldn't be motivated to find our way back to God. Emotions are among the most valuable teachers as long as we don't try to use them to validate our position and make ourselves right.

Prayer/Practice

Practice a few minutes of centering prayer or shamatha/vipassana meditation. Contemplate the way that you experienced and expressed emotions yesterday. If you need assistance in reframing emotions as teachers rather than as justifiers of your point of view, ask for the help of Raphael. If you realize that this is a particularly difficult problem, it may be a beneficial time for some therapy as well. Continue to be aware of how you express your feelings today, and what your intention is when you voice them.

October 20

Seed Thought

My second book, *Guilt Is the Teacher, Love Is the Lesson*, is about healing the emotional wounds of childhood. When that healing is done, we can more naturally express feelings in a way that does no harm. But until that time, we're like small children who truly need to be the center of constant, adoring attention. We need to know that we're still lovable even if we tell Mommy that she's so mean we wish she'd go eat worms and die. When we're little, our feelings really are sacred cows. But if our infantile feelings are respected, we will grow up secure in the knowledge that feelings are not Absolute Truth. They are reactions to the world that are valuable teachers.

Prayer/Practice

Practice a few minutes of shamatha/vipassana meditation, the egg of light or centering prayer. Retrospect the way that you expressed feelings yesterday. If you tend to use your feelings as a way to justify feeling bad, consider the possibility that you could use your feelings as guides to feeling better.

October 21

Seed Thought

My husband and our son Justin once went to a men's weekend with poet and philosopher Robert Bly. A psychologist in the audience began to wax eloquent about how he had rediscovered and befriended his inner child with whom he played each day. Bly, in his endearingly blunt manner, yelled, "Well then, it's time to kill the little son of a bitch now, isn't it?" This made the psychologist and others hopping mad. But if I heard Bly correctly (even though I wasn't there), he was making the point that after we heal our wounds, we must transcend them. Growing up ultimately means the death of the inner child and the birth of an emotionally mature adult.

Prayer/Practice

If you can, go for a mindful walk in nature today. When you're done, contemplate the state of your inner child. If it's still in the process of growing up, indulge it. If you feel like you've healed your childhood wounds and reaped their wisdom, say a prayer of thanksgiving.

October 22

Seed Thought

If old wounds are not healed before we take a mental approach to training the mind, the feeling monsters in the basement will forever be clawing on the cellar door, even as we smile and lean against the latch. This is repression of emotions, rather than the yoga of transforming the emotions. When people try the "spiritual bypass" route to accomplish emotional healing, it is generally both incomplete and unsatisfying. We cannot wish old feelings away nor do spiritual exercises for overcoming them until we have woven a healing story that transforms our previous life's experience and gives meaning to whatever pain we have endured.

Prayer/Practice

Spend a few minutes in centering prayer, shamatha/vipassana meditation or the egg of light. Contemplate whether or not you have been able to look back at the difficulties of your life and tell a story about their value in bringing forth wisdom.

October 23

Seed Thought

We have considered the "cultivation of virtue through
lovingkindness" and "doing no harm" as two of three basic
guidelines for spiritual maturity. The third guideline is "taming the
mind." The Eastern literature on meditation frequently refers to
the mind as a monkey that jumps crazily from place to place.
Perhaps you've noticed the monkeylike aspect of mind in
meditation. It can jump from prayer, to the supermarket, to unmade
phone calls, to work, to redecorating the living room, to worrying
about a loved one, to mindful awareness in just a minute or two.
The mind is both as agile as a monkey and as restless, until
trained.

Prayer/Practice

*How strong is your concentration? During the month of January,
we worked on the basic concentration exercise of counting
the breaths. On the first outbreath we concentrated on the number
four and the sensation of relaxing and letting go, on the second
outbreath we continued to relax while focusing on three, on the
third outbreath we let go into two, and on the fourth outbreath
we came to rest in one. Then we repeated the countdown for a
period of five minutes. Do this now and once again before
bed.*

October 24

Seed Thought

The Dalai Lama points out that, since even wild animals can be trained, so can our minds. He says, "If someone who easily gets angry tries to control his or her anger, in time it can be brought under control. The same is true for a very selfish person: first that person must realize the faults of a selfish motivation and the benefit of being less selfish. Having realized this, one trains in it, trying to control the bad side and develop the good. As time goes by, such practice can be very effective. This is the only alternative."

Prayer/Practice

Practice a few minutes of centering prayer or shamatha/vipassana meditation. Now think about a mind-habit that creates suffering—anger, the tendency toward hurt feelings, selfishness. . . . Enlist the help of your guardian angel in being aware of that mind-habit today. When you notice it, use your will to let it go.

October 25

Seed Thought

The untrained mind is actually quite well trained in the ways of *samsara*, the typical thought processes of fear and separation that keep us trapped in an endless cycle of unhappiness. The Tibetan Buddhist Lama Sogyal Rinpoche writes of this in his remarkable text, *The Tibetan Book of Living and Dying*.

"We are already perfectly trained by and for samsara, trained to get jealous, trained to grasp, trained to be anxious and sad and desperate and greedy, trained to react angrily to whatever provokes us. We are trained in fact to such an extent that these negative emotions rise spontaneously, without our even trying to generate them. So everything is a question of training and the power of habit."

Prayer/Practice

Practice at least ten minutes of shamatha/vipassana meditation today. This type of meditation is not only a way to calm the mind and bring it home to its own true nature of peace and wisdom, but also a way of gaining insight into how the mind works. What can you notice about your tendencies of mind during meditation? During the day today, be aware of what kind of concerns your mind is drawn into.

October 26

Seed Thought

I was driving through downtown Boulder, Colorado, during the time that I was writing this chapter. Tired out from several errands, I began to daydream about going back home for an afternoon walk in the mountains. When it was time to take a right turn into the supermarket parking lot, I was mindlessly on the left. I signaled, but the driver to my right wouldn't let me change lanes. Anger began to rise up spontaneously—out of habit. Then I became aware of it and laughed. After all, I was the mindless driver, and my inconvenience had nothing to do with anyone else. Peace or anger were my own choices. On this occasion, at least, I chose peace.

Prayer/Practice

Practice ten minutes of shamatha/vipassana meditation. Today, notice the tendency of anger and irritation to arise in your mind. As in the example above, if these emotions are just conditioned arisings from cultural monkey mind, see how quickly you can let the arisings subside, just as you do in shamatha/vipassana meditation.

October 27

Seed Thought

Psychiatrist and writer Jerry Jampolsky asks the question "Would you rather be happy or would you rather be right?" I've been working on choosing happiness for quite some time. Several years back, my husband and I were driving to the home of friends for dinner. Miron took a left, although I knew for a fact that taking a right would have gotten us there five minutes sooner. I mentioned this fact, and when he didn't turn around I mentioned it again. His point of view was, "Hey, it's a beautiful evening, enjoy the drive. A few minutes don't matter." I was so locked into being "right" that I didn't even begin to enjoy the drive until we had almost arrived at our destination.

Prayer/Practice

Practice a few minutes of shamatha/vipassana meditation. Today, be particularly aware of the ingrained habit of mind that wants to be right. When you find yourself caught up in it, ask, "Would I rather be right or would I rather be happy?"

October 28

Seed Thought

The ancient practices of mind-training are quite similar to modern cognitive-behavioral therapies. We begin to observe our thinking patterns and gradually make changes based on those observations. But for either modern therapy or ancient wisdom practices to produce results, motivation must remain strong. The basic psychological motivation that all people have in common is to be happy and to avoid suffering. Once we realize that so much suffering is created through our minds, we are motivated to change them. When there is also a strong desire to benefit others, our good intentions become extremely powerful motivators for change.

Prayer/Practice

Practice a few minutes of the meditation of your choice. Now think about the one or two specific negative mind-habits that you began working with on October 24. Contemplate how changing these habits would benefit other people. During the remainder of the month, maintain a strong intention to let these habits go.

October 29

Seed Thought

A strong motivation helps to sustain good habits as well as to let go of bad habits. Meditation is a good habit, because it trains the mind and helps part the clouds of negativity and illusion that obscure the sun of our own true nature. Nonetheless, it's a difficult habit to sustain. A friend of mine once quipped that the only bone he had to pick with God is that bad habits are so hard to break and good ones are so hard to establish. The Buddha realized this and suggested that we refresh our motivation to meditate daily by contemplating four thoughts about life that will motivate us to practice.

Prayer/Practice

Contemplate these four thoughts before you spend a few minutes in meditation:

1. *Human birth is hard to attain and extremely precious. We must do something of value with the opportunity.*

2. *All things are impermanent. The body that we are so attached to will soon be a corpse.*

3. *Karma is an immutable law. The results of our actions will return to us, so we must plant good seeds.*

4. *Samsara, the world of perpetual desires in which we have been trained to live, creates endless suffering. We must rise above it for our own benefit and the benefit of all beings.*

October 30

Seed Thought

In ancient Greece, there was a famous healing shrine in the city of Trophonius, sacred to the God Asklepias. At the conclusion of a treatment, the patient was led down a path to two springs. The first was called *Lethe*, from the Greek meaning "forgetfulness." Drinking these waters assisted patients in leaving behind bad mind-habits. The second spring was called *Mnemosyne*, from the root "remembering." These waters assisted the patients in forming new habits, remembering their insights and putting the new learnings to use in their lives.

Prayer/Practice

Get two glasses of water, one representing Lethe and the other Mnemosyne. Take a few letting-go breaths and patiently, slowly enter the place of inner wisdom. What are the mind-habits you are willing to let go of now? Acknowledge them and drink the waters of Lethe. What are the mind-habits you most want to remember and integrate into your life? Acknowledge them and drink the waters of Mnemosyne.

October 31: All Hallows' Eve

Seed Thought

All Hallows' Eve is a cross-quarter day, halfway between the autumnal equinox and the winter solstice. The earth currents continue to sweep us inward, down through the gates of death, into the womb where wisdom gestates. I once took a weeklong healing course during which we went to a graveyard and looked for a tombstone that we could imagine was our own. That act brought a sharp edge to the retrospection of our lives and gave added impetus to the desire to change. Some Buddhist meditations also take place in a cemetery, where one is brought closer to the reality of impermanence and the motivation to stay mindful, practice kindness and wake up!

Prayer/Practice

If it is possible, go for a mindful walk in a cemetery today. Find a tombstone that you could imagine might be yours. Retrospect your life from the viewpoint of what you have done to cultivate virtue, practice harmlessness and tame your mind. Give thanks to God for the fact that you are still alive, still have time to bring forth your fullness in this lifetime.

NOVEMBER

Grieving, Forgiveness and Completion

November is a month of finishing our business,
squaring the inner and outer accounts that require our energy.
One of the most important ways that we come to completion
is through grieving those who have died
and celebrating the things we have shared together and learned together.
Meditations and rituals of grieving and completion include forgiveness,
that attitude of mind that sets us free when we are able to claim
our wisdom and move on.
Forgiving ourselves and forgiving others
we pave the way for the atonement,
the At-One-Ment,
between all people and the Creator.
November completions clear the way for the birth of
Inner Light in December.
Listen to the voices of the Ancient Ones that call from the past,
from the land of the Ancestors:

November is a month
sacred to Archangel Raphael,
the Healer of God.
To heal, to be whole, is to reconcile
your accounts so that all is
in balance.
Forgiveness is the way to reconciliation,
a path made easier
because it is lighted and maintained
by the angels of grace.

November 1: All Saints' Day, Samhain

Seed Thought

All Saints' Day was originally the Celtic celebration of Samhain, the New Year. The crops were in, meat had been hunted and put by for winter, and it was time to rest in the Earth Mother's womb. Winter, after all, is a time for sitting by the fire and telling the old stories of creation and the wise and true ways of honoring the Creator. On Samhain Eve, which became All Hallows' Eve or Halloween, the tradition was to dress up in the skins of the animal brothers and sisters who gave their lives so that the tribe could eat and stay warm. Halloween honored the cycle of death and rebirth that is evident in the interconnectedness of all life. The thanksgiving celebration later this month embodies much the same principle.

Prayer/Practice

Divine Beloved, I awaken this morning with gratitude for a new mind and a new body. At this turning of the cosmic wheel, I align myself wholly with You, and your Body, the Mother Earth and all her creation. May I remember that all plants, all animals, all people are part of Your Body. Just as the cells in my body die and are replaced, one feeding on the remains of another, so does all life die and find rebirth in a new form. I give thanks today to all the plants and the animals who have nourished me and my tribe, who have provided food, shelter, clothing and shoes that we may continue our earthwalk.

November 2: All Souls' Day

Seed Thought

All Souls' Day is celebrated in many countries as a day both for remembering the dead and for celebrating the liberating aspects of death. Death is a loss as we perceive it from this reality, but for the mystic who has dedicated his or her life to union with the Divine, it is a joyful celebration—the Marriage of the Spirit that Jesus and other teachers discuss. In his autobiography, *Memories, Dreams and Reflections*, Carl Jung wrote that "when the pious Cabbalist Rabbi Simon ben Jochai came to die, his friends said that he was celebrating his wedding. To this day it is the custom in some regions to hold a picnic on the grave on All Souls' Day. Such customs express the feeling that death is really a festive occasion."

Prayer/Practice

Divine Beloved, sometimes You seem so far from us in daily life. May that gap be closed by my growing desire to be One with you now, so that at the moment of death I will fly to Your Heart on wings of awareness, forgiveness, tolerance, gratitude and the growing wish to be of service to all beings. May all remnants of negativity be burned from my heart so that the purity of love can burst forth in joy.

Spend a few minutes in the peacefulness of shamatha/vipassana meditation, centering prayer or the egg of light.

November 3

Seed Thought

November energy is conducive to rituals of completion. We began some of this work in late October, with the completion of childhood healing. Completions of grieving and of forgiveness this month help to square our accounts so that we will be able to move into the December festivals of light with clear hearts. Completion is a relative term. The spiritual metaphor to keep in mind is that of peeling an onion. Not until one layer is removed do we even become aware of the next. As each layer is explored and peeled away, we get closer to the heart of wisdom. So when working toward completion, know that we peel only the layer we can currently see.

Prayer/Practice

If possible, walk mindfully in nature today. Breathing the sun in through your head, and the earth through your feet, let them mingle in your heart. Breathe out the marriage of earth and heaven to all of nature, thankful for its gifts. When you are finished, contemplate what dreamtime has been like lately. Are you continuing September's dream practices? Look for elements in your dreams that invite you to completions.

November 4

Seed Thought

When a loved one dies, the process of grieving is a completion that allows us to honor that person's life and claim the wisdom we have gained through the relationship. As we receive the gift of understanding, it transcends time and space, simultaneously gifting the soul of the one who has passed over. Grieving is more than learning to live without a dear one. In many cases we are also required to forgive them and ourselves as we bring the story of the time we spent together to a meaningful completion.

Prayer/Practice

Great Spirit, I awaken this morning with gratitude for the gift of life that is so precious. No other place in the universe presents us with so many opportunities for growth. I am ready to enter Your wisdom through receiving the gifts of relationships that have been completed through death. I call upon the Archangel Raphael, guardian of the Gates of death and new birth, to help me in this morning's contemplation.

Take a few deep breaths and settle into the place of inner stillness. Feel Raphael's presence at your back. Contemplate your relationship with a person who has died. How do you feel about it? Have you been able to perceive the story you lived together as one of meaning and value?

November 5

Seed Thought

My father died when I was in my late twenties, my mother when I was in my early forties. By the time Mom was dying, we had given up trying to make each other over in our own images and were ready for reconciliation. We forgave one another a few hours before she died. As she passed over, my son Justin and I had the extraordinary experience of going into the Light with her, where the story of our life together was beautifully revealed. In the weeks after her death, a series of funny, pointed and luminous dreams further elucidated our relationship and brought forth its wisdom and grace. In contrast, Dad died quite suddenly. Our relationship had been extraordinarily close and loving, quite different from the constant conflict between Mother and me. Oddly, I did not cry and could not grieve. A few years after Mom's death, Dad began to come to me in the occasional dream, lonely and forgotten. I had not honored the story of his life by grieving, and began to complete that process nearly fifteen years after his death.

Prayer/Practice

Practice Metta (lovingkindness) meditation this morning (February 11–15). Send blessings to the important people in your life who have died. Speak from your heart to each of them about what they meant to you. Honor their lives. When you finish, think about how well you understand your relationship. If there is work to be done, put aside some time soon when you can write out the story of your lives together. The act of writing often reveals hidden meanings. And watch for wisdom in your dreams!

November 6

Seed Thought

One of the most important things a dying person can know is that their life has had meaning. This knowledge helps put their soul at peace. According to the extensive Tibetan Buddhist knowledge of death and after-death states, a peaceful soul is better able to distinguish the projected illusions of their mind from reality and either become enlightened in the moments after death, or be in a better position to consciously choose a rebirth. Regardless of what realm a soul is in, when we grieve as a completion, our love and wisdom reach through space and time as a help and a blessing. It is never too late to help those who have died.

Prayer/Practice

If you have any pictures of your loved ones who have died, lay them out. Light a candle to create the feeling of sacred space, and spend a few minutes in the peace of centering prayer. Open your eyes and look at the pictures of your loved ones. Speak directly to them about your love, the value of their life and what you have learned from them.

November 7

Seed Thought

The Tibetan Buddhists do a practice called *Phowa*, the transference
of consciousness. It is traditionally performed for dying people
and for the dead, particularly in the first seven weeks after their
passage. In its brief form, the practitioner imagines a form of Divine
Consciousness that the dying or dead person has felt very close to.
This might be Mary, Jesus, Buddha, Allah, the Light.... One
imagines this form of the Divine above the head of the dying or
dead person, showering them with light, and washing through
their body, carrying away any pain or illusion that obscures their
recognition of their own true nature, their heartlight or Higher
Self. One then imagines the heartlight of the dying or dead person
expanding and becoming one with the Divine Consciousness.
This is believed to help the soul recognize and remain in the sate
of Divine Union, rather than falling prey, once again, to the
ego and its projections once the experience of Light that people
describe in the near-death state is over.

Prayer/Practice

*Although Phowa is traditionally done in the seven weeks following
death, it can be done at any time. If you feel moved to try
it, follow the instructions above, and practice Phowa for someone
who has died. I like to do it on the anniversaries of the death
of my parents, a day on which Jews light a* yizkor, *or memorial,
candle. What better way to honor and remember the dead?*

November 8

Seed Thought

Remembering and honoring the dead is common to many traditions. Some religions, like Roman Catholicism, have actual prayer practices that apply back through one's lineage. I personally believe that whenever one member of a family heals, that healing goes back and forward through time and space, uplifting the whole line. A ritual of honoring our ancestors can help bring us into a more conscious relationship with our family story that promotes a healing of everyone who has ever been, or will be born into, our family.

Prayer/Practice

Practice Metta (February 11–15) for your lineage, whether these people are dead or alive. Send blessings of lovingkindness to your two parents and four grandparents. Send them to your eight great-grandparents as you know or imagine them. Imagine your blessings fanning out to sixteen great-great-grandparents and their thirty-two progenitors. If you could follow your lineage back far enough, can you appreciate how many relatives you have? Like the Native Americans, end by sending blessings to "all your relations." That, dear one, is everybody!

November 9

Seed Thought

The Apostle Paul reached the point of wisdom where he could honestly say, "I die daily." In order to greet each day with an open mind and an open heart, the accounts of yesterday need to be closed. The more unfinished business we leave, the more psychic energy goes into managing it, leaving less creativity, will and wisdom for the tasks at hand. Coming to completion with those who have died frees energy for our own life purpose. We can then turn our attention to freeing ourselves from the ghosts of our own past actions that have not yet been grieved, honored and transformed into wisdom.

Prayer/Practice

Spend a few minutes in the peace of centering prayer or shamatha/ vipassana meditation. Place your attention in back of you, at the Western Gate of your body temple. Call upon Raphael to help you in the contemplation of any regrets about mistakes you have made or projects that have not come to fruition. Today, it is enough to notice what is there, give thanks for the learning opportunity that it presents and dedicate its future working through for the benefit of all beings.

November 10

Seed Thought

When a person "cracks" during a lie detector test and tells the truth, their physiology becomes peaceful. It is a relief to confess even if it means going to jail! Studies have likewise found that people feel calmer after confessing to a shower curtain with no one behind it, or by writing out their feelings in a journal. The Catholic confessional serves a similar purpose, as does the therapist's consulting room. Confessing our wrongs is the first step toward repentance—literally rethinking—that allows us to let go of self-blame and claim the wisdom we have learned from our mistake.

Prayer/Practice

Take a few minutes to write out any regrets and confess them to God in prayer. Take a few letting-go breaths and come to rest in the inner stillness. Imagine that the Divine Light is slightly above and in front of you. Feel that loving Presence washing over you and flowing through you. Allow any regrets to flow into the Mother Earth for transformation. Let the Light wash away any pain or sadness, revealing the light that has always shined brightly in your own heart. Feel your heartlight expand and become one with the Light of God, creating a glowing egg of light around you. Send that light and a blessing to any person or situation that you are letting go of.

November 11

Seed Thought

Rituals of completion can be done alone, but are even more powerful when shared with friends. For several years a group of women in our community met weekly—and then monthly—to create rituals of healing. After a year we opened our solstice and equinox rituals to the community at large. We never knew who would come, only that they would bring an open heart and an intention to support others in healing. If you have such a group of friends, you might enjoy doing today's practice with them the next time you meet. If not, consider starting such a group and meeting regularly to enjoy the special closeness that meditation, prayer and practice with friends can bring about.

Prayer/Practice

For this ritual you will need a paper and pencil, a safe place to have a small fire, and a trowel or shovel. Begin your ritual with a centering meditation, and then think about the regret that you worked with yesterday. Contemplate what actions, if any, are needed for resolution. Now write the regret, any action plan and whatever you learned from your mistake on the slip of paper. Set it on fire, and as it burns, dedicate your experience to the liberation of all beings. Take the ashes outside and bury them or scatter them to the wind.

November 12

Seed Thought

The fourteenth-century mystic Julian of Norwich had a series of
Divine visions that were called "showings." These revelations from God
were so vivid and immediate that Julian put much more faith in
them than in Church doctrine. The showings demonstrated to
her that our sins have no ultimate reality, but are necessary devices
for us to gain self-knowledge. The remorse they cause moves our hearts
to a more sincere search for God. She reassures us that when all
is said and done there "will be no shame, but honor" in our
sins because through them we are schooled in life. Sin, says Julian,
is "behovely," the Middle English word for "necessary."

Prayer/Practice

Great Spirit, thank you for lifting the veil of shame that has so often
hidden the light within my heart. May I learn from my errors,
cultivating lovingkindness, harmlessness and strength of mind.
And above all, may the pain of remorse be transformed into an
intense longing for reunion with You, my Divine Beloved.

*Spend a few minutes in the peace of centering prayer, letting the
loving energy of God soothe your every wound.*

November 13

Seed Thought

Every religion teaches that the Love of God purifies all mistakes.
Islam is perhaps the least understood religion in the West, where
it is often judged as punitive and unforgiving. This misunderstanding
is cleared up with great beauty in the writings of Lex Hixon, who is a
scholar of comparative religions, a writer and an Islamic mullah,
or teacher. In his book *The Heart of the Koran*, he translates
the words of Mohammed: "May the healing stream of Allah's
forgiveness bathe the hearts of all human beings, cleansing every
channel in their spiritual bodies from the subtle fire of the negation
of love, the rebellion against love, the self-centered distortion of
love."

Prayer/Practice

Divine Spirit, may I feel the balm of your love restoring my soul
and washing me clean of every attitude that distorts and negates the
flow of your love through me. May my heart shine with its true
light, allowing me to see all people without judgment, so that
the great peace of your understanding can manifest in my life and
on this earth.

*Spend a few minutes in the peace of centering prayer. Place your
attention in back of you, at the Western Gate of your bodily
temple. Invoke the presence of Raphael, guardian of the Gates of
death and rebirth, wielder of the sword that cuts through the
prison of judgment and hard-heartedness. Ask for help in
maintaining an attitude of non-judgmental awareness
throughout the day.*

November 14

Seed Thought

Chronic self-criticism is one of the commonest attitudes that negates our connection to God and cuts off the flow of Divine Love. Whereas self-reflection and the honest admission of error is a step toward growth that allows Divine mercy to flow through us and reveal the wisdom heart within, self-criticism dams up the flow. The belief that we are not worthy of love from ourselves or from God is what Mohammed called "the rebellion against love."

Prayer/Practice

Divine Beloved, I awaken with a grateful heart and with a sincere desire to allow your love and forgiveness to flow through me and into the world.

Today, be aware of any self-critical thoughts and act on them with discernment. If the thought is a message from the Higher Self for you to take responsibility for your actions, do so immediately. If your thought is the tiresome voice of the ego, trying to negate God's love, quiet it by affirming, "I am One with God and completely worthy of love."

November 15

Seed Thought

The self-centered distortion of love that Mohammed referred to is
the tendency of the ego to place itself in the center of the universe.
This results in much of our thinking revolving around the idea of
"I" and "mine." The anger that arises spontaneously when we
have the thought "I have been inconvenienced" leaves little room
for thoughts of the other person and the actions and reactions
that have led to the inconvenience. When we begin to think more
about the interdependence of things, we take our place as one
more star in a magnificent universe, rather than as the sun around
which the universe revolves. Our heart grows peaceful.

Prayer/Practice

Divine Beloved, may a broader vision of the universe take root within
my mind, crowding out the limited view of love that places me and
my narrow self-interests at the center of the universe. May the stream
of your Love wash away all mind-habits of selfishness, allowing
the boundless love of the Higher Self, the part of "me" that is one
with all, to shine.

Today, be aware of how often you use the words I, me *and* mine.
*Be particularly aware of the times when self-interest
overshadows other people's points of view, leading to anger, self-
righteousness or irritation. When you notice this mind-habit,
let it go by bringing a vision of the night sky to mind, realizing
that you are part of an infinite dance of interconnected
energies.*

November 16

Seed Thought

If you've ever studied the arrangement of blood vessels in the human body, you have some idea of a network of exquisite interconnectedness. The system of flow works perfectly unless an obstruction forms. Blood cannot flow into a bed of vessels when the outflow is blocked. When I read Mohammed's teaching on the negation of love blocking the healing stream of God's forgiveness, I had the image that we are all cells in the body of God. When any one of us blocks the flow of love through unforgiveness, the entire body feels those effects. It is said that when any one person overcomes a block toward growth, the consciousness of the Whole is uplifted. Your commitment to forgiveness is a gift given to all.

Prayer/Practice

Great Spirit, as our hearts look forward to the festivals of Light next month, we have an ideal of peace on earth and goodwill toward all. May that ideal inspire me to claim my own inner peace through forgiveness, and, in so doing, help to bring a more peaceful world into being.

Spend a few minutes in the peacefulness of centering prayer, the egg of light or shamatha/vipassana meditation.

November 17

Seed Thought

Jesus taught his followers a prayer that has come to be called the
"Our Father." More precise translations from the original Aramaic
are closer to "Oh Cosmic Birther" than to "Father." Scholar Neil
Douglas Klotz has translated this prayer very carefully, revealing
a deeper beauty and wisdom than the traditional version. The part
of the prayer that usually translates "Forgive us our debts as we
forgive our debtors" retranslates, "Loose the cords of mistakes binding
us as we release the strands we hold of others' guilt." In this way we
clear the vessels of the Divine Body from obstructions and enable
the whole to rise free in the Light of the heart.

Prayer/Practice

Oh Cosmic Birther, Father/Mother God, please teach me the
sacrament of forgiveness so that in forgiving others I can finally
forgive myself and help all beings attain the freedom of a peaceful
heart.

*Take a few letting-go breaths and slowly, patiently come into the
inner stillness, the Holy of Holies. Contemplate the strands you are
holding of other people's guilt. Do you really want to keep holding
on and making their errors into your burdens? Consider how
it might feel to let go of their guilt. If you wish to begin or
accelerate this process, ask for the help of Raphael.*

November 18

Seed Thought

An interesting metaphor for the interconnectedness of all souls comes from the psychiatric literature. In multiple personality disorder, most personalities or "alters" are unaware of the existence of the others and the effects of their actions upon them. There is one personality, however, called the Inner Self Helper, that is aware of the entire constellation of apparently separate selves. This personality claims to be birthless and deathless, a conduit for wisdom and Divine Love. Perhaps we are all "alters" of the Divine One.

Prayer/Practice

Spend a few minutes in the peacefulness of centering prayer or shamatha/vipassana meditation.

Today, whenever you look at another person, entertain the possibility that they, like you, are an "alter" of God. Once we become self-aware and aware of our connectedness to others, we will experience the atonement. At-One-Ment of spirit will occur for humanity as a whole, just as it does for individuals who "integrate" their multiple personalities. Forgiveness is the key to the atonement.

November 19

Seed Thought

In our usual perception, there is an order of difficulty to forgiveness.
The guy who cut us off in traffic is relatively easy to forgive.
The uncle who raped us is much, much harder. Hitler, for many
people, is unforgivable. The timeless wisdom of *A Course in
Miracles* teaches that a miracle is a shift in perception. Once that
shift has occurred, there is no order of difficulty in miracles.
Forgiveness is a shift in perception out of "us" versus "them"
thinking into "we" thinking. If we view Hitler as an aspect of
ourselves, one more "alter" of God, the miracle of forgiveness
becomes possible. But even if we are willing to accept forgiveness
as a possibility, we need powerful techniques to change our perception
and make it a reality.

Prayer/Practice

Divine Beloved, I am grateful for the gradual awakening that will
allow the miracle of atonement to take place within my heart. Please
help me consider the possibility that there are no unforgivable acts
and that repentance is one of the most important ways that
souls grow. Help me also to remove myself from the position of
judge and jury, for I can never know if another person has truly
repented in their heart.

*Spend a few minutes in the peace of centering prayer or shamatha/
vipassana meditation. If your heart is troubled, place your
awareness in back of you, at the Western Gate of your bodily
temple, and call upon the Presence of Raphael for guidance
and healing.*

November 20

Seed Thought

The Dalai Lama has been interviewed many times about the holocaust
in Tibet in the 1950s. The Chinese killed one sixth of the
population, torched 6,000 monasteries and tortured many of the
monks and nuns. The beautiful Tibetan plateaus are now nuclear
dumping grounds and the great herds of wildlife extinct. I am
always moved when the Dalai Lama responds with compassion
for the ignorance and pain of the Chinese that must underlie their
actions. He practices a form of meditation called *tonglen* for
their benefit. Taking on their pain, he gives them his happiness
and joy. This extraordinary meditation of giving and receiving
has been very helpful in bringing about forgiveness in my own life.

Prayer/Practice

*Before we learn to practice tonglen on behalf of others, we will
learn to do it for ourselves. Begin by bringing back the
memory of a holy moment, a time when your heart was open
to nature, a child, a pet, to beauty. Now imagine that you
are sitting, facing yourself. Look into your eyes and see the beauty
of who you are, and the pain that keeps you out of touch
with that beauty. Imagine that your pain is like a thick, black
smoke covering your heart. Inhale that smoke into your own
heart, and exhale the peace, love and happiness of your own true
nature. Continue this meditation of breathing in pain and
breathing out happiness. If breathing in black smoke bothers you,
substitute dark clouds.*

November 21

Seed Thought

People sometimes fear that tonglen will harm them when they imagine breathing in pain, ignorance or illness. The Tibetan lamas say that the only thing we can harm with tonglen is our ego and its self-grasping, which will dissolve in the intention of compassion. Nonetheless, until you are comfortable with tonglen, perform it only for yourself or loved ones. When you feel more secure, you can extend it to strangers whom you feel judgments about, or feel sympathetic to, and then to others about whom your judgments are stronger. In time, you can extend it to your worst enemies, creating peace and compassion where there was pain and fear. Tonglen is truly a yoga that transforms pain into forgiveness.

Prayer/Practice

When I was sick, my mother used to say that she wished she could take on the sickness for me. This motherly care and compassion is the basis of tonglen. Today we will do tonglen for a loved one. Take a few letting-go breaths and slip into the place of inner silence. Bring to mind a memory of a holy moment, a time when your heart felt open. Bring a loved one to mind and imagine any pain, confusion, illness or unhappiness they might be experiencing as a black smoke around their heart. Breathe that smoke into your own heart and return your peace and happiness. Continue to do this for a few minutes until you feel a sense of completion. Complete the practice by praying for your loved one.

November 22

Seed Thought

The Tibetan lama Geshe Kelsang Gyatso speaks of the importance of praying for the awakening of compassion in our heart. As our heart opens, the power of tonglen naturally increases, as does the desire to practice it. If you are a Christian, think of Jesus' many teachings on compassion and pray sincerely for its inner experience. If you are a Jew, think of all the teachings on kindness and the practice of mitzvot. Pray for an inner awakening to these teachings. No matter what your beliefs, pray for the *experience* of compassion.

Prayer/Practice

In his book, Universal Compassion, *Geshe Kelsang Gyatso suggests this contemplative prayer. It is based on the interconnectedness of all beings; the realization that at some time we have all parented one another:*

Having considered how all these tormented beings have been my mother, and raised me in kindness again and again, I seek your blessings to develop genuine compassion, like that of a loving mother for her only child.

Addressing God in your own way, pray for genuine compassion.

November 23

Seed Thought

Have you ever felt overcome with pity at the plight of a stranger?
Writer and teacher Stephen Levine says that when our fear touches
another person's pain we feel pity, but when our love touches
another's pain we feel compassion. And only love and compassion
have the power to change this world for the better. When you feel
frightened, and therefore pity someone's plight, you can use
tonglen to respond with love instead. I once saw a news clip of a
Bosnian mother keening her grief over the dead body of her
teenage son. Thinking of my own sons, my heart broke open. Instead
of feeling helpless or fearful, I practiced tonglen for that mother.
My heart stayed open, rather than closing.

Prayer/Practice

*Today, if it feels right for you, practice tonglen for a stranger
whom you might otherwise pity. Whether it's a homeless person
or someone you read about in the paper or see on the news,
imagine breathing in their pain in the form of black smoke.
Take it into your heart and return your happiness to them.*

November 24

Seed Thought

Tonglen is one of the most powerful practices of forgiveness and compassion that one can learn. It is useful to encourage not only the type of forgiveness that addresses specific hurts and injustices, but also the attitude of forgiveness that does not condemn or judge in general. Being critical of others is a conditioned mind-habit that arises with little or no provocation. The snap judgments we make about people and situations are powerful negations of love that reinforce the ego's sense of fear and separation. Throughout the year we have practiced owning the projections that form the basis of the way we judge others. Tonglen is a wonderful way to extend that practice and erode the very sense of "us" versus "them" that underlies the tendency to judge.

Prayer/Practice

Today, be aware of the judgments you make. Whenever you catch yourself judging someone, imagine that you are breathing in their pain in the form of black smoke. Breathe your happiness back to them.

November 25

Seed Thought

Tonglen is an extremely useful tool for transforming negative emotions. A pattern that I had found particularly painful occurred when, as an author, I would go into a bookstore and discover that my books weren't being carried. I would walk around and see stacks of books that I judged not nearly as good as my own. Jealousy would rear its ugly head, and soon I would feel miserable. So I learned to do tonglen for myself, breathing the terrible pain of jealousy into my heart, and breathing out happiness to myself. It worked. I'm happy in bookstores now, whether or not they carry my books!

Prayer/Practice

Today, be aware of any negative emotions that arise. If the emotions have a message to give you, make sure that you attend to it before you use tonglen to transform the emotion. Begin by getting in touch with just how miserable your anger, jealousy, spite or sadness is making you feel. Then take a few deep breaths and do your best to bring back the memory of a holy moment when you felt connected with the universe. Then practice tonglen for yourself.

November 26

Seed Thought

As I retrospect my life, it is clear that the people from whom I have learned the most were once my enemies. These were the people who confronted me with ethical difficulties and made me think hard about the notions of right or wrong. In many cases, they were reflections of my own self-righteousness, paranoia or fear. In other cases, they did me real and tangible harm. In a few instances forgiveness came easily, and in others it was a process that spanned many years. The instances in which forgiveness took the longest, and was the most difficult, have turned out to contain the most valuable teachings.

Prayer/Practice

Today we will begin the practice of tonglen in behalf of our enemies (and ourselves, of course, since forgiveness ultimately sets the forgiver free). It's best to begin with a "minor enemy" unless you have a strong wish to let go of a more vibrant resentment. Begin, as always, with the memory of a holy moment when your heart was open and you felt connected with the universe. Now bring your enemy to mind. Imagine the pain and ignorance that led them to behave in a way that was hurtful. See it as a thick black smoke that obscures the true Light in their heart. Breathe the smoke into your own heart's Light, and return your Light to them. Continue until the Lights in your two hearts touch.

November 27

Seed Thought

One of the most moving stories in the New Testament is that of the Prodigal Son. The "good" son stays at home and manages the family farm. The "bad" son squanders his inheritance on wine and women in a foreign land. He finally crawls home broke and penitent. Word of his son's approach overjoys the father, who orders that a party be made and the fatted calf slain. The "good" brother feels very angry, self-righteously jealous that no parties have been held for him. The father explains that he has always rejoiced for the good son, but that the other was lost and now is found, a cause for the greatest joy. The father had already forgiven the prodigal son, and his child had only to repent to feel his father's love. The harder task was for the "good" brother to give up his judgments and jealousy and learn to forgive as did his father.

Prayer/Practice

Spend a few minutes in the peace of centering prayer or shamatha/ vipassana meditation. Read the story of the Prodigal Son in the New Testament. You will find it in Luke 15:11–32.

November 28

Seed Thought

The process of self-forgiveness is complete when we let go of what we have done and celebrate what we have become. The process of forgiving others is complete when we let go of what they have done and celebrate the wisdom we have gained through the difficult experience they have facilitated for us. We can claim our freedom independently of their actions. Likewise, the decision to forgive specifies no particular action on our part. We may decide not to see or speak to a hurtful person again. Forgiveness is an attitude of mind rather than a particular action.

Prayer/Practice

Great Spirit, I arise this morning with a heart made clean by my intentions to find true compassion through forgiveness. This is a difficult task which can be accomplished fully only through your grace. I pray for that grace to flow down upon me and wash my heart clean.

Spend a few minutes in centering prayer or shamatha/vipassana meditation. Then imagine the Divine One slightly above you and in front of you, and feel the Loving Light of God washing you clean of resentment and revealing the purity of your heart.

November 29

Seed Thought

The sixteenth-century mystic Saint Teresa of Avila used mental prayer as a way of coming closer to God. One of the prerequisites for this prayer was to have "love for one another." Without forgiving her sisters in the convent for all kinds of petty grievances that occurred in cloistered life, Saint Teresa realized, her heart was not free to join with God. Instead, she would spend her prayer time stewing about the injustices that had transpired. She discovered that the easiest way to forgive was to truly develop love for her sisters, since "there is nothing annoying that is not suffered easily by those who love one another."

Prayer/Practice

The ability to love all people is increased when we practice the ancient wisdom of trying to see the God in one another. Today, whenever you meet someone, bow to them mentally in your heart. The Sanskrit word Namaste *sums up this viewpoint. It means, essentially, "The light in me sees and acknowledges the light in you." Another way to accomplish this, in the words of psychiatrist Jerry Jampolsky, is to see another person's light rather than their lampshade. The light is always lovable.*

November 30

Seed Thought

As November comes to an end and we complete the squaring of our inner accounts, the time comes for squaring outer accounts. This means making amends to those we may have hurt, returning things we may have borrowed and forgotten, and setting our financial records straight so that we can discharge or minimize debt and enter the holiday season with clarity about our resources and what we can prudently spend. On the other side of the ledger, November is the time to settle up with those who may owe us something. Clarity in matters that may seem difficult or embarrassing is often a relief to both parties.

Prayer/Practice

Spend a few minutes in shamatha/vipassana meditation and then contemplate what needs to be done to square your accounts. This may entail some time at your desk. If you have any problems managing money, this is the time to master the skill. Ask for any help you might need, not only from the angelic realm, but from friends or experts. Being accountable financially is an important aspect of spiritual maturity. Remember that you only need to take one step at a time to make movement toward completion.

DECEMBER

Kindling the Light Within

December is the month in which all the forces of nature
are aligned to help us give birth to the Light within.
Midwinter has cast a spell over the land,
and all of nature sleeps.
Members of the human tribe gather
by the fire to hear the old stories
by which the soul awakens
and finds its way back home.
We will use the stories of the Christ Child in a universal sense
as a source of December contemplation.
Those stories are timeless reminders of the heart's true light—
compassion and forgiveness.
Listen to the voices of the Ancient Ones who call from the
deepest core of your being:

Guided by the Northstar
and the Archangel Michael
The great festivals of Light—
Solstice, Hannukah and Christmas—
Beckon us to gather round
and witness the birth of love
within one another.
The earth turns, and a mantle of peace
Falls ever so gently over the land
blessing all creatures
great and small.

December 1

Seed Thought

We are entering the season of darkness during which we partake in the most ancient of miracles, giving birth to the Light. We are ready to bear witness to the renewal of the world and the renewal of our souls. In this season of blessing, the ancient ones celebrated winter solstice as the turning point when darkness births Light. The Jews celebrated the miracle of Light at Hannukah, when due to a war, the oil lamp in the Temple was about to go out. Miraculously, it continued to burn for eight days until new oil was found. Christians celebrate the same miracle of Light with the story of Jesus' birth.

Prayer/Practice

Great Spirit, I give thanks this morning for the velvety darkness that covers the world like a blanket of mystery. With humility and a pure heart, I offer myself as a vessel for the rekindling of the Divine Light. May I be made new this December, bringing forth the Light of compassion, peace and wisdom more fully into this world.

Spend a few minutes in the peace of centering prayer, the egg of light or shamatha/vipassana meditation.

December 2

Seed Thought

As the cosmic wheel turns to the moment of rebirth, an almost preternatural sleep has fallen over the land. The bears slumber in their dens and the grasses lie asleep in the frozen fields. The voices of the Ancient Ones call through the crystalline silence to the hearts of the people: "Arise now and trim your lamps. It is time to enter the Kingdom." Will you hear the inner voice that calls you to awaken this season, or will you allow the frenzy of the outer world to distract you?

Prayer/Practice

Practice a few minutes of shamatha/vipassana meditation or centering prayer. Contemplate the need to put aside time for your inner life this month, in spite of the constant outward pull of the holiday rush.

December 3

Seed Thought

The earth energy draws us inward in December, while the cultural energy draws us outward to shop and prepare for the holidays. Magazines abound with articles on holiday stress, and I've often wished that someone would send all the Santas home and cancel the outer Christmas so that the Christ Child could more easily be born within. For years our children called me the Grinch. Nonetheless, we usually manage to celebrate Hannukah, Christmas and Solstice in a way that allows time for reflection in the weeks preceding them, and gives rise to meaningful rituals that make the holidays Holy Days.

Prayer/Practice

Now is the moment to plan time for rest and reflection, time for shopping and cooking, time for visiting, and time to meet with family and friends to prepare joyful, meaningful holiday rituals. Without careful planning, celebrations of the Light can become dark, stress-filled weeks and lost opportunities for joy and inner awakening.

Practice a few minutes of centering prayer or shamatha/vipassana meditation. When you get up, find your calendar and begin to make a plan for the Holy Days.

December 4

Seed Thought

People often ask how a nice Jewish girl like me became interested in the life of Jesus and in the Christianity, which for better or worse, emerged from his teachings. I reply that Jesus, of course, was a rabbi, a Jewish teacher. If you pay attention to what he taught, it will make you a better Jew, a better Muslim, a better Buddhist, a better Hindu, a better Christian and an overall better person whether you can relate to the culturally Christian elements that grew out of his lifestory or not.

Prayer/Practice

Great Spirit, I awaken this morning with an open mind and an open heart, willing to receive Your teachings from all sources *and thank the Son of Peace for your gradual awakening.* that I can receive the wisdom of the man who was called Jesus, whose life is a pattern for awakening to the light within.

Practice a few minutes of centering prayer or shamatha/vipassana meditation. Invoke the presence of Jesus and ask for inner revelation of the Mystery of Christ.

December 5

Seed Thought

The philosopher Martin Heidegger defined a person as an opening or clearing through which the Absolute can manifest. In *The Gospel According to Jesus,* poet and scholar of comparative religions Stephen Mitchell discusses how the Absolute can manifest through purity of heart, "If we compare God to sunlight, we can say that the heart is like a window. Cravings, aversions, fixed judgments, concepts, beliefs—all forms of selfishness or self-protection—are, when we cling to them, like dirt on the windowpane. The thicker the dirt, the more opaque the window. When there is no dirt, the window is by its own nature perfectly transparent, and the light can stream through it without hindrance."

Prayer/Practice

Great Spirit, throughout the year I have worked to clean the windowpane of my heart, to let go of the attachments and aversions that obscure your Light. May any residues of fear, unkindness and ignorance be washed away by Your grace in this season of the realization of Inner Light, and may I be inspired by the Great Stories of those who have already awakened. May all the benefits of my prayer and practice be for the enlightenment of all beings.

Spend a few minutes in the silence and peace of centering prayer or shamatha/vipassana meditation.

December 6

Seed Thought

Stephen Mitchell quotes from a letter that Thomas Jefferson wrote to John Adams, "In the New Testament there is internal evidence that parts of it have proceeded from an extraordinary man; and that other parts are the fabric of very inferior minds. It is as easy to separate those parts, as to pick out diamonds from dunghills." In *The Gospel According to Jesus*, Mitchell has attempted to pick out the "largehearted" diamonds of Jesus from the "bitter, badgering tone" of the passages added by the early church. When reading the Bible or any other source, purity of heart—kindness, forgiveness, inclusivity rather than exclusivity—is a good yardstick by which to measure the authenticity of the teachings.

Prayer/Practice

Contemplate the purity of heart in this teaching, paraphrased from the Gospel of John, chapter 8:3–11.

A group of priests trying to discredit Jesus brought a woman who had been caught in the act of adultery. According to the law of Moses, she was supposed to be stoned. They asked Jesus, "What do you say about her?" Jesus bent down and wrote on the ground. When he stood up he said, "Let him who is without sin among you be the first to throw a stone at her."* Once more he bent down to write upon the ground, and beginning with the eldest, one by one the accusers walked away. Jesus looked up at the woman and said, "Woman, where are they? Has no one condemned you?" She said, "No one, Lord." And Jesus said, "Neither do I condemn you; go and do not sin again."

*In all the stories that I tell from the Gospels, the words of Jesus are taken directly from the Revised Standard Version of the Bible and are indicated by quotation marks.

December 7

Seed Thought

For thousands of years, the nomadic tribes out of which the Jews
sprang celebrated the realization of the inner Light at Solstice.
When it proved too difficult to stamp out this "pagan" ritual, Solstice
became the Hannukah celebration. In Christianity, this same custom
got transmuted into Christmas, even though Jesus was most likely
born in the spring. As to the virgin birth, almost all cultures
have had a similar legend. But the factual nature of the Christmas
story is not an issue. Rather, the story of Jesus' birth and his
life is a pattern for human awakening; his words a guide to cleaning
the windowpanes of our hearts.

Prayer/Practice

*Meditate for a few minutes and then enjoy the story of Mary
Magdalene and her sister Martha. At the age of thirty, Jesus
began teaching his gospel of lovingkindness and forgiveness. One
day, he and his disciples came to a small village, and a
woman named Martha invited him to teach at her house. Martha
bustled around serving, while her sister Mary sat rapt at the
Master's feet. Exasperated, Martha finally asked Jesus if he cared
that her selfish sister had left her to do all the work. Jesus
replied, "Martha, Martha, you are anxious and troubled about
many things; only one thing is needful. Mary has chosen the
good portion, which shall not be taken away from her."*

*As you make your Holy Day preparations, notice whether you
are assuming the role of Mary or Martha.*

December 8

Seed Thought

Winter is the time to sit by the fire and tell stories. For the last two thousand years, an inspiring Christmas story has been told concerning an archangel and a young Jewish woman called Miriam whose name has come down to us as Mary. She lives in a small, rural village in Judea—the kind of place where everyone knows their neighbor's business. The religious customs of the region are harsh. Adultery (which applies to betrothal as well as marriage) requires stoning. Mary is just a teenager, betrothed to a carpenter by the name of Joseph, when Gabriel shows up at her door with an amazing and—in light of the times—potentially distressing announcement.

Prayer/Practice

Imagine you are Mary. A splendid angel bursts onto the scene and says, * *"Hail, oh favored one, the Lord is with you! Do not be afraid, Mary, for you have found favor with God. And behold, you will conceive in your womb and bear a son, and you shall call his name Jesus. He will be great, and will be called the Son of the Most High. . . ." And Mary said to the angel, "How shall this be, since I have no husband?" And the angel said to her, "The Holy Spirit will come upon you, and the power of the Most High will overshadow you; therefore the child to be born will be called holy, the Son of God."*

If you were Mary, back in her times, how would you feel about the angel's visit, and about breaking the news to Joseph?

*This account of the annunciation is taken from Luke 1:28–35.

December 9

Seed Thought

Six months before Gabriel appeared to Mary, a similar visit had
been made to Mary's cousins, Elizabeth and Zechariah. They were an
elderly, childless couple until Gabriel announced that Elizabeth
would become pregnant in her old age with a son to be named
John. John, said the angel, would grow into an ascetic holy man
who would live in the desert until the Son of God appeared, for
whom he would prepare the way. Mary went to visit Elizabeth shortly
after hearing that she was to become the mother of Jesus. At
the sight of her, Elizabeth was "filled with the holy spirit." The
babe jumped for joy in her womb, and she greeted Mary as the
"Mother of the Lord." Mary's response, called The Magnificat, is
one of my favorite New Testament passages.*

Prayer/Practice

*Take a few letting-go breaths and slowly, patiently enter the place
of inner stillness, the "Holy of Holies." Contemplate what it
means to be "filled with the holy spirit." Then contemplate Mary's
response to Elizabeth's rapture: "My soul doth magnify the
Lord and my spirit hath rejoiced in God my Savior; for he hath
regarded the low estate of his handmaiden; for behold, from
henceforth all generations shall call me blessed. . . ."*

*Whenever you hear a story, regard it as a dream and as a
revelation from Your Higher Self. If each character is a part
of you—Elizabeth, Mary, John leaping for joy in the womb, and
Jesus just beginning to take human form—how can you
understand the story?*

*The Magnificat appears in Luke 1:48–55.

December 10

Seed Thought

John the Baptist was an Essene, one of a small band of Jews who
withdrew from the community to find God by practicing a life of
meditation and asceticism. Some scholars believe that Jesus' teachings
were inspired by the Essene community, in which he was said
to have lived. In the 1940s, the Dead Sea Scrolls were discovered in
Qumran by a shepherd. These contain the Essene doctrines—
a kind of post-Jewish/pre-Christian thinking, called Gnosticism. At
nearly the same time, other Gnostic manuscripts were unearthed
in the Egyptian desert town of Nag Hammadi. They had been buried
there by Christian monks to preserve them from destruction by
the early church, which considered them heretical. The Nag
Hammadi manuscripts contain many gospels that were not
included in the New Testament. When we read apocryphal scriptures
like these, once again our best guide to their authenticity as
"the word of God" is the purity of heart that they demonstrate.

Prayer/Practice

*Take a few deep breaths, and contemplate this teaching of Jesus
from the Gospel of Philip, published in the Nag Hammadi
Library: "Light and darkness, life and death, right and left, are
brothers of one another. They are inseparable. Because of this
neither are the good good, nor the evil evil, nor is life life, nor
death death. For this reason each one will dissolve into its
earliest origin. But those who are exalted above the world are
indissoluble, eternal."*

December 11

Seed Thought

The Gospel of Philip, as well as the other Gnostic writings, contain many of the same stories found in the Old and New Testaments, but with a decidedly psychological twist. Carl Jung became a student of the Gnostic writings when a series of dreams that he discusses in his autobiography, *Memories, Dreams and Reflections,* synchronistically revealed some of their subject matter and their relation to the growth of the soul. Jung had posited that within the unconscious of every woman there is a male principle; and within every male a female principle. In the language of the spirit, these two parts unite within us in the bridal chamber of our heart, and when the two become as one, they are transcended and bring us back to the original state of Wholeness or Union with God.

Prayer/Practice

Practice a few minutes of centering prayer, shamatha/vipassana meditation or the egg of light. Now contemplate these two exerpts from the Gospel of Philip from the perspective we just discussed.

When Eve was still in Adam, death did not exist. When she was separated from him, death came into being. If he enters again and attains his former self, death will be no more.

If the woman had not separated from the man, she would not die with the man. His separation became the beginning of death. Because of this, Christ came to repair the separation . . . and again unite the two.

December 12

Seed Thought

There is a Christ Principle within every human being that longs to overcome the separation into good and evil, up and down, male and female, that constitute the phenomenal world. This Christ Principle is birthless and deathless and always pure, regardless of what we may have experienced. It has never been separated from the Wholeness of God. This Higher Self has never given up on us, never ceased its efforts to bring us into the bridal chamber in which the opposites are reconciled. The birth of the Light that the coming of Jesus symbolizes in our own lives is the realization of that Higher Self that will bring us to Divine Union. Jesus is the outer personification of the inner teacher.

Prayer/Practice

Contemplate this song, which according to the Gnostic Apocryphon of John, Jesus sang to his disciples at the last supper. These few verses about the reconciliation of opposites are from a longer teaching:*

I would be saved; and I would save. Amen!
I would be broken; and I would break. Amen!
I would understand; and I would be understood. Amen!
I would be at-oned; and I would at-one. Amen!
I am a lamp to thee who seest me. Amen!
I am a mirror to thee who understandest me. Amen!
I am a door to thee who knockest at me. Amen!
See thyself in me who speak.

*These verses come from the version of the Apocryphon of John published in Jung and the Lost Gospels, *by Stephen Hoeller. (Quest Books, 1989.)*

December 13

Seed Thought

I remember sitting in church one Christmas about twenty years ago.
The minister said that we were never meant to worship the
Christ; we were meant to become the Christ. To become the Christ
was, in itself, the greatest act of worship that a human being
could aspire to. Jesus told his disciples that "if you had faith as a
grain of mustard seed, you could say to this sycamine tree, 'Be
rooted up, and be planted in the sea,' and it would obey you."* All
the powers of the Christ are ready to be born within us.

Prayer/Practice

*Contemplate the story of Jesus' birth adapted from the second
chapter of the Gospel of Matthew.*

*Jesus was born in Bethlehem during the rule of the Roman King
Herod. Just after his birth, three wise men from the East arrived
in Jerusalem, searching for a holy child—a great king—whose
birth had been forecast by astrological portents. Herod was
concerned for he did not want the Jews to have a strong king who
might rebel against the Roman occupation. He told the wise men
to search out the child so that he, too, could come pay his respects.
The star they had followed to Jerusalem led them to Bethlehem. Knowing
that a Great Light had been born into the world, they fell on their
knees and offered gifts of gold, frankincense and myrrh. Having
been warned in the dream to avoid the villainous Herod, they left
for home by another route.*

*If this story was a dream, and all the characters, including the Christ
Child, were parts of you, what might it mean for your awakening?*

*Matthew 17:5

December 14

Seed Thought

Even the Christ Child had to grow up and connect with the wisdom that was already present within before he could turn water into wine, heal by the laying on of hands, and bring the dead to life again—awaken them to their own true nature. In Jesus' case it took thirty years to come into his power. Then, as now, an outpouring of Divine Grace was required to rend the veil over his heart and allow Jesus to come fully into his authenticity, owning his power and his mission.

Prayer/Practice

Take a few letting-go breaths, and slowly, patiently, enter the inner silence. Now let's continue our winter's story.

When Jesus was thirty, he heard of a great priest called John the Baptist who, in the ritual of washing the soul clean by water, could call down the Holy Spirit and ignite the spark of God within. So Jesus went to this wild, powerful Essene preacher for baptism. John immediately recognized Jesus, and although he protested that it was Jesus who should baptize him, he dutifully dunked his Master beneath the water and lo! a light descended from heaven, and a white dove appeared over Jesus' head. A great hush fell over the crowd, and a voice came from heaven saying, "This is my beloved son in whom I am well pleased."

Contemplate this story as if it were a dream, and all the characters, including the voice of God, were part of you.

December 15

Seed Thought

As Jesus' story progresses, he, like the rest of us, has to face and vanquish the unseen darkness within in order to fully own the light. All mystics speak of suffering the "dark night of the soul" and the painful exorcism of inner demons. The dark night is a trial by fire, or, in the words of Stephen Mitchell, a scouring of the heart with steel wool. It is a confrontation with the shadow, or in the picture language of the unconscious, a meeting with the Devil.

Prayer/Practice

Contemplate this story that I have adapted (quite freely) from the third chapter of the Gospel according to Matthew:

Shortly after his baptism, Jesus was led into the wilderness, where he was tempted by the Devil. He fasted for forty days and forty nights, leaving every vestige of his prior life behind. The Great Tempter came to him, saying, "If you are the Son of God, command these stones to become loaves of bread." Jesus responded, "Man shall not live by bread alone, but by every word that proceeds from the mouth of God." Then the devil took him to the pinnacle of the temple and dared him to jump, since if he was truly the Son of God, the angels should catch him. Once again, Jesus resisted the temptation to exercise power. Finally the devil took him to the top of the world and offered it to him as his kingdom, if Jesus would just bow down. Once again, Jesus declined.

If this were a dream, and both Jesus and the Devil were parts of you, how could you relate it to the events of your life?

December 16

Seed Thought

When we are in the throes of a dark night of the soul we have indeed descended through the Western Gate of Death. If we can surrender to our passage and own the lessons of the underworld, rebirth is sure to follow.

Prayer/Practice

Contemplate this story, which I have adapted from the eleventh chapter of the Gospel according to John.

Mary Magdalene and her sister Martha had a brother named Lazarus who became very ill. They sent for Jesus, whose reputation for healing was known throughout Judea. He told his disciples, "This illness is not unto death; it is for the glory of God, so that the Son of God may be glorified by means of it." When Jesus came to Lazarus, he explained, "Our friend Lazarus has fallen asleep, but I go to wake him out of sleep." Lazarus, meanwhile, had been lying in his tomb for four days. Jesus said, "I am the resurrection and the life; and he who believes in me, though he die, yet he shall live, and whoever lives and believes in me shall never die. Do you believe this?" He then called, "Lazarus, come out," and the dead man came forth.

If this were a dream, and all the characters were parts of you, what would the famous statement "I am the resurrection and the life" mean to you?

December 17

Seed Thought

An ego-death is a crisis of monumental proportions. After we die to
who we were, there is a period of time that must pass before we awaken
to who we have become. This period is a kind of no-man's-land,
a period when we are neither here nor there. The Jews wandered
for forty years in the wilderness after they left the bondage of slavery
to the Egyptian pharaohs. Lazarus rested for four days in a tomb.
Persephone languished for six months in the underworld. The
caterpillar rests in apparent death while the miracle of
transformation proceeds in the silent darkness of the cocoon. This
period of transformation requires faith. The great Christian mystic
Meister Eckhart summed up the necessary attitude in his teaching
that in the time of darkness we have never been closer to the
light.

Prayer/Practice

*Take a few deep breaths and slowly, patiently slip into the inner
silence. Contemplate the notion that the most important aspect
of the Christmas story—Joseph's story—concerns the faith that
sustains us in dark nights. In* The Gospel According to Jesus,
*Stephen Mitchell points out that Mary's pregnancy is a big test of
faith for Joseph. His working through the doubt, hurt, and shame of
her pregnancy—and his emergence into forgiveness—would
become "an undoing, a redoing, a regeneration of the male
myth of Adam and Eve, a myth in which the serpent seduces Eve,
and man blames her ever afterward for his expulsion from
Paradise. (Actually the moment when Adam blames Eve is the
moment when he is expelled)."*

---

*Stephen Mitchell, *The Gospel According to Jesus*, p. 96.

December 18

Seed Thought

Every spiritual tradition stresses the need to be reborn. Rebirth is a miracle in which we perceive that peace and safety come not through blame and self-righteousness but through forgiveness. This is the Christmas Miracle that the birth of Jesus symbolizes. In forgiveness we enter the Promised Land. In forgiveness we return to the Garden.

Prayer/Practice

Contemplate this story that I have adapted from chapter seven of the Gospel according to Luke.

Jesus had been invited to dinner at the home of an influential priest. Mary Magdalene, who had been a prostitute, heard that her Master was in town and rushed to see him. Her heart was so full of gratitude that she knelt before Jesus at the table and washed his feet with her tears. She dried them with her hair and then anointed them with precious ointment from an alabaster jar. This humble act aroused a self-righteous tirade from the priest who wanted to know what kind of second-rate prophet would fail to know that a harlot was touching him. Jesus responded with a parable: "A certain creditor had two debtors; one owed five hundred denarii, and the other fifty. When they could not pay, he forgave them both. Now which of them will love him more?" The priest answered, "The one, I suppose, to whom he forgave more."

If this were your dream, and all the characters were parts of you, how would it apply to your own life?

December 19

Seed Thought

Mary Magdalene is one of the most important characters in the New Testament. In Jesus' response to the priest who criticizes him for letting her wash his feet he continues, "Do you see this woman? I entered your house; you gave me no water for my feet, but she had wet my feet with her tears and wiped them with her hair. You gave me no kiss, but from the time I came in she has not ceased to kiss my feet. You did not anoint my head with oil, but she has anointed my feet with ointment. Therefore I tell you, her sins which are many, are forgiven, for she has loved much; but he who is forgiven little, loves little." And he said to her, "Your sins are forgiven. Your faith has saved you; go in peace."

Prayer/Practice

Great Spirit, I awaken this morning with such love and gratitude for Your forgiveness. I understand that sin—the sense of separation from You—is the very path back to Divine Union. May the same forgiveness that is in you, awaken within me, that I may embody the heart of the Christmas Mystery.

Spend a few minutes in the deep peace of centering prayer. If Mary Magdalene's story were your dream, and all the characters were part of you, how would it apply to your life?

December 20

Seed Thought

One of the Gnostic manuscripts in the Nag Hammadi Library is the
Gospel of Mary (Magdalene). It dates back to the second century,
and unfortunately the two copies (one in Greek and one in Coptic)
that have been found are both fragmentary. It is estimated that
only eight of eighteen pages survived. Part of what was lost,
unfortunately, are teachings that Mary received from Jesus in a
vision after his death. Peter, whom the other disciples called a
hothead, did not at first believe Mary's vision. The other disciples
reprimanded him, reminding him that since Jesus loved Mary more
than all the rest of them, why should he not have blessed her
with special wisdom?

Prayer/Practice

*Spend a few minutes in centering prayer or shamatha/vipassana
meditation. Contemplate these words of Jesus, written in the
Gospel of Mary Magdalene: "Peace be with you. Receive my peace
to yourselves. Beware that no one lead you astray, saying,
'Lo here!' or 'Lo, there!' For the son of man is within you. Follow
after him! Those who seek him will find him. Go then and
preach the gospel of the kingdom. Do not lay down rules beyond
what I appointed for you, and do not give a law like a
lawgiver lest you be constrained by it."*

December 21: Winter Solstice

Seed Thought

Peace be with you. The darkest day of the year has dawned, and the Great Medicine Wheel has shifted from the West to the North. We have descended to the deepest levels of archetypal wisdom, and on this day we come to rest. The silence of winter covers the land, and even the waters are still and frozen. Their clarity reflects the purity of heart that we are claiming in this season. Their mirrored surface reflects our insight and understanding. North is the pole of wisdom and the province of the Archangel Michael.

Prayer/Practice

If possible, take a mindful walk outside today. Feel the energy of the North and the deep rest of the natural world. As you walk, bridge earth and heaven in your breath. Breathe the life of the Earth Mother in through the soles of your feet. Breathe the blessing of Father Sun in through the top of your head. Let the two streams mingle in your heart, and breathe out a blessing to all God's creatures: "May there be peace on earth and goodwill towards all."

December 22: Rebirth of the Light

Seed Thought

The time has come for celebration, for the Light has been reborn!
The animals feel the stirring of the lifeforce deep within their dens.
The seeds begin to stir within the womb of Mother Earth, and we
know that the cycle of life will continue for another year. Rejoice,
for today the time of light is greater than the time of darkness.
Rejoice, for today the Christ Principle is born within.

Prayer/Practice

Welcome the Divine Light today. Take a few letting-go breaths
and relax into the inner stillness. In the space above you and
slightly in front of you, imagine Jesus, Mary, the Buddha, a Great
Light or whatever symbol of the Divine you feel especially close
to. Give thanks for the rebirth of the Light within yourself and in
the world. Now imagine that a Living Light is flowing from
the Divine to you, showering over you and entering through the
top of your head. Let the Light penetrate all your cells,
awakening them from their ancient sleep, and washing away
any darkness that obscures the Sun within your Heart. See
your heartlight, the Christ Principle within, shining as bright as
the star over Bethlehem. Allow it to grow brighter and brighter,
uniting with the light of God, surrounding you in a glowing egg
of light. Send the light out into the world with the Metta blessing,

"May there be peace on earth, may the hearts of all beings be open,
may all be reborn in forgiveness, may all creation reflect the
Glory of God."

December 23

Seed Thought

Jesus came from the "root of Jesse," the House of David. David himself was a model of rebirth through repentance and forgiveness. Smitten with the beautiful Bathsheba, he contrived the death of her husband. For years David wrestled with his guilt, which was compounded by the death of the son Bathsheba bore to him. In confronting his sin—which in Hebrew means "to miss the mark"—David came to the at-one-ment. He understood the nature of forgiveness. Out of his hard-won wisdom came the psalms. As is true for the sayings of Jesus, some ring true because of their purity of heart; some are clearly the work of "inferior minds."

Prayer/Practice

Contemplate this portion of the one hundred and thirty-ninth Psalm of David. The beautiful verses below are a true song of the Higher Self, the Inner Light. The last six verses, should you want to look them up, are surely the addition of someone's most unhappy ego!

Whither shall I go from thy Spirit?
    Or whither shall I flee from thy presence?
If I ascend to heaven, thou are there!
    If I make my bed in Sheol (the grave)
Thou art there!
If I take the wings of the morning
    and dwell in the uttermost parts of the sea
even there thy hand shall lead me,
    and thy right hand shall hold me.

December 24

Seed Thought

The dawning of the Light is accompanied by a new cycle in the maturity of our faith. The growing ability to discriminate the fearful messages of the ego from the loving communications of the self allows us to walk the path of Jesus, the Buddhas and the great Masters who have come to awaken us and bring us back to the heart of wisdom. The twin flames of wisdom and trust continue to burn away any obscurations to our awareness of love's presence until we come to abide in the understanding that we are always cared for, always loved, always cheered on, regardless of the difficulties we may be experiencing.

Prayer/Practice

Take a few letting-go breaths and slowly, patiently enter the inner stillness. Contemplate the faith that shines through the twenty-third Psalm.

The Lord is my shepherd, I shall not want; he makes me lie down in green pastures. He leads me beside still waters; he restores my soul. He leads me in paths of righteousness for his name's sake. Even though I walk through the valley of the shadow of death, I fear no evil; for thou art with me; thy rod and thy staff, they comfort me. Thou preparest a table before me in the presence of my enemies; thou anointest my head with oil, my cup runneth over. Surely goodness and mercy shall follow me all the days of my life; and I shall dwell in the house of the Lord forever.

December 25: Christmas

Seed Thought

You are the light of the world. A city set on a hill cannot be hid.
Nor do men light a lamp and put it under a bushel, but on a stand,
and it gives light to all the house. Let your light so shine before
all men, that they may see your good works and give glory to
your Father who is in heaven.

—The Sermon on the Mount,
Matthew 5:14–16

Prayer/Practice

*This is a day to let your light shine in the true spirit of compassion
and forgiveness that is the heart teaching of all religions.
Practice Metta meditation as instructed on February 11–15.*

And peace be with you.

December 26

Seed Thought

Although the Light has been reborn in our hearts more brightly because of the past year's cultivation of compassion, tolerance, humility, humor and kindness, more growth is yet to come. More difficulties are yet to arise and lead us through the next spiral of awakening. In this year to come, remember the Buddhist practice called "making difficulties into the path." If we use all our trials, all our fears, all our disappointments to spur ourselves on, just think of all the fuel we'll have for the journey!

Prayer/Practice

Practice a few minutes of centering prayer or shamatha/vipassana meditation. The following is a Tibetan Buddhist prayer that you might like to remember:

Grant that I may be given appropriate difficulties and sufferings on this journey so that my heart may be truly awakened and my practice of liberation and universal compassion be truly fulfilled.

December 27

Seed Thought

It is said that the spiritual journey is like a razor's edge. We balance on that very fine line between the pairs of opposites that make up the phenomenal, relative world in which we live. The need to stay aware of our growing edges so that we can use them as fuel for the journey, while maintaining a gentle attitude of forgiveness toward our shortcomings, is one such example of the razor's edge.

Prayer/Practice

Spend a few minutes in the peace of centering prayer or shamatha/ vipassana meditation. Contemplate these words of Peace Pilgrim, a woman who crisscrossed the United States seventeen times carrying no money, no bags, no possessions—only a message of peace and forgiveness. She said:

Every good thing you do,
every good thing you say,
every good thought you think,
vibrates on and on and never
ceases. The evil remains only
until it is overcome by the good,
but the good remains forever.

December 28

Seed Thought

A Course in Miracles is a living testimony to the words of Jesus and all the Great Masters. It distills the essential teachings into a simple idea: Make forgiveness your primary function and peace of mind will naturally follow. Another way to think about this is to make peace of mind your primary goal. Forgiveness then follows as the most reasonable path to that end.

Prayer/Practice

Spend a few minutes in the peace of centering prayer or shamatha/ vipassana meditation. Now contemplate this magnificent prayer of Saint Francis of Assissi:

Lord make me an instrument of thy peace.
  Where there is hatred, let me sow love.
  Where there is injury, pardon.
  Where there is doubt, faith.
  Where there is despair, hope.
  Where there is darkness, light.
  And where there is sadness, joy.
O, Divine Master, grant that I may not
  so much seek to be consoled as to console;
  to be understood, as to understand;
  to be loved, as to love;
  for it is in giving that we receive,
  it is in pardoning that we are pardoned,
  and it is in dying that we are born to eternal life.

December 29

Seed Thought

I was cleaning the kitchen over the Christmas Holy Days one year while writing this book. Our son Justin, then in his mid-twenties, was visiting with me in the kitchen. I began to wax eloquent on the virtues of cooking food from scratch, since it was obviously the better way—more nutritious, more delicious, lots cheaper. The corollary of virtuous cooking, I explained, was virtuous refrigerator husbandry. Leftovers, in particular, were a precious resource always to be used up, never thrown out. Perish the thought of wastefulness. Justin's reply? "Have you applied for sainthood yet, Mom?" A monk was once asked what they did up there in the monastery all the time. He replied, "We fall and get up again. Fall and get up again. Fall and get up again." It's good not to take yourself too seriously.

Prayer/Practice

If possible, go for a mindful walk outside today. In the words of Thich Nhat Hanh, do nothing, just practice "being peace." Do the same thing in your interactions with other people. If a sudden fit of "setting people straight" comes over you, withdraw your application for sainthood and refrain from the urge to lecture.

December 30

Seed Thought

> In the secret recesses of the heart
> beyond the teachings of this world
> calls a still, small voice
> singing a song unchanged
> from the foundation of the world.
> Speak to me in sunsets and in starlight
> Speak to me in the eyes of a child
> You Who call me from a smile
> My cosmic beloved
> Tell me who I am
> And who I always will be.
> Help me to remember.

—J.B.

Prayer/Practice

Great Mystery, I awaken this morning with deep gratitude for the gift of life. May the renewal of faith in this season be the ground from which perfect peace will grow. May that peace extend as a blessing to all beings. And may the light in my heart pour through my eyes and touch the world with wonder. May I be present in this moment, and in every moment, so that I may remember Who I really am and meet this world with the kindness and grace of Your Spirit.

Spend a few minutes in the peace of centering prayer. Contemplate the gifts of this year and of these Holy Days.

December 31: New Year's Eve

Seed Thought

As the season of the Festivals of Light draws to a close, may this
old Gaelic blessing light your way into the New Year.

Deep peace of the running wave to you.
Deep peace of the flowing air to you.
Deep peace of the quiet earth to you.
Deep peace of the shining stars to you.
Deep peace of the watching shepherds to you.
Deep peace of the Son of Peace to you.

Prayer/Practice

*Take a few letting-go breaths and slowly, patiently, enter the place
of deep peace. Place your awareness in front of you, and
thank Uriel and the peace of the shining stars for the fiery changes
that have transformed you this year. Place your awareness
on your right side, and thank Gabriel and the peace of the quiet
earth for your growth. Place your awareness behind you, and
thank Raphael and the running waves for the healing you have
given and received this year. Place your awareness on your
left, and thank Michael and the flowing air for the wisdom and
insight you have gained. Place your awareness in your heart,
and thank the Son of Peace for your gradual awakening.*

RESOURCES

BOOKS

There are a number of books which have had a profound effect on my gradual awakening. Each one is like a jewel and comes very highly recommended. I am grateful to these authors for all they have taught me, much of which is revealed in the pages of *A Pocketful of Miracles*.

Meditation

Being Peace. Thich Nhat Hanh. Parallax Press, 1987.

Centering Prayer: Renewing an Ancient Christian Prayer Form. Basil Pennington. Image Books, 1982.

A Gradual Awakening. Stephen Levine. Anchor Books, 1979.

A Guide to Walking Meditation. Thich Nhat Hanh. Fellowship Publications, 1985.

The Miracle of Mindfulness! A Manual of Meditation. Thich Nhat Hanh. Beacon Press, 1976.

Open Mind, Open Heart. Thomas Keating. Element Books, 1986. (One of my all-time favorite books on meditation.)

The Sun in My Heart: From Mindfulness to Insight Contemplation. Thich Nhat Hanh. Parallax Press, 1988.

The Tibetan Book of Living and Dying. Sogyal Rinpoche. Harper San Francisco, 1992. (The classic text on Tibetan Buddhism as a practice that can enrich all spiritual paths.)

Universal Compassion. Geshe Kelsang Gyatso. Tharpa Publications, 1988. (A marvelous book on the practice of tonglen.)

Prayer

The Art of Spiritual Healing. Joel S. Goldsmith. Harper San Francisco, 1959.
(A classic on healing prayer.)

*Earth Prayers From Around the World: 365 prayers, poems and
invocations for honoring the earth.* Edited by Elizabeth Roberts and
Elias Amidon. HarperCollins, 1991.

Gratefulness, The Heart of Prayer. Brother David Steindl-Rast. Paulist Press,
New York, 1984.

The Healing Light: The Art and Method of Spiritual Healing. Agnes Sanford.
Macalester Park Publishing, 1947. (A classic on scientific prayer—the
art of spiritual healing.)

Healing Words: The Power of Prayer and the Practice of Medicine. Larry
Dossey. HarperCollins, 1993.

Peace Pilgrim; Her Life and Work in Her Own Words. Friends of Peace
Pilgrim. 43480 Cedar Avenue, Hemet, CA 92344. Write for a free copy!

Recovering the Soul: A Scientific and Spiritual Search. Larry Dossey.
Bantam Books, 1990.

The Perennial Philosophy

The Doors of Perception. Aldous Huxley. Harper and Row, 1954.

The Varieties of Religious Experience. William James. Mentor Books, 1958.

Judaism

The First Step: A Guide for the New Jewish Spirit. Rabbi Zalman Schachter-
Shalomi. Bantam Books, 1983.

Jewish Meditation: A Practical Guide. Aryeh Kaplan. Schocken Books, 1985.

Jewish Mystical Testimonies. Louis Jacobs. Schocken Books, 1976.

The Wisdom of Jesus

The Coming of the Cosmic Christ. Matthew Fox. Harper and Row, 1988.

A Course in Miracles. Foundation for Inner Peace, 1975.

The Gospel According to Jesus. Stephen Mitchell. HarperCollins, 1991.

Prayers of the Cosmos: Meditations on the Aramaic Words of Jesus. Neil Douglas-Klotz. Harper and Row, 1990.

Gnostic Thought

The Gnostic Gospels. Elaine Pagels. Vintage Books, 1981.

Jung and The Lost Gospels. Stephan A. Hoeller. The Theosophical Publishing House, 1989. (Insights into the Dead Sea Scrolls and the Nag Hammadi library.)

The Nag Hammadi Library James M. Robinson, General Editor. Harper and Row, 1988. (The full translations of the Gnostic Gospels found at Nag Hammadi.)

Spiritual Traditions of the World

Answers. Mother Meera. Meerama Publications, 1991.

Atom from the Sun of Knowledge. Lex Hixon Nur al Jerrahi. Pir Publications, 1993. (A marvelous book on Islam.)

Enduring Grace: Living Portraits of Seven Women Mystics. Carol Lee Flinders. HarperCollins, 1993.

Heart of the Koran. Lex Hixon. The Theosophical Publishing House, 1988. (A magnificent book that reveals the heart of Islam.)

How to Know God: The Yoga Aphorisms of Patanjali. Swami Prabhavananda and Christopher Isherwood. Mentor Books, 1953.

Introduction to Tantra: A Vision of Totality. Lama Yeshe. Wisdom Basic Books, 1987. (A fine introduction to Tibetan Buddhist practice.)

The Orthodox Way. Father Kallistos Ware. St. Vladimir's Seminary Press, 1979.

A Policy of Kindness. The Dalai Lama. Snow Lion Publications, 1990.

The Song of God, Bhagavad Gita. Swami Prabhavananda and Christopher Isherwood. Mentor Books, 1944.

Voices of Our Ancestors: Cherokee Teachings From the Wisdom Fire. Dhyani Ywahoo. Shambala Books, 1987.

Psychology and Religion

Forgiveness: A Bold Choice for a Peaceful Heart. Robin Casarjian. Bantam Books, 1992.

Memories, Dreams and Reflections. C. G. Jung. Vintage Books, 1965.

A Path With Heart; A Guide through the Perils and Promises of Spiritual Life. Jack Kornfield. Bantam Books, 1993.

Practical Jung: Nuts and Bolts of Jungian Psychotherapy. Harry A. Willmer. Chiron Publications, 1987.

Stages of Faith: The Psychology of Human Development and the Quest for Meaning. James W. Fowler. Harper and Row, 1991.

Practical Instruction for the Inner Life

Dreamwork: Techniques for Discovering the Creative Power in Dreams. Jeremy Taylor. Paulist Press, 1983.

Exploring the World of Lucid Dreaming. Stephen La Berge and Howard Rheingold. Ballantine Books, 1990.

Lucid Dreaming: Dawning of the Clear Light. G. Scott Sparrow. A.R.E. Press, 1976.

which you can order a variety of music CDs and cassettes, selected videos, posters of Miroslav's mandalas, calendars, and Joan's books and tapes. Please write or call for a newsletter:

Mind/Body Health Sciences, Inc.
393 Dixon Road
Boulder, CO 80302-7177

(303) 440-8460 phone
(303) 440-7580 fax

APPENDIX OF
MEDITATION PRACTICES

BELLY BREATHING

Awareness of breath is the cornerstone for developing control of the bodymind. When breath is shallow and fast, body responds with an increase in heart rate, blood pressure and fear hormones. Mind responds with fantasies of loneliness, unworthiness and negativity. When breath is long and slow, body becomes peaceful and relaxed. Mind stops churning and comes to rest.

Become aware of your breathing now. Is it shallow and irregular or deep and slow? Take a big breath in and let it go slowly, like a sigh of relief. Let the next breath come in slowly and feel how your belly expands. When you exhale, feel how your belly relaxes. As you breathe diaphragmatically from your belly, notice how both mind and body come to rest.

COUNTING THE BREATHS

Take a letting-go breath, a big sigh of relief. Now shift to belly breathing. On the next outbreath, mentally concentrate on the number four. On the next outbreath, three, then two and one on successive outbreaths. Start counting down from four again and continue for five minutes. Whenever thoughts come to mind, just notice them and let them go as soon as possible, returning your attention to breathing and counting.

Repeat this exercise two or three times today.

BREATH OF BRIDGING EARTH AND HEAVEN

Meditate outside if possible when first learning this meditation. Sit with your feet solidly upon the earth, close your eyes and begin with a minute of belly breathing. Now place your awareness at the bottoms of your feet, and either feel or imagine the energy of Mother Earth. Breathe

*that energy into your heart, and breathe out a sense of compassionate
awareness. . . . Now either feel or imagine the energy of Father Sun shining
down on you. Breathe it in through the top of your head, taking it into
your heart. Breathe out a sense of compassionate awareness. . . . Now breathe
in the sunlight from above and the earth energies from below and let
them meet and marry in your heart. Breathe out the creative, loving
energies of earth and sky that have been blessed by your being. Let each
outbreath expand to caress all creation. Continue for as long as you
like. I practice this breath with eyes open for much of the day.*

BASIC CONCENTRATION MEDITATION

Meditation is a form of mental martial arts. If we resist thoughts they will
overpower us. But if we just step lightly out of their way, letting them
come and go like birds flying overhead, we can use their energy to further
focus our minds.

*Take a big letting-go breath and take up concentration on breathing
and counting as outlined above. Let part of your awareness watch
for thoughts, and when they arise, just let them subside, continuing to
focus on breathing and counting. Continue for five minutes and repeat
once or twice more during the day.*

STRETCHING

Mind and body are so intimately related that they form a bodymind unit.
When the body is relaxed, the mind slows down. When the mind slows
down, the body relaxes. Before meditation and throughout the day, remembering
to stretch the body allows the mind to be spacious. Before prayer and meditation,
and throughout the day when you feel stressed or fatigued, take a moment to
stretch.

*Inhale and gently stretch back, then exhale and round your back
forward, dropping your chin to your chest. Inhale and stretch your
arms above your head, then exhale and let them float down as if you*

were making a snow angel. Gently move your head from side to side, then drop it front to back. Stretch your face with a big yawn.

Notice how your body feels two or three times each day. Then stretch and observe how your body and mind respond to your attention.

CENTERING PRAYER

Centering prayer is a form of meditation that is a conscious letting go of small mind and its continuous self-centered fantasies. In this form of prayer, popularized by Father Thomas Keating, we shift awareness away from the thoughts that Keating compares to boats floating down the river of consciousness, to the river itself. The river is Big Mind, Divine Presence.

Focus your mind by counting back from four to one on successive outbreaths. Continue for two or three minutes. Now let go of counting and let your awareness focus on the feelings of peace and tranquility that naturally arise as small mind quiets down. When you begin to think, mentally repeat a word or phrase of your choice—a prayer word. Thank you, peace, shalom, Kyrie Eleison . . . are examples of prayer words. As soon as your mind quiets down again, let go of the word. Your intention is just to sit quietly in the peace of God's Presence. Continue for as long as you like.

HOLY MOMENT MEDITATION

Take a few letting-go breaths and remember a time when you felt present in the moment—absorbed in a sunset, marveling at fresh-fallen snow, enchanted by the smile of a baby . . . enter the memory with all your senses . . . remember the sights and colors, the smells, the position and movement of your body, the emotional or felt sense . . . Now, let the memory go and meditate for a few minutes on what remains—the stillness and joy of your awareness of the Divine Presence. Every moment that you are in the present is a holy moment. I often begin periods of meditation or centering prayer by recalling a holy moment.

THE EGG OF LIGHT

In the space before you and slightly above you, imagine a great star
of light or whatever form of the Divine you relate to most easily.
Feel streams of Divine Love and Light flowing down over you and
washing through your body, carrying away any fatigue, fear, or negativity.
As all the darkness washes out of the bottoms of your feet, imagine that
the light in your heart shines more and more brightly, filling you
and extending around you like an egg. Allow the egg of light that you
are to merge and become one with Light of the Divine Presence. Rest for a
few minutes in that Presence.

You may also wish to say the Unity Church Prayer of Protection while
in the egg of light:

The light of God surrounds me,
The love of God enfolds me,
The power of God protects me,
The Presence of God watches over me.
Wherever I am God is
And all is well.

LOVINGKINDNESS (METTA) MEDITATION

Begin by taking a few letting-go breaths, and then enter the inner
sanctuary of stillness. Imagine a great star of light above you and
slightly in front of you, pouring a waterfall of love and light over you.
Let the light enter the top of your head and wash through you, revealing
the purity of your own heart, which expands and extends beyond you,
merging with the Divine Light. See yourself totally enclosed in the
egg of light, and then repeat these lovingkindness blessings for yourself
with all the respect and love that you would have for your only child:

May I be at peace, May my heart remain open,
May I awaken to the light of my own true nature,
May I be healed, May I be a source of healing for all beings.

Next bring a loved one to mind. See them in as much detail as possible,
imagining the loving light shining down on them and washing through

them, revealing the light within their own heart. Imagine this light growing brighter, merging with the Divine light and enclosing them in the egg of light. Then bless them:

May you be at peace, May your heart remain open,
May you awaken to the light of your own true nature,
May you be healed, May you be a source of healing for all beings.

Repeat this for as many people as you wish.

Next, think of a person whom you hold in judgment, and to whom you're ready to begin extending forgiveness. Place them in the egg of light, and see the light washing away all their negativity and illusion, just as it did for you and your loved ones. Bless them:

May you be at peace, May your heart remain open,
May you awaken to the light of your own true nature,
May you be healed, May you be a source of healing for all beings.

See our beautiful planet as it appears from outer space, a delicate jewel hanging in the starry vastness. Imagine the earth surrounded by light—the green continents, the blue waters, the white polar caps. The two-leggeds and four-leggeds, the fish that swim and the birds that fly. Earth is a place of opposites. Of day and night, good and evil, up and down, male and female. Be spacious enough to hold it all as you offer these blessings:

May there be peace on earth, May the hearts of all people be open to themselves and to each other, May all people awaken to the light of their own true nature, May all creation be blessed and be a blessing to All That Is.

DEDICATING THE MERITS OF ANY MEDITATION PRACTICE

By the power and the truth of this practice
May all beings have happiness and the causes of happiness
May all beings be free from sorrow and the causes of sorrow
And may all live in equanimity without too much attachment
*   and too much aversion*

And live believing in the equality of all that lives.

(Adapted from *The Tibetan Book of Living and Dying,* by Sogyal Rinpoche.)

MINDFULNESS

A man who had a near-death experience following a heart attack returned
to his body, and the first thing he saw in his hospital room was a rose.
He experienced seeing a rose as for the first time, realizing that he was
intimately connected to that flower. Now, when he walks through the forest,
he feels as though he is one with the trees. He has realized directly his
participation in the web of life. The secret of happiness, he says, is twofold:
to realize that all things are interconnected and to send love along those
connections. This attitude leads directly into the experience of mindfulness—
the curious, openminded observation of life that characterizes children.

*Keeping your eyes open, take a deep breath and let go, feeling your
body and mind begin to relax. Shift your attention to belly breathing.
Look around and select an object to contemplate. Keeping an awareness
of your breathing, see the object with the eyes of a child, as if you were
seeing it for the first time. See with wonder, delight and absorption. This
is mindfulness, or moment-by-moment, non-judgmental awareness.*

*Several times each day, stop and take a letting-go breath. Enter the
moment with all your senses, taking time to taste and smell, hear
and see, feel and move. Feel your connectedness with all things. Begin
with a moment of mindfulness right now.*

MINDFULNESS EXERCISES

We can extend the practice of mindful awareness and spaciousness beyond
the period of sitting meditation into the rest of life. The Vietnamese
Buddhist poet, peaceworker and meditation teacher Thich Nhat Hanh has
written a beautiful book called *The Miracle of Mindfulness.* With true simplicity
and beauty he reminds us that we can wake up in the ordinary activities

of life by bringing our full attention to eating, washing the dishes, smelling the roses, walking, making love.

Mindful Eating: *Today, choose a piece of fruit and eat it mindfully. Be aware of its look, smell and feel. Notice the way that your mouth fills with saliva in anticipation of its flavor. Be aware of each bite moving down your throat into your stomach. To be mindful is to be present in your higher self rather than your ego.*

Mindful Activity of Your Choice: *Choose one activity, like taking a walk, washing the dishes or taking a shower, and commit to doing it as mindfully as possible. You will really enjoy yourself!*

Mindfulness Blessings (Brachot): One of the most beautiful practices that I have retained from my Jewish roots is the recitation of blessings, called *Brachot*, which are prayers of gratitude. Judaism is similar to Greek Orthodoxy in being a tradition of gratitude. In Judaism there are over a hundred blessings that express our gratitude to God for every kind of natural wonder—things that grow, stars that shine, rainbows, food we eat, even the natural functions of elimination that keep our bodies healthy! Brachot naturally bring us into mindfulness.

The bracha is a blessing of God for all that has been created. You can say an impromptu blessing whenever you notice something of wonder or beauty: *Blessed art Thou, Creator of the Universe, who has given us the first star of evening, or the light of the moon, or the smile of babies.* After each one, spend a minute or two in mindfulness. Be aware of the way in which the lifeforce awakens in your body through gratitude and mindful attention.

Mindful Walking: *Place your attention lightly on the flow of your breathing. At the same time, notice how your body moves, how the weight shifts from one foot to the other. Perhaps you can coordinate your footsteps with your breathing, two or so steps to each inbreath and outbreath. The sensation of breathing and walking is like the anchor for your attention. When you feel focused in breathing and walking, open your senses to everything around you. The breath is like a bridge between*

you and everything you see, touch, smell and sense. If your mind wanders,
return to the sensation of breathing and walking. Enjoy!

HEALING THROUGH THE GAZE

There is a subtle channel, like a vein in which energy flows, that extends
from the heart out through the eyes. You can communicate great love
through your gaze, speaking directly to your own soul or the soul of another
person.

Get a mirror and look into your face. See yourself without judgment. Forget
the wrinkles, the freckles, the beauty or its lack that small mind is
attracted to or repelled by. See yourself through the eyes of a child, without
judgment. See yourself as a child, the Divine child who is always worthy
of your love and respect. Look deeply into your eyes and tell yourself silently,
"I love and respect you." Tell yourself whatever else you would most
like to hear from a person who truly wishes you to awaken and find the
Divine within your heart and in your life. As you go through the day,
speak to others through your heart, allowing respect and love to flow out
of your eyes and into their soul.

SHAMATHA/VIPASSANA MEDITATION

The Tibetan Buddhist practice of shamatha/vipassana, which means the
meditation of calm abiding and insight, is a basic practice for seeing
with the Higher Self, rather than through the eyes of the ego.

Sit in your seat with great dignity, back straight and eyes open. Look directly
in front of you, eyes down slightly, without particular focus. Become
aware of your breathing—how breath comes in and fills you and how
breath moves out into space. Keep about 25 percent of your attention
on breathing and the other 75 percent on the feeling of spaciousness. When
thoughts arise, just let them go by. Sogyal Rinpoche, a Tibetan Buddhist
lama, compares the thoughts that arise in meditation to waves that rise
from the ocean. It is the ocean's nature to rise. We cannot stop it, but, as
Rinpoche says, we can "leave the risings in the risings."

PHOWA—THE TRANSFERENCE OF CONSCIOUSNESS

The Tibetan Buddhists do a practice called *Phowa,* the transference of consciousness. It is traditionally performed for dying people and for the dead, particularly in the first seven weeks after their passage. In its brief form, the practitioner imagines a form of Divine Consciousness that the dying or dead person has felt very close to. This might be Mary, Jesus, Buddha, Allah, the Light.... One imagines this form of the Divine above the head of the dying or dead person, showering them with light, and washing through their body, carrying away any pain or illusion that obscures their recognition of their own true nature, their heartlight or Higher Self. One then imagines the heartlight of the dying or dead person expanding and becoming one with the Divine Consciousness. This is believed to help the soul recognize and remain in the state of Divine Union, rather than falling prey, once again, to the ego and its projections once the experience of Light that people describe in the near-death state is over.

Although Phowa is traditionally done in the seven weeks following death, it can be done at any time. If you feel moved to try it, follow the instructions above, and practice Phowa for someone who has died. I like to do it on the anniversaries of the death of my parents, a day on which Jews light a yahrzeit, or memorial, candle. What better way to honor and remember the dead?

TONGLEN—THE MEDITATION OF GIVING AND RECEIVING

The Dalai Lama has been interviewed many times concerning his feelings about the Chinese holocaust in Tibet in the 1950s. They killed one sixth of the population, torched 6,000 monasteries and tortured many of the monks, nuns and lamas. The Chinese rape and pillage extended to the land. The beautiful Tibetan plateaus are now nuclear dumping grounds and the great herds of wildlife extinct. I am always moved when the Dalai Lama responds with compassion for the ignorance and pain of the Chinese that must underlie their actions. In his compassion he practices a form of meditation called *tonglen* for their benefit, taking on their pain, and gives them his happiness and joy. This extraordinary meditation of giving and receiving has been very helpful in bringing about forgiveness in my own life.

People sometimes fear that tonglen will harm them when they imagine breathing in pain, ignorance or illness. The Tibetan lamas say that the only thing we can harm with tonglen is our ego and its self-grasping, which will dissolve in the intention of compassion. Nonetheless, until you are comfortable with tonglen, perform it only for yourself or loved ones. When you feel more secure, you can extend it to strangers whom you feel judgments about, or feel sympathetic to, and then to others about whom your judgments are stronger. In time, you can extend it to your worst enemies, creating peace and compassion where there was pain and fear. Tonglen is truly a yoga that transforms pain into forgiveness.

Before we learn to practice tonglen on behalf of others, we will learn to do it for ourselves. The first step is to open our hearts so that we have something good to give. So begin by bringing back the memory of a holy moment, a time that your heart was open to nature, to a child, to a pet, to beauty. Now imagine that you are sitting, facing yourself. Look into your eyes and see the beauty of who you are, and the pain that keeps you out of touch with that beauty. Imagine that all your pain is like a thick, black smoke covering your heart. Inhale that smoke into your own heart, and exhale the peace, love and happiness of your own true nature. Continue this meditation of breathing in pain and breathing out happiness. Since you can only experience love and joy by giving it away, this meditation is a form of "wise selfishness." It will make you happy.

Next, bring a loved one to mind and imagine any pain, confusion, illness or unhappiness they might be experiencing as a black smoke around their heart. Breathe that smoke into your own heart and return your peace and happiness. Continue to do this for a few minutes until you feel a sense of completion.

Next, if it feels right for you, practice tonglen for a stranger whom you might otherwise pity. Whether it's a homeless person, someone you read about in the paper or see on the news, imagine breathing in their pain in the form of black smoke. Take it into your heart and return your happiness to them.

Next, bring to mind someone that you hold in judgment. Imagine the pain and ignorance that led them to behave in a way that was hurtful. See it as a thick black smoke that obscures the true Light in their heart. Breathe the smoke into your own heart's Light, and return your Light to them. Continue until the Lights in your two hearts touch.

You can do tonglen for areas of the world where there is war, famine or other suffering, for all the people who are grieving, for those who are sick. . . . The practice is universally applicable to all pain and sorrow.

TONGLEN TO TRANSFORM EMOTIONS THROUGHOUT THE DAY

During the day, be aware of any negative emotions that arise. If the emotions have a message to give you, make sure that you attend to it before you use tonglen to transform the emotion. Begin by getting in touch with just how miserable your anger, jealousy, spite or sadness is making you feel. Then take a few deep breaths and do your best to bring back the memory of a holy moment when you felt connected with the universe. Then practice tonglen for yourself.

MEDITATION ON THE ANGELS

Close your eyes and take a few letting-go breaths. Center yourself in belly breathing or the breath of bridging earth and heaven.

Place your awareness in the space in front of you, the Eastern Gate of your body temple. Ask for the presence of the Archangel Uriel, whose name in Hebrew means "the light of God." Stay centered and notice whatever you can about Uriel's presence. Review your current situation, thinking of areas where you need more clarity. Ask Uriel for any help that you need in making decisions or in discrimination.

Place your awareness to your right, the Southern Gate of your body temple. Ask for the presence of the Archangel Gabriel, whose name in Hebrew means "the strength of God." Stay centered and notice whatever you can about this presence. Gabriel is the angel who helps us to overcome fear so that we may bring forth our creative gifts for the benefit of all. Review your current situation and ask for the removal of fear, as well as for help in realizing your creativity.

Place your awareness in back of you, the Western Gate of your body temple. Ask for the presence of the Archangel Raphael, whose name in Hebrew means "the healer of God." Stay centered and notice whatever you can about Raphael's presence. Review your current situation, thinking of any emotional, physical or spiritual healing you may need. Ask Raphael for that healing. Think, too, about the healing that you can bring to others, and ask for any help you might need.

Place your awareness to your left, the Northern Gate of your body temple. Ask for the presence of the Archangel Michael, whose name in Hebrew means "how like unto God." Michael is the pure presence of love, forgiveness and wisdom. Stay centered and notice whatever you can about this presence. Review your current situation, thinking of any areas in which love or forgiveness needs to flow. Ask also for any insights you require.

Now become aware of a star of light above your head and slightly in front of you. Feel the Divine Light wash over you like a waterfall and flow through you the way that a river flows through the sand at its bottom. Let the light wash every cell clean, carrying away any fatigue, dis-ease, heaviness or pain. As the light flows through you, imagine that it is dissolving any darkness from around your heart, allowing the Sun within you to shine forth brightly as a blessing to all beings.

Conclude your meditation anyway you like—with Metta, tonglen, centering prayer, shamatha/vipassana or a heartfelt prayer of thanksgiving.

ACKNOWLEDGMENTS

Heartfelt thanks to all those who have been teachers in the traditional sense:
Hadassah Blocker, Reverends Chris and Joan Williamson, Swami
Chidvilasananda, Dhyani Ywahoo and Sogyal Rinpoche.
And to those friends, the circle with whom I've shared the journey:
The magical, mystical Mother Goose—Celia Thaxter Hubbard.
Robin Casarjian, Peggy Taylor, Rick Ingrasci, Steve Maurer,
Olivia Hoblitzelle, Beth Lawrence, Joan Drescher, Loretta LaRoche,
Alan Shackelford and Ursula Reich-Henbest,
Kristi Jorde, Gordon and Julie Burnham, Leslie Kussman,
Tricia Stallman, Renee Summers, Carolina Clarke and Roxanne Daleo.
With great admiration I thank those teachers whom I have not had the
benefit of studying with directly, but whose work and being have
deeply inspired my thinking, practice and living:
His Holiness the Dalai Lama, Brother David Steindl-Rast, Matthew Fox,
Mother Meera and Thich Nhat Hanh.
The work of Jon Kabat-Zinn, Jeremy Taylor, Stephen Mitchell, Stephen
Levine, Elaine Pagels and Carol Lee Flinders
have enriched both this book and my life.
Miroslav Dmitrivitch Borysenko,
my partner, not only contributed the beautiful mandalas to this book
but endures with some grace the vicissitudes of living with a woman whose
nose is often either in a book or in the Other World.
But it is to our children, son-in-law and grandchild that I am most indebted.
Justin, Andrei, Natalia, Shawn and Alexsandr—
you have provided the opportunity for me to learn what it is to nurture,
encourage and love. I am still learning.
Thanks to Helen Rees, my wonderful agent, and to
Joann Davis, an editor with a vision,
for providing the opportunity for me to follow my heart
in the varied book projects they have midwifed.
And finally I give thanks to the two Miriams—Jewish mothers both.
Mary the Mother of Jeshua and Mary the Magdalene.
Your time is at last at hand.

ABOUT THE AUTHOR

Joan Borysenko has been described as a rare jewel: respected scientist, gifted therapist and unabashed mystic. She completed a doctorate and three postdoctoral fellowships at the Harvard Medical School where she did research in cancer cell biology, psychoneuroimmunology and behavioral medicine. She is also a licensed clinical psychologist and the cofounder and former director of the Mind/Body Clinic at Boston's New England Deaconess Hospital. In 1988 she defected from academia and clinical practice to teach, write and found Mind/Body Health Sciences, Inc. Her guiding vision is to bridge medicine, psychology and the great spiritual traditions of the ages. Author of *Minding the Body, Mending the Mind; Guilt Is the Teacher, Love Is the Lesson; On Wings of Light*; and *Fire in the Soul*, she is currently at work on a novel (a revisionist history) about the life of Jesus as told through the eyes of the women. She lives in the mountains northwest of Boulder, Colorado, with her husband Miroslav, stepdaughter Natalia, son-in-law Shawn, grandson Alexsandr, a houseful of plants, the Noble Maxwell (her 115-pound devoted Rottweiler) and two feuding cats, Pudgie and Foxie. She likes skiing, hiking, gardening, laughing and an occasional outstanding piece of chocolate cake.